CHILD AND FAMILY ASSESSMENT

D0223571

Child and Family Assessment provides a practical, thoughtful and systematic guide to the theory and practice of family assessment. It combines a clear summary of current knowledge with practical, detailed and adaptable procedures for practitioners to use, such as a script for a family interview.

Not only does it contain clear and specific guidance for practice, but the materials are discussed within a broad theoretical context. Written from an eclectic point of view in a clear and precise style using common-sense terms, it is an essential summary of key concepts and methods for assessment.

The book is written in three parts: on theory, practice and current issues. Part I traces the development of important theoretical ideas which are relevant to assessment with children and families. Part II shows what results when these principles are applied in practice, and how information gained from the assessment can be used to determine a therapeutic strategy. Part III considers the relationship between science, assessment and clinical practice, and the book concludes with a set of brief clinical guidelines for child and family assessment which summarize the approach described.

Child and Family Assessment will be an essential guide for practitioners who work with children and their families, and will be an invaluable aid for practitioners and students in all disciplines in the helping professions.

Ian Wilkinson is a Consultant Clinical Psychologist at South Tees Community and Mental Health Trust and co-founder of the Marion Family Centre in Darlington. He has also worked as an academic tutor for the University of Newcastle upon Tyne doctoral course in clinical psychology, and his work on child and family assessment has received wide recognition.

CHILD AND FAMILY ASSESSMENT

Clinical guidelines for practitioners

Second edition

Ian Wilkinson

London and New York

First published as *Family Assessment* 1993
by Gardner Press

Second edition published 1998
by Routledge
11 New Fetter Lane, London EC4P 4EE

Simultaneously published in the USA and Canada
by Routledge
29 West 35th Street, New York, NY 10001

© 1993, 1998 Ian Wilkinson

Typeset in Goudy by RefineCatch Limited, Bungay, Suffolk
Printed and bound in Great Britain by
TJ International Ltd, Padstow, Cornwall

British Library Cataloguing in Publication Data
A catalogue record for this book is available from the British Library

Library of Congress Cataloging in Publication Data
Wilkinson, Ian, 1953–
Child and family assessment : clinical guidelines for
practitioners / Ian Wilkinson. – 2nd ed.
p.   cm.
Includes bibliographical references and index.
1. Family assessment.   I. Title.
RC488.53.W56   1998
616.89′156–dc21   97–26566

ISBN 0–415–16806–6 (hbk)
ISBN 0–415–16807–4 (pbk)

CONTENTS

TABLES AND FIGURES

Tables

Figures

ABOUT THE AUTHOR

Ian Wilkinson was born and brought up in the north-east of England, where he returned to work as a psychologist. He studied at Nottingham University and then worked at a community school for children and as a research assistant with the elderly, before completing his clinical psychology training in Edinburgh. He then helped to establish and develop the Marion Family Centre in Darlington, and made other contributions to the development of children's services within the northern region of England. His work on child and family assessment has received wide recognition and he has also worked as academic tutor for the Newcastle-upon-Tyne University doctoral course in clinical psychology. He currently works at the Roseberry Centre in Middlesbrough, is a national assessor for the BPS, and is respected for encouraging co-operation and teamwork between professions. He also has personal experience of family life in various forms. His hobbies include reading literature, watching films, cooking, creative writing and photography. He was also a keen soccer player and is mad about the Boro.

ACKNOWLEDGEMENTS

A full list of acknowledgements would fill this book: but thanks are due first to all my colleagues past and present at the Marion Centre and the Roseberry Centre; to the Darlington Memorial Hospital League of Friends, the Darlington Round Table, the Northern Regional Research Committee, and the Khan Fund, who all provided funds to support aspects of the original research work; and to the many individuals and families who have taught me by sharing their experiences with me.

On a wider basis I would like to thank the various experts in the UK and abroad who have helped and encouraged me, again too numerous to list but all warmly remembered.

This work is dedicated to my father, my mother, my brothers and my sister, but especially to my children, Emma and Adam, and also to Sheila, Nick, Catherine and Dominic.

1

INTRODUCTION AND OVERVIEW

Fools rush in where angels fear to tread
Alexander Pope, *An Essay on Criticism* (1711)

This book stems from twenty years' experience as an applied psychologist fulfilling a variety of roles. Mostly this has been in clinical practice, but it has also included experience of teaching and training with my own and other professions, supervision, consultation, professional representation and developing teamwork in multi-disciplinary teams. Looking back, my initial reaction to child work in the British National Health Service was one of abject dismay, if not horror, at the general disorganization and chaos – the lack of attempts to develop a systematic understanding of problems, and practices which seemed to be more defined by personal preferences of the therapist than patient need. This book is the result of what I have learned in my struggle to find a different path.

I clearly remember the anxiety when I first started working with families together, and how confused I felt; the confusion of trying to listen to five people at once and then the confusion of trying to work out who everyone was in a large case conference. After a while I began to have a sneaky feeling I was not alone in my confusion.

My initial efforts to remedy this were somewhat naïve, in that I assumed that the solutions lay in methods and the practical application of good psychometric principles. But I began by observing the practice of others and trying to define what seemed good practice, and studying what others had written. It soon seemed clear to me that there was something ethically odd about intervening in families without assessment – rather like a tradesman who is asked for an estimate and instantly starts to knock holes out of the wall. Many parents insisted: 'We really just want to know what the problem is'. I began to be interested in process, negotiation, the patient's view, contract, and empowerment by giving the assessment back to the patient and family in a careful and respectful manner. Only fools rush in where angels fear to tread. On the other hand, I can appreciate that to some it may seem equally foolish to try to assess something as complex as a person and their family context, so perhaps I have been the one who rushed in . . .

The experience during this work has taught me a lot. My views about the general disorganization of children's services have not changed, but this is partly due to the relative infancy (in historical terms) of children's services: plus the inherent complexity and lack of coordination of the multiplicity of agencies and professions involved in child work. They have grown haphazardly, owing to limited funding and lack of planning. This has strengthened my belief in a need for rigorous and systematic approaches to the work, and for more developmental content in training for all professions. My views of what constitutes 'science' have also changed considerably. A useful scientific approach must be a pluralistic scientific analysis (one that uses a variety of theoretical perspectives) and must be explicitly taught as such. The explicit use of several perspectives helps to give trainees a way of thinking about the complexity of development and family life, and helps them understand links between different problems on different levels in terms of either linear or circular causality. Multiple perspectives also help to understand individual differences and different needs. Their use also encourages a flexible approach to therapy, treatment, or problem-solving, tending to generate choices rather than single answers. Families should have choices and this is a key issue for public services.

Gale (1985) discussed the characteristics of applied research in terms of a process which is best understood using the metaphor of a journey. As you travel, the question changes and so does the destination. The literature and the process of self-evaluation force researchers to revise their views. Thus my question changed from 'Can we develop a scientific measuring instrument?' to 'Is it possible to develop a system for assessment which is simple enough to use for training beginners, but which adequately reflects the complexity of psychological work with children and their families?' In more recent times I have also used the questions 'Do we know what we are doing? Can we find out?' Perhaps they are the simplest but most eloquent way of describing the aims of this book.

Summary of the contents of this book

This book is intended to provide a practical but systematic guide to the assessment of the family which will be useful for trainees and practitioners of all disciplines in the helping professions, i.e. doctors, nurses, social workers, psychologists, counsellors and psychotherapists. Although much has been written about family therapy in the last couple of decades, the topic of assessment has been sadly neglected. This book will attempt to cover the topic in common-sense, non-jargon terms. It will also integrate views of the individual and the family, and aim to give practical advice to the mainstream practitioner.

This introductory chapter summarizes the contents and briefly describes important social trends and developments which underpin this work; it also relates these developments to other general trends in science, society and health care.

The rest of the book is written in three parts. Part I (Chapters 2 to 4) traces the development of important theoretical ideas which are relevant to assessment with children and families. The family structure in relation to patterns of attachment, the nature of the power hierarchy, and communication processes (particularly emotional communication) are important. The cultural context, life stages, transitions and events also need to be considered. Finally, the perceptions and beliefs of the family members must also be considered carefully, since family members construct (multiple) views of reality. In relation to therapeutic methods available for working with both individuals and families, each method makes certain assumptions about the precise nature of the problems and what the role of the therapist should be in solving them. Certain key concepts and skills can be identified, but there is no cure-all; in addition certain methods will suit certain people and not others. Users have a right to be involved in the choice about the range of options available; since family situations also present difficult ethical dilemmas for therapists in relation to confidentiality and privacy, this makes work with children and families very complex. Child and family assessment is a relatively recent activity handicapped by gaps in the knowledge base and splits among and between the various groups concerned, but principles for good practice can be identified, and Chapter 4 traces their origin and development in the literature.

Part II of the book shows what results when these principles are applied in practice. In order to present assessment as a set of practical and adaptable procedures, each chapter in this section concentrates upon a different aspect of the assessment process. The presentation is intended to emphasize practical explanation and discussion whilst also highlighting the principles which have guided the development of the approach.

Chapter 5 outlines the framework of ideas used to conceptualize family problems. The framework uses four perspectives upon the family, with a set of problem dimensions for each perspective. This helps to develop links between problems so that causal effects between individual and relationship difficulties can be perceived more easily. The developmental perspective is used to gain an overview which gives an understanding of the history and origin of problems as well as the type of broad pattern.

Chapter 6 examines the topic of preparation for family assessment. This is complex because family members often have different views, and the first part of the chapter examines ways to understand and work with patient views and motivations. Ethical dilemmas include dealing with privacy boundaries and conflicts of interest, welfare versus confidentiality, and dealing with unrealistic expectations. The wider system also has to be considered, and principles for convening family members are summarized. It is argued that an initial interview understanding patient and family views which prepares for a contractual assessment (utilizing formal assessment methods as the practitioner thinks appropriate) has a number of practical and ethical advantages. Effectively, this preliminary client-centred interview can be used to select more specific assessments if required. Finally, practical policies and procedures for preparation of families are specified.

Chapter 7 discusses the application of a family interview schedule and an accompanying rating scale which can be used to obtain a broader, comprehensive view of the child and family. This broader view is important because the level of public awareness about children's health problems (particularly mental health) is low, leading to a high rate of unrecognized problems. The interview has three key principles: the use of normalizing statements, which facilitate disclosure, prior to the probe questions; an emphasis on seeking permission to make enquiries; and a sequential progression into more sensitive areas.

Chapter 8 considers the use of other assessment procedures. It begins by describing the use of the original Darlington Family Assessment System package in a research project and the lessons that were learned for clinical practice from its use. The advantages and disadvantages of formal assessments are summarized. The second part of the chapter considers the issue of communication with children as a special topic and gives a summary of the main principles for effective communication. Finally the use of other more specific assessment procedures is considered and useful methods for clinical practice recommended. A selective and informed use of these methods can form the basis for a skilled and professional approach to assessment with children and families.

Finally, Chapter 9 examines the central issue of how information gained from the assessment can be used to determine a therapeutic strategy for a particular practitioner interacting with a family. Six stages are proposed as a framework for choosing a therapeutic strategy, which take into account the individuality of both practitioner and family. Each stage is considered in turn, with examples and guidelines for the practitioner. Giving an assessment back to the family in a collaborative, contractual, and empowering way is also very important. The use of a written report, using plain English and avoiding jargon, to follow up verbal discussions is recommended.

Part III of the book considers the relationship between science, assessment and clinical practice. Traditional scientific approaches to family assessment are difficult to apply because of the complexity of the variables involved, and the need for a pluralistic analysis. The assessment ideas and methods in this book are intended to provide this kind of analysis and function as an aid to training. The concept of clinical guidelines can be considered as a bridge between science and practice. Clinical guidelines are intended to summarize the literature in relation to good practice and good professional ethics, to be based upon the evidence about what procedures are effective, preferably to be applicable by multiple professions, and to encourage standardized practices. The book concludes by presenting a set of brief clinical guidelines for child and family assessment which summarize the approach described.

Historical overview

One purpose of this first chapter is to place this work in a wider context. As I write these words we are rapidly approaching the dawning of a new millennium which is, according to astrology, the age of enlightenment. Hopefully this will have begun by the time some of you read this. It seems to me that one of the things we are headed for is a more explicit and wider acceptance that our reality is infinitely complex and that there is no single thread of truth or theory that can help us in all circumstances. Human theories are limited by our own mental capacity and by the context in which they develop. It is helpful to bear this in mind in relation to the history and philosophy of science, psychology and therapy. Kuhn (1962) argued that science must be understood as a social activity in which disciplines develop their own (social) rules of practice. Observations are not simply made in a neutral, non-judgemental way; in fact they are profoundly influenced by the observer's preconceptions and underlying theoretical assumptions. Kuhn gave the name *paradigms* to these assumptions and the term has proved an enormously useful tool with which to compare different theories.

For a short and readable summary of the history of philosophy there are few better books than the novel *Sophie's World* by Jostein Gaarder (1996).

The implications for psychology of a more modern philosophical approach were summed up by Manicas and Secord (1983). They concluded that:

- theories merely represent the world
- the world is best viewed as a set of interacting, interwoven structures
- events are always the outcome of complex causal configurations at the same and at many different levels
- events are not predictable with certainty in the real world
- explaining the behaviour of a particular person requires not only psychological theory but also situational, biographical, and historical information.

In clinical psychology there has been a gradual shift over the last twenty years from purely 'objective' models based on learning theory towards cognitive, ecological and social models utilizing subjective and system theory concepts.

In fact what has been termed 'postmodernism' would take us much further. Postmodernism is a reaction to traditional conceptions of science which takes the view that objective knowledge is impossible; that every theory is relative, socially constructed and value-ridden. It has tended to result in a rejection of traditional methods to the extent that, for example, family therapists and others have had little interest in assessment because of the dominant idea that families socially construct their worlds. However, this throws the baby out with the bathwater. Traditional science certainly has limitations, and we need to be acutely aware of these limitations upon how accurate and confident we can be in our opinions and judgements about people and their families. Nevertheless to abandon the process of assessment completely is foolish, and also disrespectful to our clients or patients. Health problems do exist and are not always socially constructed. Consumer surveys also show that many people come wanting an *opinion about what the problem is*, rather than 'therapy'. Although we can never be totally certain of our opinions, in practice they are often helpful to others if they are based on knowledge, experience and sound and tested clinical assessment procedures. Although our reality and theories may be socially constructed, we cannot even begin to test and evaluate them if we abandon traditional science completely. The real lesson is that traditional science and postmodernism both contain some truth and have some flaws, and they can both be useful tools for the helping professions. I have to admit that I have viewed the avoidance of assessment by family therapists with some irony, particularly when the justification has been that of new knowledge. The paradigms of social constructivism can be seen all too clearly in cognitive therapy, which is nothing new. Twenty years ago clinical psychology abandoned assessment for a decade in its rush towards the role of therapist. The tide of history is such that trends are often repeated in different ways.

There are special difficulties to overcome within health and mental health. Bopp and Weeks (1984) pointed out that psychotherapy itself emerged in an era when mechanistic and reductionist assumptions were prominent and that most activity in the helping professions is still laden with those values and assumptions. Treacher (1984) has also pointed out how, from the end of the last century, psychiatry in particular and medicine in general have focused upon individual pathology following the 'miraculous' discoveries of the bacteriologists Koch and Pasteur. For many years this led to a total lack of consideration of the social and economic factors that influence illnesses. Only in relatively recent years have social factors again been given real consideration, and even then this knowledge has been ignored by a government whose ideology did not accept the evidence. For many years economic and political factors discouraged social medicine, and the impact of market forces in a capitalist society ensured that medicine remains geared to pathology and not to prevention.

However, other changes occurring within Western societies have created an ideological and political need to consider how the mental health of individuals relates to the forms of social organization available to the person. Greater geographical mobility resulting in a loss of extended family support;

changes in traditional gender roles; increasing divorce rates; and a developing awareness of child abuse have all contributed to a demand for knowledge of how families function and cope with their problems. Furthermore, a growing concern over the problems of large institutions has led to efforts to use the family and the community as resources in health care. The sheer economic cost of maintaining a palliative rather than preventive health system has become too much, so that a genuine effort is being made to shift to prevention rather than cure. Services are encouraged to listen to users. A big push is being made for services to incorporate knowledge and evidence into their practice rapidly, by developing and using clinical guidelines – otherwise it usually takes about twenty years for research evidence to become common practice. These trends are exemplified in current policies for mental health and learning disability. Therefore in a very clear way this work is problem-driven, since the psychology of the family has been much neglected. As health care models move to the community, the impetus to properly understand and assess families becomes stronger. This book was always intended as a set of clinical guidelines, and it is timely.

Similar trends can be seen in social policy. Recognition of children's rights has led to a concern for the welfare of children who suffer abuse or have other special needs, and the balancing of needs for family support and child protection has proved to be a very difficult one for social agencies and the law. Current procedures in the UK call for the coordination of health and social service agencies, which is difficult without a greater common ground in knowledge base and practical methods. The courts are generating a level of demand for high-quality assessment which far outstrips the supply of more specialist professions. The need for family assessment skills is therefore significant.

One final concept related to the process of change is worth mentioning. Bopp and Weeks also stressed how the development of knowledge often occurs through 'dialectics'. A dialectic refers to a process in which knowledge evolves through developmental transformations, often involving a struggle which occurs between interactive and often polarized concepts. For example, conflicts between behavioural and psychodynamic views of therapeutic endeavour have led to the growth of cognitive analytic psychotherapy which acknowledges and combines both views in a rather more sophisticated way. In a similar way, this work contains several dialectics. It seeks to build a bridge between science, academic theory and the practice of family assessment by presenting methods which are practical but which also relate to the knowledge base. It seeks to present psychological theory in a common language that can be used by other professions. It discusses the dialectic between individual and family models of psychotherapy and seeks to build a bridge between the two. I hope you, the reader, will find the effort worthwhile.

Part I

THEORETICAL
BACKGROUND

The next three chapters review the literature which is relevant to family assessment in three ways. Chapter 2 explores the concept of the family in order to illustrate why it is important to try to understand and work with family groups as well as with individuals. After considering the links between the development of individuals and families using the concept of the family life cycle, other models of family functioning are described and their implications for family work examined. The literature on families under stress is then surveyed, before examining the relationship between mental health and social relationships. A number of themes emerge; in particular that child development, family characteristics, and social relationships are intricately linked; that the family acts as a powerful mediating factor in determining how its members cope with a wide range of health and other problems; and that certain kinds of family characteristics can be delineated which appear to be useful for understanding whole family difficulties.

Chapter 3 examines how theories of 'psychotherapy' have changed and developed according to the key assumptions or paradigms (Kuhn, 1962) which underlie each particular theory. Understanding the paradigms that shaped a particular theory helps to grasp its main purpose and how it compares to other theories. In particular, after a brief description of general system theory some of the more common approaches to 'family therapy' are described in terms of their own particular paradigms. Each theory emphasizes different aspects of a problem. Similarly, there are a number of complex pragmatic issues that emerge in relation to therapeutic work with families. It is suggested that in order to overcome these pragmatic difficulties some rational means of matching particular problem situations to particular therapeutic approaches is required. This is the purpose of a proper assessment.

Having thus argued a case for working with families and outlined some of the difficulties of doing so, Chapter 4 concludes the review section by examining the current state of the art of child and family assessment. It is apparent that there is a paucity of systematic methods available for clinical and training purposes. This is for several reasons:

- the relative newness of the study of the family
- the family has tended to fall between traditional academic boundaries
- trends in professional psychology and family therapy
- the divide between academics and clinicians

The review concludes by discussing principles for better family assessment.

2

PSYCHOLOGICAL PROBLEMS, SOCIAL RELATIONSHIPS AND MENTAL HEALTH

The first part of this chapter contains a review and discussion of several theoretical models of family functioning. Most of these models contain an implicit assumption that it is impossible to understand psychological problems without reference to social relationships and therefore to the family. Evidence supporting this paradigm will be considered in the second half of the chapter.

Definition of the family

a group of people – united by ties of blood, marriage or adoption; who form a single household; in which they perform their respective roles of husband and wife, son and daughter, mother and father, brother and sister; creating a common culture

(North, 1980)

Sociologists tend to consider the family in terms of its functions in relation to society as a whole rather than to the individuals within it. In particular, the role of the family in the process of socialization of young children (developing general social controls by the internalization of social rules) has been well documented. In addition, cross-cultural studies show how roles and family structure vary according to cultural beliefs and customs. In contemporary Western society, there has arisen an acute awareness of the changing structures and roles within families in recent times. Greater social mobility arising from the industrial revolution has led to a sharp distinction between 'nuclear' and 'extended' families. Changing sex roles, greater longevity, and a greater diversity of values seem to have led to rising divorce rates and consequent increases in the numbers of single parent and step-families. Since 1976, even within the small population of the UK at least 150,000 children per year witness their parents' divorce, and will therefore spend some of their life with a single parent (HMSO, 1987). Finally, immigration into the UK has resulted in a multi-racial and multi-cultural society. The current diversity of family structure and function within post-industrial UK is enormous. In the next section, some perspectives upon the family will be presented which rely upon a normative viewpoint. Because of the cultural variations this is an over-simplification of extremely complex issues, but it is none the less very important.

Normative development : the family life cycle

The concept of the family life cycle derives from Erik Erikson who pre-sented a psychosocial theory of human development which emphasized 'the unity of the human lifecycle, and the specific dynamics of each of its stages, as prescribed by the laws of individual development and of social organiza-tion' (1963, 1980). In his theory Erikson attempted to link the development of the individual personality with socialization by describing eight stages of life. He described each stage in terms of the successful characteristic that is assumed to result from a proper resolution of the stage versus the problem-atic characteristic that results from difficulties encountered at this stage of life. The stages are summarized as follows:

STAGE 1: TRUST V. MISTRUST

Infants learn either a sense of basic trust in those who meet their basic needs for warmth, nourishment and protection – or a sense of basic mistrust in others if the needs are not met.

STAGE 2: AUTONOMY V. SHAME AND DOUBT

During the second and third years of life, the effectiveness and quality of parental control will determine whether the child learns to be confident and self-sufficient in basic activities, such as walking, feeding, toileting and talk-ing; or whether the child learns to doubt their own ability and to feel shame at any setbacks or failures.

STAGE 3: INITIATIVE V. GUILT

Once basic skills have been mastered then the capacity to act and develop a sense of initiative is required as children begin to copy more adult-like activ-ities. If the child is not encouraged, or is even actively discouraged from learning skills, a sense of guilt develops.

STAGE 4: INDUSTRY V. INFERIORITY

As the child enters a larger social world with the advent of school, a sense of industry and usefulness should develop if the child continues to receive proper encouragement. Difficulties at this stage are characterized by a sense of failure and feelings of inferiority relative to others.

STAGE 5: IDENTITY V. ROLE CONFUSION

With the advent of puberty and adolescence, the person begins to develop a recognizable self-identity in terms of sexual, personal and activity-related roles. How much these roles are supported by significant others determines the clarity and strength of self-identity versus role confusion.

STAGE 6: INTIMACY V. ISOLATION

This stage of young adulthood is usually characterized by a need to seek greater degrees of intimacy with peers, which normally leads to the finding of a sexual partner. The characteristic tension experienced between freedom and security is most often resolved when a suitable partner is chosen on a more permanent basis. Difficulties at this stage are therefore characterized by social isolation.

STAGE 7: GENERATIVITY V. STAGNATION

Middle adulthood is characterized by a period of productiveness, both in terms of work and often also of raising a family or teaching future generations in some way. Problems here are therefore reflected in a general loss of direction and energy.

STAGE 8: INTEGRITY V. DESPAIR

This final stage refers to later life where people generally try to make sense out of their lives, either coming to terms with what has happened to them or despairing at goals that have never been reached and questions never answered.

Although Erikson's theories were originally formulated from an individual perspective, subsequent writers have elaborated and developed them in relation to the life cycle of the family as well as the individual. The concept of the family life cycle has become a central one in many traditions of family therapy. Carter and McGoldrick (1980) published a classic collection of papers about the family life cycle which examined the applicability of the concept in relation to different life stages and types of families, as well as other special issues such as the impact of death and illness. In the same way that the individual life cycle can be divided into stages, so can the life cycle of families. A typical division simplified into six stages in relation to families with children would be:

1   Couple or family formation (marriage).
2   Birth of (first) child.
3   Individuation of the young child; going to school.
4   Individuation of the adolescent; puberty and sexual development.
5   Leaving home (separation from the family of origin by the children).
6   Older adulthood: for the parents, the 'empty nest' syndrome.

This particular scheme is a typical one which might be used to represent the family life cycle from the point of view of child-rearing. (Those working with the elderly would obviously require a radically different scheme.) For each stage of the life cycle, the family group as a whole has a number of basic issues which need to be resolved and which set the group as a whole, and the individuals within it, certain tasks. For a typical representation of the issues, tasks and typical problems encountered at five of the above stages of the family life cycle see Table 1.

The particular usefulness of the concept of the family life cycle is that it does give a clear standard against which to evaluate individual families. This uses the same principles as those used to evaluate a child's cognitive development by comparison with age-related normal abilities, although the comparisons are more complex. Hence, the family life cycle is a key concept with which to understand the psycho-social development of families and of the individuals within them. The way that the concept is presented in terms of the emphasis and elaboration of different life stages depends very much upon the interests of the presenter. Both Erikson, and Carter and McGoldrick, were more preoccupied with children's development than adults'. Levinson *et al.* (1978) elaborated the stages of adult psycho-social development, albeit in relation to men in particular. Sheehy (1976) popularized their ideas, and also added a female perspective, so that adult psycho-social development has now also been described in this way (see Table 2 for details).

Life is never quite that simple, however. For many families formed by second marriages, the whole concept of the family life cycle must be radically reformulated. Emily and John Visher (1980) pointed out in their classic work how much more difficult the life-cycle stages and tasks become for step-families, based on their own personal and professional experiences. The additional complexities of resolving separations and forming new boundaries with ex-spouses' families of origin, together with the complexity of forming new relationships with new spouses and their family of origin, makes the family situation fraught with problems. A growing percentage of British families are single-parent and step-families. Clearly the nature of the tasks at different stages of single-parent families will also vary considerably –

Table 1 The family life cycle

Stage of couple formation

MAJOR TASKS FOR FAMILY

Both partners move away from families of origin and towards each other to form the basis for a new family unit. This involves:

a) Balancing loyalties to partner, friends, families of origin and own needs.
b) Acceptance of some loss of individuality/freedom: which is replaced by a sense of belonging (complementarity).

Practical tasks

a) Renegotiate boundaries with previous social worlds so that the new social world is acceptable to both partners (preferably avoiding too much loss).
b) Adjust to a variety of unexpected differences and unmet expectations, caused by differences between the families of origin.

PARTICULAR TASKS FOR COUPLE

1 Establish sufficient intimacy to meet each other's emotional needs without 'smothering' the partner.
2 Resolve fundamental issues of power and dominance.
3 Accept, understand and tolerate the different emotional responses and style of partner.

Practical tasks

a) Ensure that personal space is available for communication between the couple.
b) Divide up responsibilities in a mutually acceptable way.
c) Establish a workable means of conflict resolution with partner.

COMMON PROBLEMS

1 Loyalty conflicts including
   a) Cutting off/rejection scenes.
   b) Intra-family conflict =
      'He's not good enough for you'
      'I'm going home to mother'.

2 'Grown-ups' who don't like the role
   e.g. Continuing assumption of responsibility for the couple or one partner by one or both sets of in-laws,
   or Spouse whose behaviour does not change after marriage.

3 Formation problems
   a) Closeness and distance: feeling lonely, frustrated, jealous or smothered.
   b) Power conflicts: overt conflict (chronic bitching) or covert conflict (tense atmosphere).
   c) Affective communication: e.g. affectional needs unmet, leading to accusations of selfishness versus demandingness.

Table 1 continued

Stage of the birth of the first child

MAJOR TASKS FOR FAMILY

Adjust to arrival of a new person and balance loyalties to self, partner and child.

Practical tasks

1 Reorganize nearly all patterns of family functioning.
2 Again renegotiate boundaries with social world (families of origin, friends and work).

PARTICULAR TASKS FOR PARENTS

1 Maintain intimacy in marriage while meeting the needs of the child.
2 Adjust to new role and responsibility as parent with resulting change in identity – plus implications for 'freedom', career, etc.
3 To love the infant, accept its biological dependency and its emotional responses.

Practical tasks

a) Coping with physical demands, tiredness, learning new skills, while retaining some personal space with partner.
b) Coping with extra responsibility, worries and establishing acceptable division of work with spouse.
c) Resolving differences in parenting style towards the child: and learning to understand the child's expression of needs, feelings and desires.

TASKS FOR CHILD (INFANT)

1 Formation of primary bonding with parents.
2 Implicit learning of family rules, particularly regarding social and emotional behaviour.
   N.B. Subsequent children born will require elder children to adjust to changes in the sibling system – and cope with

   a) jealousy,
   b) roles as elder sibling and the responsibilities that may go with this, and
   c) changes in emotional behaviour expected due to loss of status as 'baby of family'.

COMMON PROBLEMS

1 Loyalty conflicts
   Overt
   a) Complaints that the spouse is under- or over-involved with child or neglecting partner.
   Covert
   b) Complaints of decreased marital satisfaction (social activity, sex, communication or intimacy).
2 Coping with responsibility
   a) One or both parents depressed and overwhelmed by parenthood.
   b) Grandparents take over parenting.
3 Neglect of infant needs by one or both partners, e.g. husband escapes parenting by going out every night.

Table 1 continued

Stage of individuation of young child

MAJOR TASKS FOR FAMILY

1 Balancing the growing autonomy of the child with a sense of loyalty and belonging.
2 Maintaining a reasonable level of control – not burdening the child with responsibility ('missions') or expecting too little from child.
3 Allowing the child to experience and express a range of emotions so that the child recognizes the needs of self and others.
4 Encouraging the child to develop some independent behaviour and social activity outside the home.

PARTICULAR TASKS FOR PARENTS

1 Facing a sense of separation from the child – loss of intimacy and fears about welfare.
2 Both parents must establish clear age-appropriate rules and work together to
   a) regulate the child's behaviour,
   b) give a sense of value and achievement.
3 Encouraging the child to recognize others' needs but also to develop self-esteem so that the child does not sacrifice itself for others.

Practical tasks

a) Recognising and encouraging individual strengths and skills.
b) Encouraging play activity within and outside the home at an age-appropriate level.
c) Encourage acceptance of gender identity.

TASKS FOR CHILDREN

1 Facing the fears of new situations and gradually increasing separations from parents.
2 Adjusting to different rules and expectations of behaviour from peers and other adults.
3 Balancing own needs and desires with those of others: accepting and giving pain and anger.

Practical tasks

a) Learning to contribute and take responsibility at age-appropriate level.
b) Developing relationships outside family.
c) Accepting gender identity.
d) Resolving jealousy and rivalries.

COMMON PROBLEMS

1 Separation Problems. The child is commonly presented as the problem, although a parent may also present as anxious, lonely or depressed. Issues of loyalty and responsibility to parents may lead to school refusal: other children may present as regressed or psychosomatic.
2 'Power' Problems. A small child may be presented as a stubborn, rebellious 'little monster' or as too powerful in some other way – often when the parents covertly disagree.
3 Conduct Problems. Low expectations of the child and inconsistent control may lead to behaviour which ignores the needs of others.

Table 1 continued

Stage of individuation of the adolescent

MAJOR TASKS FOR FAMILY

1 Maintaining a degree of mutual loyalty, trust and respect between adolescent and parent(s) despite increasing distances in relationships: compensate for this by developing greater intimacy in peer group relationships.
2 Redefining issues of autonomy, control and responsibility.
3 Acceptance and facilitation of the changes in emotional behaviour required in movement from childhood to adulthood.

Practical tasks

a) Encouragement of greater freedom and privacy for adolescent.
b) Acceptance of puberty and impending sexual maturity.

PARTICULAR TASKS FOR PARENTS

1 Acceptance of the loss of the 'child' – loss of closeness, being needed and availability of adolescent.
2 Acceptance of loss of control – may include overt rebellion.
3 Tolerating disturbances in emotional behaviour as adolescent learns a new set of rules.

Practical tasks

a) Allowing the adolescent to make his own mistakes; encouraging autonomy.
b) Acceptance of adolescent's peer group.
c) Tolerating 'differences' which adolescent uses to differentiate self from family and parent identities.

TASKS FOR ADOLESCENT

1 Accept loss of parents as 'protectors' – cope with fears of loneliness, responsibility, sexuality, identity and autonomy.
2 Learning to assert oneself with peers and adults and to take responsibility for important decisions.
3 Learn to express emotions and needs in adult way – 'new rules'.

Practical tasks

a) Development and acceptance of sexual identity.
b) Completion of tests and 'rites of passage' in adolescence.
c) Develop confiding relationships with peers.

COMMON PROBLEMS

Struggles for autonomy:

> *Overt*
> Commonly a rebellious, poorly performing, or conduct disordered teenager is presented by parent(s) with the request to 'fix him'. The adolescent may resist or sullenly comply – but is usually fearful and ambiguous about growing up. He may be labelled as a 'changed personality'.
>
> *Covert*
> Here the teenager is tied to the family by loyalty or mutual consent. The problem may present as 'psychiatric', psychosomatic, school refusal, eating disorder or in a wide variety of ways. The symptom is best viewed as a way of expressing frustration while the teenager remains loyal to the family on the surface.

Family legacies and missions: Expectations about careers, responsibilities, and 'substitution' effects commonly create problems in adolescence.

Table 1 continued

Stage of departure of the children

MAJOR TASKS FOR FAMILY

1 To separate without breaking relationships.
2 Acceptance of greater equality between the parent(s) and offspring.
3 Developing some mutual understanding of what is owed and expected between the parents and the departed offspring.

Practical tasks

Re-organization of intra-family boundaries: this climaxes with the departure of the last child to leave home.

TASKS FOR PARENTS

1 Facing the pain of loss of offspring and 'empty nest'.
2 Acceptance of greater equality with offspring.
3 Re-examination of needs and limitations of self and marriage. Development of new focus or purpose may be required.
4 Learning to accept children's choice of partners as potential or actual relative 'in-law'.
5 Acceptance of probable new roles as grandparents.

TASKS FOR (ADULT) CHILDREN

1 Letting go of family of origin – facing loneliness and fear.
2 Coping with the responsibilities of housing, work and the social world independently.
3 Putting one's own development and needs before family loyalty.

Practical tasks

a) May involve adjusting to new rules if living with others.
b) Coping with mature social and sexual relationships.
c) Developing identity and priorities; choosing a style of life which suits their own needs.

COMMON PROBLEMS

'Binding': The young adult may present with vague neurotic or social problems, sometimes returning home repeatedly or simply unable to leave.
'Expelling': The young adult is thrown out and attempts are made to sever family relationships.
'Delegating': Another problematic form of leaving home in which the offspring is allowed to leave but only on condition they fulfil a 'mission'.

Parental Problems

Commonly the parent most involved with parenting presents with anxiety and/or depression. However, long-standing but covert marital problems often surface at this time.

Table 2 The adult (normative, heterosexual) life cycle – normal stages and crises in adulthood

Age or stage	General comments	Men	Women	Couples
20s 'TRYING OUT A LIFESTYLE'	After the internal turmoil of adolescence, there is a shift towards sorting out the exterior details of one's life – as part of the process of trying out a particular lifestyle. How this has been chosen, particularly in relation to one's parents' roles, is often significant. Often we attempt to be different, but the outsider can sometimes see a lot of similarity in basic roles, or assumptions about life.	For most men, this period is bound up with 'career' issues – or simply sorting a role as a worker and provider. Traditional cultural pressures to be strong and tough may conflict with changing expectations of males as partners and fathers. (Biological drives will lead to the majority trying out sexual roles and finding a partner by the end of this decade.)	Women may also be bound up with career issues in the 'educated classes'. However, traditional roles as care-givers are also influential, and are likely to cause internal or external conflict. Some women develop roles as care-givers explicitly with children, others implicitly with partners and others. Pressures to conform to this role expectation are intense.	Early marriage can signify a rapid transfer of dependency. (People who feel unable to pursue their own ambitions often attach themselves to a stronger person whom they can 'piggy-back'.) After the 'honeymoon' period, marital satisfaction can go through troughs and peaks if marital problems are faced – or gradually deteriorates if they are not acknowledged. Unacknowledged difficulties, or simple mistakes, can lead to separation rapidly after children arrive – (divorce peak 1). Mutual expectations of power, intimacy, and communication style are critical.

Table 2 continued

Age or stage	General comments	Men	Women	Couples
EARLY 30s 'RESTLESSNESS AND RESTRICTION'	A restless vitality wells up at the beginning of the 30s – usually to do with feeling restricted by the roles we have chosen for ourselves during the twenties. Parts of ourselves that we have 'hidden away' begin to make their presence felt, and many people 'change direction' in their career or family lives. People feel energetic and restless: others channel this energy into existing roles (e.g. by working harder). Unattached men and women begin to experience fears of 'ending up alone'.	For 'traditional' men, their previous preoccupation with career and 'strong' roles often means that they begin to be conscious of feelings of loneliness and vulnerability. Some men turn more towards their wife (wanting her to be a 'friend as well as a wife') and children. Others push these feelings away, and throw more energy into work or career: hence the stereotype of the intense, driven, careerist. Those more in touch with feelings will discover new creative channels for their energy – outside of work, sometimes in a positive way as a parent.	For 'traditional' women, their previous preoccupation with satisfying others' needs means that they suddenly become conscious of their own. They may feel an acute loss of contact with the world outside the family, a loss of confidence, and resentment to partners. Many women start or re-start work after children go to school, which can be a time of growth and development. Others are starting families as a 'mid-career' break.	Often the man's preoccupation with his own internal needs clashes with the woman's need to look outward and explore her own potential: conflict can result. Extra-marital affairs are common as restriction and restlessness is blamed on the partner. Marital conflicts put on one side because of young children may also surface.

Positive aspects can be that couples discover or rediscover each other as unique individuals rather than stereotyped expectations. |

Table 2 continued

Age or stage	General comments	Men	Women	Couples
MIDDLE AND LATE 30s 'ROOTING & EXTENDING'	Provided that the difficulties of the 'restlessness and restriction' phase have been faced and acknowledged, the adult moves through into a new phase of growth as they accept 'their other half', i.e. in themselves they acknowledge secret ambitions and wishes – their partners are accepted as complex individuals with needs of their own (not assumed to be the same).	For many men this phase of life is concerned with looking into the family and discovering a much greater capacity for intimacy and caring. Sometimes this feels 'too late', but many will become 'paternal' in work relationships as a compensation. High achievers who have continued to focus on work may face crises through neglect of other parts of their lives.	By contrast, women look more outward and as the children grow older they rediscover their enjoyment of an outer social world. Many more go back to work, or take up new work during this period. Hidden 'potential' in the female can surface with unsettling results on the partnership. Feminist issues can also surface as the woman gains maturity and confidence. It can be a liberating, and painful, time.	For many couples, intimacy is regained or rediscovered as the children grow older. A sexual life re-emerges, other past pleasures are rediscovered and often there is a greater acceptance of self and partner as they are ('warts and all'). For many others, this is a period of discovering, in a second partnership, that it *can* work after all! For a third group, the children growing up allows the issue of separation to be faced up to.

Table 2 continued

Age or stage	General comments	Men	Women	Couples
40s 'MID-LIFE CRISIS'	Biological changes and the realization that one is 'past half-way' begin to signal a need for psychological change. (Often the death of parents can also begin this process.) The tasks required to continue development are the acceptance of one's mortality, letting go of unrealistic dreams and obtaining a realistic view of one's achievements. Buried parts of ourselves demand to be included – and unresolved problems from earlier stages often surface. Sometimes they surface with a bang! (= CRISIS)	Many men experience a sense of 'time running out' as they struggle to resolve their hopes and dreams with reality. Suddenly there is a sense of fear and danger as one becomes the 'next in line' for ageing and death. Some men 'escape back to youth' by taking a new and younger partner. Others switch to teaching and helping others as a way of 'passing on' the hopes and ambitions they cannot fulfil. Others are forced to face what they have been avoiding.	Women, too, experience the problems of accepting the loss of youth. They may also experience a sense of 'too much time' as children leave home creating a void. Those women who can resolve this loss, and accept the loss of their bodies' creativity, may find a new outlet of creative energy. This is easier for those with jobs or careers, and those without either may suffer badly from the 'empty nest' syndrome.	The stress of this period, and diverging patterns of life, can often lead to 'temporary' separations. If there are long-standing differences the children's departure will allow divorce to occur. (2nd divorce peak) Other couples who resolve these issues successfully will find a new level of intimacy with each other as partners; as genuine friends, for life (now that there is greater awareness of what that means).

Table 2 continued

Age or stage	General comments	Men	Women	Couples
50s and 60s 'ACCEPTANCE AND RETIREMENT'	Continuing physiological changes create the need for changes of activity, habit, and lifestyle. However, (provided health is retained) this period usually signals a period of greater freedom from child-caring responsibilities. The role of grandparent is likely to be accepted. Finally, the formal retirement from work is likely to complete this succession of external changes that, essentially, prepare the person for old age.	Many men will find a new sense of freedom, and enjoy this greatly – and also enjoy a new companionship with their spouse as a result. Others will experience a profound loss of role and identities. Men may be more conscious of anxieties over health because of greater male mortality in this age range.	Many women will also experience a phase of liberation where freedom from other commitments can be used and enjoyed to the full. Health issues can be crucial as the menopause is faced. Women may also experience disappointment if their idyllic hopes of 'life together at last' are not fulfilled. Fears for their partner's health are likely to be stronger in women as men die earlier.	Couples who have negotiated the difficulties of the mid-life period together well may enter a phase of affectionate companionship in which they discover a new and greater closeness. Other couples manifest clearly unresolved problems, but their inter-dependence prevents or hinders separation. Increasingly, some couples choose to have 'semi-independent' lives rather than separate completely.

Table 2 continued

Age or stage	General comments	Men	Women	Couples
70s and beyond 'OLD AGE'	As the ageing process accelerates the tasks that have to be faced are: 1. Accepting a loss of strength and independence. 2. Accepting increasing bereavements among one's friends. 3. Accepting a degree of dependency upon others without becoming a burden. 4. Facing increasing vulnerability.	For men, facing their vulnerability is often difficult. For both sexes, this is a time for looking back over life and dealing with 'unfinished business'. Some find a new tranquillity.	For women, they are more often called upon to carry on living alone after the loss of their spouse, in increasingly difficult conditions. Nevertheless, many do – and find new strength in this independence.	Accepting and coping with increasing inter-dependency, especially if one spouse becomes chronically ill, is the major difficulty for couples.

depending upon such factors as the reason for loss or separation, how well that separation or loss is resolved, and the ages of the children at which it occurs.

Mrazek and Mrazek (1981) pointed out a further complication. They have observed how the impact of the birth of the first child upon the parents is very different depending upon the age and life-cycle stage of the parents (i.e. adolescence, young adulthood, or middle age). They describe differences in the development of the family arising from the effects of developmental changes in the children upon the parents. For example, when the children themselves begin to experience sexual awareness in puberty this may trigger very different responses from the parents depending upon the parents' own ages and feelings about sexuality at that point in time.

A number of authors (e.g. Jurkovic and Ulrici, 1985) have pointed out that early theorists adopted a rather undue emphasis upon separation processes in adolescent development. They point out that work with non-clinical families suggests that normal adolescents remain quite connected to their family. Although they may experience some family discord in early adolescence, the evidence is that they rarely 'separate' but rather become increasingly influential in decision making within the family, especially regarding decisions about the regulation of their own behaviour.

Other writers such as Carpenter (1986) have pointed out sub-cultural variations in family life cycles. He argued, in response to an article about intimacy as the core principle in marriage, that many working-class marriages in the context of dangerous occupations lack intimacy, primarily because a greater degree of solidarity among the workers themselves is adaptive for safety reasons (e.g. soldiers or coal miners). As we noted at the beginning of the section, cultural differences are also very significant. Hence there are a number of complicating factors which must be taken into account when using the life-cycle concept with individuals and families.

Nevertheless the transition point between each life-cycle stage represents, for a family, a natural developmental crisis at which considerable changes are demanded. Consequently, several writers (e.g. Barnhill and Longo, 1978) have suggested that families may present for help to professional agencies as a result of not being able to make the particular changes required by these transition crises. The issue of why some families cope with such changes and others do not is an interesting one. Boss (1980) pointed out that particular stress in families occurs whenever family boundaries and structure are reorganized after the acquisition or loss of a family member, and that family structures are constantly changing across time in order to facilitate task accomplishment while maintaining family boundaries. Like Haley, she concluded that an ambiguity in the power hierarchy resulting from all these changes was often a key factor leading to presentation for help. It is certainly widely accepted that, for certain kinds of problems such as those occurring in adolescence, an understanding of the normative role changes required is essential. Hence despite all of the above complexities the life-cycle concept is increasingly seen as important and relevant to therapeutic work. The concept has become such a fundamental one that L'Abate and Bagarozzi (1992) stated in their review of family assessment that any instrument used for diagnostic assessment with families should have its roots in a theory of family development across the life cycle. They also suggest that the instrument needs to be multi-dimensional in order to cope with the complexity of the issues that needed to be considered.

Other models of family functioning

There are a number of other models of family functioning. Walsh (1982) provided a comprehensive review of models of normal family processes. The word normal can be interpreted in a number of ways, so she began her review by pointing out four definitions of normality. These were in terms of:

- health or the absence of pathology
- a Utopian vision of the ideal or optimally functioning family
- a statistical average
- normal processes (e.g. the family life cycle).

As a further cautionary note she emphasized that what is functional for an individual may not be for the family; that what is functional at one stage of life may not remain so in the next; and what is normal within one family may be abnormal within a sub-culture or society; and that cultural norms may often lag behind events in a particular family which may reflect ongoing social changes. She then went on to review models of normal family functioning which have been widely used in clinical work and the following paragraphs incorporate her conclusions.

Psychodynamic psychotherapy and transgenerational models of family therapy both carry an explicit assumption that the parents' capacity to relate to each other and to their children adaptively is a consequence of childhood relationships in their own family of origin. Patterns of unmet needs and other kinds of implicit or unconscious 'relationship bargains' influence a person's choice of partner, their style of parenting, and their ongoing relationship with their partner. In these models there is a strong emphasis upon historical and cultural issues, and the unconscious transmission of values and problems from one generation to the next. Early attachments are assumed to be of crucial importance in determining patterns which are unconsciously repeated in subsequent relationships, and attachment theory (which will be described later in this chapter) has been influential. Although in these models the ideals of health or normality are not well defined, the critical aspects seem to be: first, to be lucky enough to have a stable and loving early life; and second, to develop an ability to recognize, accept (in oneself and others) and express a range of needs and emotions in order to cope effectively with life events. Hence there are implicit models of normative psychological growth and development within which the role of the emotions is crucial but which is also quite compatible with the life-cycle concept.

One of the clearest and most detailed models of normal family functioning provided by clinical theorists was the structural model. Minuchin (1974) defines the family as 'an open socio-cultural system in continuous transformation', i.e. undergoing development over time, through stages that require restructuring of the family. As such the family life-cycle concept is a central idea, and he also emphasizes that normality is not the absence of problems, by clearly illustrating the normal difficulties that occur and must be overcome in family life. Minuchin emphasizes the characteristics of families using the terms of system theory and in particular lays heavy emphasis on families differentiating and accomplishing tasks through sub-systems. He stresses the importance of power hierarchies, balanced closeness and distance in relationships, and the executive (decision-making) function of the parental sub-system. Although he states that no particular family style is inherently pathological the theory has implicit assumptions that an ability-related (thus, age-related) hierarchy is required. Additionally there are functional criteria which are summed up in Minuchin's statement that the task of the therapist is to create a 'workable reality'. Walsh concluded that this is an optimal model of normality, defined in terms of functional accomplishment.

The strategic models of family therapy generally assume that normal families are more flexible than clinical families, i.e. they use a larger repertoire of problem-solving behaviours. With this exception, strategic therapists attempt to adopt a 'non-judgemental' position with relation to normality. In other words, they suggest that each family should define what is normal and healthy for themselves, and that it is ethically wrong for a therapist to label a family as 'pathological'. However, many strategic therapists such as Haley (1976) clearly utilize normative concepts such as the family life cycle and acknowledge the importance of system theory in their understanding of family functioning. Haley himself suggests that certain family characteristics are more relevant to change (i.e. power, organization and hierarchy) and thus more useful for therapists. He stresses that this is not a theory of normality, but one of change. In doing so he argues that there is simply too much diversity among normal families to make clear statements about what characterizes normality. This absolute rejection of normative comparisons is also associated with some of the more recent brief therapy schools, such as solution-focused therapy (de Shazer, 1985). Although the ethical position appears attractive, the danger for therapists is that by avoiding normative comparisons completely they may blind themselves to real health problems which can only be detected using a knowledge of what is normal and what is unusual.

Early behavioural therapists also paid little theoretical attention to the question of what was normal in families – treating this more as an empirical question. They implicitly assumed a functional approach, in terms of whether behaviour was adaptive or not. A clear and sophisticated version of a behavioural approach to families was provided by the McMaster model (Epstein and Bishop, 1981) which utilizes six main dimensions of family functioning – problem-solving, communication, roles, affective responsiveness, affective involvement, and behavioural control (plus a global dimension termed general functioning). For each of these dimensions adaptive behaviours are defined, for example verbal communications may be clear or masked, and direct or indirect. Most effective and least effective behaviours are specified within the model (in this case, clear and direct verbal communications are most effective; masked and indirect, least). These operational definitions correspond to a description of an optimally functioning versus a multi-problem family. What made this model unusual was that it is founded upon a classic empirical study of non-clinical families. Westley and Epstein (1969) described the results of this study of 1,100 college students and their families, undertaken in the previous decade at McGill University, Montreal, as *The Silent Majority*. Their most important conclusion was that children's emotional health in these 'normal' families was most closely related to the quality of the emotional relationship between their parents. If the parents had a healthy relationship with each other (i.e. they met each other's needs and had clear identities) then this seemed to insulate the children from problems even when the parents had psychological problems themselves as individuals. They also attempted to measure a number of variables relating to individual family members and family life as a whole (using interviews, questionnaires and observer ratings) and concluded that the organizational, structural and transactional family pattern variables were more powerful in determining the behaviour of family members than were the intrapsychic variables that they measured. These conclusions emphasized the importance of relationships and shifted behavioural therapists to adopt more social perspectives.

In summarizing the clinical models, Walsh (1982) originally concluded that there is quite a lot of agreement among clinicians about what is adaptive. She suggested that the differences among models reflect a selective emphasis or focus on particular issues and that very few theorists explicitly refute or imply the reverse of another. In particular she stated that 'those who posit a model of optimal functioning are not in disagreement about the distinguishing features'. Although she was not very explicit about what these features were, the life cycle is a common theme among the descriptions which can integrate historical perspectives, current structure and functioning within the family, developmental perspectives on the individual and the family, and responses to life events.

A more recent edition of this work (Walsh, 1993) acknowledges that research over the last decade has led to a greater appreciation of the diversity of family life, and the importance of the social constructions of both family members and therapists. She points out the need to take a historical and cultural perspective which shows us that the nuclear family has rarely been the norm; changes such as dual earner families, increased frequency of divorce, and changing sex roles have to be considered. Also, social relationships and family networks are what we each believe them to be, rather than having an objective reality which is the same for everyone. Families can be said to consist of multiple perceptions of reality, engaged in complex developmental struggles. Nevertheless she argues that therapists cannot be neutral and must understand their own perceptions and bias rather than ignoring the question or pretending they do not exist. She suggests that there are three key domains which are family organization, communication processes, and beliefs.

Walsh also reviewed models derived from non-clinical theories and investigations. Another classic empirical study which compared a total of 103 normal and clinical families was published by Lewis *et al.* in 1976. In their conclusions they summed up the implications of their study for clinicians (p. 218):

> perhaps the primary finding of general concern was the affirmation of the clinician's need to be pluralistic in his conceptual bases, and in his observational methods and techniques of intervention.

The study itself began with the definition of the normal family in terms of not having an emotionally ill member; however, as the data were collected the writers moved to a definition of an optimally functioning system based upon the data they had collected. Their overall conclusion was that there was no single factor which was readily identifiable as critical for health and several dimensions needed to be considered. Within this text Beavers presented a chapter on the theoretical basis for family evaluation which he later elaborated and modified to produce an explicit model of family functioning using the concepts of competence and style (Beavers and Hampson, 1990). This model has been extensively used in clinical work and training. The competence dimension is intended to assess a global quality of health/competence, which is then applied to several dimensions and sub-dimensions:

- STRUCTURE of the family, including power, parental coalition and closeness
- MYTHOLOGY (beliefs and perceptions of the family)
- NEGOTIATION (in relation to problem solving)
- AUTONOMY, including clarity of expression, responsibility, and openness
- AFFECT, including range of feelings, mood and tone, conflict, and empathy.

The family style concept characterizes family systems as either centripetal (inward looking and internalizing in their beliefs, values, views and actions) or centrifugal (outward looking with tenuous boundaries, tending to look outside the family for key values, separate more readily, and act more as individuals). This is an interesting blend of systemic theory and practice-based ideas.

While clinically based workers derived models from their practice, many academic family researchers derived models based on theoretical ideas applied to large psychometric samples of normal or college populations. Moos and Moos (1976) produced a good example of a statistically derived normality based on questionnaire responses. Their 'typology of family social environments' utilized three main dimensions: relationships, personal growth, and system-maintenance dimensions (with a total of ten sub-scales subsumed under these). Even using this relatively simple typology, a cluster analysis on a sample of a hundred families identified six distinctive clusters of family types with a number of possible sub-clusters. The result might be interpreted as underscoring the variability of different family types, but the fact that these (and many other) results are derived purely from self-report data must necessitate some caution. It can only be concluded from these studies that the way families *see themselves* differs widely, and it cannot be assumed that these differences are observable.

Olson, Sprenkle and Russell (1979) produced another questionnaire-based statistical typology of family systems which has been updated on a number of occasions (e.g. Olson, 1986). This is known as the circumplex model which rests mainly on two orthogonal dimensions of cohesion and adaptability. The cohesion dimension refers to closeness and distance in personal relationships and ranges through disengaged, separated, connected and enmeshed relationships. The adaptability dimension refers to decision-making and problem-solving behaviours and ranges from chaotic through flexible and structured to rigid at the other extreme. Because the dimensions are assumed to be orthogonal, each with four anchor points, a typology of sixteen types of families is thus created. This model is probably the most clinically relevant of the theory-derived models. (A third 'facilitating dimension' of communication is also included in the later versions of the model and it is clear that this dimension has been superimposed in an effort to counter some criticism.) Although superficially neat and attractive, the model was described by Walsh as 'premature typologizing' or begging the question.

Perhaps what is really at issue here is the different purposes underlying different models of assessment. While Olson as an academic is searching for a general law (a model that can describe everyone in the population in the same terms) Walsh as a clinician is searching for a model which will help to describe and understand particular idiosyncratic behaviours (a model that can delineate individual differences). This paradigm difference underlies many divisions between researchers and clinicians. With such fundamentally different aims, it is perhaps not surprising that clinicians and researchers often disagree.

The importance of beliefs was mentioned earlier. Studies of normal families also show that there are wide differences in shared belief systems which affect behaviour. Reiss and Oliveri (1980) examined the ways that non-clinical family members constructed reality in a series of laboratory studies using family tasks with a sample of 400 American families of mixed race and class. In particular, they identified three major kinds of variation among families in the way that they approached the tasks. The first was their general openness to influence from outside of the family (supporting Beavers' concept of family style, and the distinction between open and closed family systems). A second significant variation that Reiss and Oliveri discovered was differences between families in the way that they relied upon individual, as opposed to group, efforts in problem-solving activities. The third major source of variation among families was the level of conviction that the problems could indeed be solved (optimism v. pessimism). Reiss and Oliveri explained these differences in family behaviour in terms of underlying paradigms which family members shared. In this work the paradigms are inferred from observations rather than reported directly. Nevertheless, assuming these inferences are correct, then each of these shared beliefs would have major implications for clinical workers in their problem-solving activity with families.

Wertheim (1975) summed up one of the critical theoretical issues involved in understanding idiosyncratic aspects of family systems. In considering families from a system point of view, she stressed the need to look at higher-level system rules within the family. The concept of the idiosyncratic 'family rule' appears to be an extremely useful one with which to compare different families. Ford (1983) also wrote about the importance of shared family rules in shaping behaviour within the family. He suggested that these shared rules can be considered to be one of the most important ways to understand the differences between family systems. In their classic work, Watzlawick *et al.* (1967) pointed out that when assessing communication it is sensible to concentrate upon rules which govern the expression and regulation of 'meta-communications', as these rules will in turn govern the kinds of social transactions occurring in the family. Emotional communication appears to play a central role in this respect. Middleberg and Gross (1979) devised a procedure to assess family rules about emotions in samples of clinical and normal families. Their results supported the notion that emotional rules could be measured and that they tended to be shared within families.

Walsh concluded her first review (1982) by stating that:

- an immense diversity existed among normal families
- experience of non-clinical families underscores the need for multiple

dimensions to be used in order to understand families and their functioning

- there are distinctions between well-functioning and dysfunctional families but that these are exceedingly complex.

The more recent conclusions (1993) add that:

- family functioning and structure, communication processes, and family members' perceptions and beliefs all need to be considered
- the therapist also constructs reality but we should be aware of what we are doing rather than blinding ourselves to our own bias.

The literature also has a recurrent developmental theme in which the family life cycle is used to understand important processes in relation to the individual and the family.

The characteristics of families under stress

The impact of these disorders and even the ensuing treatment can have profound and disrupting effects on the psychological well-being of the family of the chronically sick child.

(Fielding, 1985)

This section will examine the evidence regarding the effects of various kinds of stresses upon families in order to demonstrate the importance of considering family phenomena, and also draw some conclusions regarding the types of phenomena that most clearly identify distressed families.

One of the most severe stresses that a family can suffer is that of chronic illness. In her review of the psychological effects of chronic illness in children Fielding concluded that the degree of family reorganization required by the illness is often profound, affecting financial, time, school and peer group issues as well as emotional and interpersonal ones. Some families appeared to cope with these problems fairly well, but in others problems occurred which were related to three factors – the nature and fluctuating course of the illness, the nature of the family, and the developmental age of the child and consequent nature of the developmental tasks disrupted by the illness. Pless, Roghmann and Haggerty (1972) studied a sample of 1,756 American families of mixed race and class who had school-age children with chronic physical disorders. They found that the frequency of psychological maladjustment, as assessed by self, parent and teaching ratings, was found to be 10–15% greater among the chronically ill than among healthy controls. Furthermore, they found that those among the chronically ill group who were at highest risk for psychological difficulties could be identified by consideration of the quality of family life as measured by an index of family functioning. Hence the ongoing quality of family life can be considered as a clear vulnerability factor in terms of how well people cope with chronic illness conditions.

Other authors have emphasized the important relationships between the family and disease processes in different contexts. For example Litman (1966) described the importance of the family in aiding the physical rehabilitation of orthopaedic patients suffering an accidental and sudden onset of some kind of handicap. Chen and Cobb (1960) reviewed the evidence linking health and disease with adverse family circumstances. They pointed out a striking association between, for example, tuberculosis and both childhood deprivation and current marital status. It would be naïve to infer direct causal links, but one would certainly expect that disease in a family member would have an effect upon the family system, and conversely that the strengths available in the family system will partly determine an individual's ability to resist or cope with the disease process.

Meissner (1966) reviewed family dynamics and psychosomatic processes and concluded that the 'evidence for the association of emotional maladaption and physical illness is overwhelming'. Grolnick (1972) also suggested that families with a greater rigidity of structure were associated with increased psychosomatic illness and perhaps with chronicity of illness. One of the best theoretical articles on this topic was written by Rosen, Kleinman and Katon in 1982. They presented an excellent model of the relationship between illness conditions and psychological and family factors which they termed a 'biopsychosocial approach'. As General Practitioners, they begin by pointing out the high proportion of time taken up in primary care by patients with psycho-social complaints. They suggest that this is because for some people somaticization is often the only legitimate and culturally sanctioned means of seeking and receiving care from the family, social network and medical system. In their discussion of the socialization processes which lead to this state of affairs, they point out that initially infants will not distinguish between physical and psychological distress. It is only through the reaction of adults that the language to label distress is learned. In some families distress may be labelled entirely in somatic terms. Furthermore, in some families somatic ills may elicit nurturance while emotional distress will elicit little, or even a negative response. As a result, emotional and physical problems can become confused within the child, a psychological language for internal mood states may not develop, and emotional problems may be constantly somaticized.

Families whose children are handicapped from birth also suffer severe stresses. Clearly a child with severe developmental delay cannot be expected to progress through the normal changes of the life cycle. If they are to remain together the family must adjust to this. Foster and Berger (1985) reviewed the research on families with handicapped children with particular reference to the psychology of the families. Unfortunately they report that the research is characterized by a number of basic methodological weaknesses (such as a lack of prospective studies) and that most research has focused so much upon the individual that it cannot stand conceptually as family research. What evidence is available is somewhat contradictory – for instance, random samples of families with handicapped children have generally found minimal differences from appropriate control groups. However other clinical studies have reported weak parental sub-systems, parent–child coalitions, marital distress, reality distortion in reference to the handicapped child, and other problems. Similarly, while some studies have reported themes of stress and frustration and identity problems in the siblings of handicapped children, others have reported that siblings can be quite well adjusted with findings of greater maturity, responsibility, and increased concern for others. It, therefore, seems quite probable that most families cope but some do not, and that the nature of the family organization prior to the problem of handicap is a crucial factor which determines the family's coping ability. Research on the processes within families which lead to positive and negative outcomes is required. In general, Foster and Berger conclude that a comprehensive view of families with a handicapped child should take into consideration the family's ecological context, its organizational structure (including the sub-systems and their pattern of organization) and aspects in relation to the family's life cycle.

Drug abuse is a problem which has come to be accepted as having little association with individual psychopathology (HMSO, 1982). However in a detailed study Stanton et al. (1980) examined the characteristics of the families of heroin addicts before and after structural family therapy. They concluded that addict families, compared to normal families, showed rigid stereotyped patterns of interaction characterized by open conflict. In addition, the pattern of structural roles within the family tended to be that of a peripheral father and a central, dominant mother. As a result of therapy, the families apparently became more cooperative and less conflictual, with the fathers generally becoming more involved in the family following therapy. Furthermore, they demonstrated a link between successful therapy outcome and observed changes in family interaction patterns. Coleman, Kaplan and Downing (1986) have also suggested that heroin addiction is associated with problems of separation and loss in the life cycle, since many addicts repeatedly separate from and return to their families.

Berger (1985) reviewed the available evidence on the characteristics of child-abusing families. As with the work on handicap, there were numerous methodological flaws in much of the research; but she drew the following conclusions:

- although a number of characteristics of the parent have been identified (such as personality or psychiatric problems; a tendency to view the children's behaviour as intentional; and high expectations of the child) none of these characteristics are necessary or sufficient. It is important to examine the family as a whole.

- parent–child interactions are often characterized by less reciprocation between mother and infant, higher verbal and physical aggression between parent and child, and higher rates of coercive behaviour by the parent accompanied by non-compliant responses from the child. In general, there is a clear tendency towards punitive control of the child's behaviour. She concludes that abuse 'may occur within the context of certain types of ongoing interactive patterns within the family that escalate into abusive episodes'. Patterns of child rearing are often inconsistent, with positive reinforcement for aversive behaviour.
- in terms of marital relationships the most common characteristics are conflict or patterns of dominance and submissiveness, although again these are not necessary or sufficient conditions.
- the family relationship with the environment is characterized by isolation of the nuclear family unit, a tendency to suffer environmental stress, and negative life events. The best research also considers the interactional effects between these factors, e.g. that a life crisis has a stronger impact on a parent who experienced punitive discipline in childhood.
- although the notion of intergenerational transmission of child abuse is often accepted as axiomatic, the evidence is not strong. It is suggested that this is only one of a constellation of variables that need to be considered.

Berger concludes that abusing families are a heterogeneous population and that there should always be a very careful assessment of which particular variables are involved in a given situation.

Despite Berger's scepticism about its universal applicability, for certain families the concept of 'the cycle of deprivation' (HMSO, 1973) seems to be quite appropriate. The concept is a very interesting one in that it is effectively a systemic concept suggesting a repeating circular causality from one generation to the next. Jenkins (1983) termed this kind of family as 'underorganized' and outlined the usefulness of a family life-cycle framework in working with such families. In addition, his very use of the term makes it clear that he thinks the structural disorganization of deprived and abusing families is critical in understanding their problems.

Perhaps the most serious problem of all is family violence (since the majority of murders occur within a family system). Interestingly, Kirkland (1982) concluded that recent research findings in the area of family violence suggest that, although many factors may be involved, violence is most often a product of the learning history of the batterer rather than a product of current marital or family system dysfunction. Hence individual historical information should never be overlooked when assessing families under stress.

There are, therefore, a number of themes which emerge from the literature about the characteristics of families under stress. First, it seems beyond doubt that the quality of family relationships can mitigate the effects of a whole number of different life problems upon the family system as a whole and its consequent ability to cope with the problem. Some kinds of family characteristics which appear to be important to consider in this respect are:

- characteristics regarding the family structure, both in terms of the patterns of attachments within the family and also the nature of control, authority and power.
- the rules governing communication within the family appear to be of crucial importance; rules about emotional communication appear to play a central role in the somaticization of problems.
- a number of authors also underscore the importance of understanding the family system in relation to the wider environment, to developmental stages (the family life cycle) and to other historical information about family members.

Social relationships and mental health

Neither the traditional medical assumption (mental illness is purely within the individual – a biological or psychological matter) nor the sociological assumption (social factors are primary) should be adopted. The relative importance of individual, biological, and social factors must be studied in each case.

(Sanua, 1985)

This section is a difficult one because there is a veritable quagmire of semantic confusion associated with two key issues.

The first issue surrounds the question of whether various phenomena such as anxiety, depression and schizophrenia can be appropriately conceptualized as 'mental illnesses'. In this respect, it is worth examining the logic of Akiskal and McKinney (1975) who elaborated a holistic model for depression. In doing so they pointed out that problems can be approached at various levels of analysis (i.e. at a biological, an individual psychological or intra-psychic level, a social psychological level, and a sociological level). They pointed out that for each individual person, there are likely to be a number of factors operating at *each* of these levels which will contribute to produce the particular problems of an individual case. Furthermore, it is erroneous to assume that in all cases one level has any *general* primacy over another. (Although for a certain case one factor on a particular level may be very important, perhaps more important than all the factors operating at other levels.) It is also sometimes erroneous to presume *causal* assumptions between factors operating at different levels, for example that physiological disturbances in depression are 'caused' by cognitive phenomena or vice versa. By using the concept of levels of analysis, it is clear that the same event may be manifested in different ways at different levels – each of which utilizes different *types* of descriptions. It is important to consider for each individual situation what factors are operating on different levels (see below) and how they relate to each other. Good historical detail is necessary to do this.

Level	Examples of factors
BIOLOGICAL	Genetics, illness
INTRA-PSYCHIC	Temperament, personality, internal conflicts, cognitive schema
FAMILY	Attachment patterns, communication, power hierarchy
SOCIO-CULTURAL	Peer relationships, sub-culture, stigma and persecution

The second issue arises from the assumption of Cartesian dualism which is implicit in most medical and psychological theory. The success of the physical sciences has led to an assumption that somehow objective physical models of reality are more valid than psychological ones. Perhaps the best challenge to this implicit assumption was made by Bateson (1970) who pointed out that the mind, unlike the brain, is not contained within the skin (see the next chapter).

Both psychology and psychiatry tend to use language and paradigms which focus upon physical and intrapsychic events and in doing so tend to overlook interpersonal and communicational phenomena. This makes it inherently more difficult to demonstrate the links between social relationships and mental or psychological health.

However, perhaps the single most influential theory in this respect has been that of attachment theory. Bowlby (1988) summed up the implications of his theories for clinical work in a modest way but his ideas have profound implications for health and education. He argued that attachment behaviours are a distinct internal motivational control system which is as important and powerful in biological terms as feeding and mating. The goal of this motivational system is perceived security (and the safety of the organism from a biological point of view) since parents protect their young from danger. The attainment of a secure base and healthy attachment allows the infant to indulge in exploratory behaviour (play, learning and adaptive development). Thus a homeostatic balance occurs between attachment, perceived as security in a relationship with a carer, and adaptive development, perceived as exploration. This allows healthy individuals to develop to their full potential. To put it another way, human beings are genetically programmed to seek and maintain mutually satisfactory social relationships in order to develop to their potential. Bowlby also explored the effects of separations from the primary attachment figure and suggested that these normally led to emotional disturbance such as chronic anxiety or angry behaviour. He emphasized the importance of internalized models which regulated the attachment process and subsequent behaviours. For example, an attachment figure who gave comfort appropriately would be perceived as loving and because of the reciprocal nature of the relationship the child would perceive himself as worthy of love. A parent who did not comfort would be perceived as rejecting but the child would also perceive itself as unworthy of love. This was the mechanism by which early experiences played a significant part in the development of the personality and contributed to adult problems. Bowlby also discussed the effects of a subjective experience of loss (which might be due to a lack of care from a parent figure, and not necessarily a bereavement) in causing sadness and depression. The severe impact of loss results from the internal models needing to be resistant to dramatic change (because of an inherent biological need for stability). Clearly attachments need to be strong for survival reasons, but this means that the organism will suffer when attachments are disturbed or broken. Over the course of time, Bowlby's theories have been modified in the light of later evidence and criticism. Certain basic parts of the theory have required qualification. The theory was derived after the Second World War at a time when it was politically important (to men) to encourage women to go back to child rearing. It is now accepted that every separation does not necessarily involve bond disruption and the two cannot be regarded as synonymous. Although there is normally one main bond, children usually develop bonds with several people. The main bond may not be with a biological parent, nor even with the chief caretaker, and it certainly need not be a female. Children also have fathers. Furthermore, Lewis and Rosenblum (1975) underscored the importance of peer attachments from an early age in the development of sociability.

However, given these and certain other qualifications it is clear that Bowlby's ideas have a lot of support from ethological, animal laboratory, and human studies (such as Harlow's research with rhesus monkeys in 1958 and mother–infant studies such as Belsky, Rovine and Taylor in 1984). Bowlby argued that the nature and stability of early attachments was of crucial importance to normal psychological development and mental health in adulthood. Strong evidence for his ideas was provided by Ainsworth with studies of infants in the 'strange situation' (Ainsworth et al., 1978) and this was followed by a proliferation of research which has eventually led to ways of understanding attachments in adults as well as children (Main and Goldwyn, 1984). Bretherton and Waters (1985) reviewed the evidence in support of attachment theory and listed a variety of evidence derived from studies of adaptation, maladaptation, maltreatment, intergenerational transmission and cross-cultural studies of infant-rearing patterns. The most powerful evidence derives from studies utilizing the 'strange situation' procedure, which enables classification of a child as securely attached, avoidant or resistant. A number of studies have shown not only that these patterns of behaviour are predictable from earlier styles of interaction between the mother and the child as an infant, but also that classifications of children's attachment as toddlers (12–18 months) is predictive of a whole variety of cognitive, emotional and social aspects of behaviour at 4–5 years of age and probably beyond. Recent work in attachment theory emphasizes the importance of internalized models which regulate the attachment process and influence the development of defensive processes and behaviours. For example, Crittenden (1992) gives detailed descriptions about how various types of attachment processes and defensive behaviours manifest themselves in pre-school children. In an earlier article (1981) she also describes a coding system which can differentiate abusing, neglecting and other mothers on the basis of their interaction with infants less than two years old. Some of the clinical implications of attachment theory were summarized in a collection of work edited by Belsky and Nezworski (1988). Steele and Steele (1994) have attempted to develop connections between adult and child attachment patterns and this clearly has important clinical implications for work with parents. A recent collection of work on the assessment of parenting (Reder and Lacey, 1995) presents powerful arguments that link attachment behaviours to the family system via circular patterns of behaviour within family relationships which are assumed to originate from attachment regulation processes. This is a very productive field which is beginning to influence ways of working preventively with parents and with families at risk.

C. Murray Parkes (1972) echoes much of what Bowlby suggests about the effects of loss in his work describing the various stages and manifestations of the adult grief reaction in bereavement. Indeed in recent times the effects of unresolved grief in producing problems many years after the event has become publicly recognized in relation to peri-natal deaths, emphasizing the power of attachments in adults as well as children.

One key feature of Bowlby's ideas is that in a healthy parent–child attachment, there should be a balance of alternating closeness and distance behaviour. The care-giver has a dual role which is to be available and responsive as and when needed to give protection, nurturance and emotional care to the child; and also to encourage exploratory behaviour yet be available to intervene judiciously should the child be heading for trouble. This feature of healthy relationships (closeness and care-giving alternating with respect for individuality and autonomy) relates to a number of other clinical concepts. For example, Minuchin's terms of enmeshment and disengagement can easily be understood in attachment terms as representing respective polarities whereby only attachment-seeking and exploratory behaviour respectively are encouraged. Several authors have made explicit links between family systems and attachment theories. Heard (1982) used a concept of the 'attachment dynamic' to explain a number of properties of families as systems, and L'Abate (1985) used the concept to suggest how an attachment process could result in distance regulation within families. He suggested that consistent negative interchanges following unsuccessful attachment-seeking behaviour helped to create a fear of intimacy, but also brought other members of the family together to comfort each other following the negative interchange. More recently John Byng-Hall (1995) has produced a definitive text relating attachment theory to clinical work involving families.

In summary, there is a great deal of evidence for the basic contentions of attachment theory although the theory has had to be qualified in many ways over the years. The theory appears to form a useful basis with which to conceptualize family phenomena as well as offering the clearest model of how loss and disrupted social relationships can lead to problems in psychological and social development, with consequent implications for 'mental health'.

Although there have been some trends towards using social models in psychiatry, resistance to social models has been quite intense because of the prevailing culture of diagnosis by category in medicine. One of the more significant acceptances of the necessity for social aspects to be incorporated into psychiatric models occurred in child psychiatry when Rutter, Shaffer and Shepherd produced a multi-axial classification scheme for psychiatric disorders in childhood and adolescence as long ago as 1975, consisting of five axes:

1 Clinical psychiatric syndrome
2 Specific delays in development
3 Intellectual level
4 Medical conditions
5 Associated abnormal psycho-social situations.

The use of a psycho-social axis within formal psychiatric classification provides an explicit acknowledgement by the psychiatric profession that a child's mental health cannot be considered properly without reference to family social relationships.

In relation to general behaviour problems in children, Richman, Stevenson and Graham (1982) made a five-year follow-up study of a large sample of three year olds. First, they found that severe behaviour problems in young children were not only common but extremely persistent (61% of those identified at the age of three were still having problems five years later). Furthermore, they found that currently disturbed family relationships were the strongest predictor of behavioural problems in children. Although social disadvantage was not a significant predictor on its own, when it was combined with family relationship disturbance then this combination was highly predictive of behaviour disturbance in the children.

Steger and Kotler (1979) reviewed the relationships between children's problems and the quality of family life. They stressed the importance of resources (in terms of work, relatives, friends, the extended family and the general socio-economic context) as critical factors in determining whether problems are coped with or produce a developing spiral of emotional disadvantage and conflict. As well as these current factors, they also suggested that interpersonal difficulties or conflict in the lives of the parents before marriage could severely constrain the parents' own psychological development. This would in turn affect the personal resources which are available in coping with the marriage and other critical stage transitions and life events in later stages of their life cycle. The breadth of their article makes it difficult for them to justify all their conclusions in detail but they represent a neat integration of a number of themes in the family literature.

In the field of adult psychiatry, Brown and Harris (1978) demonstrated the overwhelming importance of a confiding relationship in protecting women from vulnerability to depression. They also demonstrated a number of other factors which predisposed women to depression, including social class, and their work forms one of the most powerful pieces of evidence supporting the importance of social factors in mental health. In a follow-up study Brown and Prudo (1981) found that in rural settings integration into a traditional way of life was a greater protective factor than social class in the normal sense. Caplan (1981) reviewed a number of studies of stress involving both mental and physical illnesses and concluded that social support was crucial in enabling individuals to overcome the original stress. He concluded that 'empirical researchers confirm that exposure to high stress by individuals receiving adequate support does not increase the risk of mental and physical illness'. The theme that social support in the form of a satisfactory network or family can insulate individuals against the most negative effects of physical and mental health conditions is an extremely important one. In stating the case for the importance of social relationships in this way, the trap of erroneous or extravagant cause–effect assumptions is avoided. Claims about what really causes problems is a source of much professional conflict between psychology and psychiatry. Psychological models have been more warmly welcomed in relation to physical health problems – what has come to be termed behavioural medicine – where causative factors are not claimed or implied by psychologists, so that they do not threaten the basic role of physicians in the same way as they may be viewed in psychiatry.

Even in conditions such as schizophrenia, the need to consider social factors in treatment has been demonstrated. Studies of communication deviance in families with psychiatrically ill members initially demonstrated links between psycho-social phenomena in relation to serious psychiatric illness. Singer and Wynne (1963) published a classic study in which the parents of psychotic offspring were reliably differentiated from those of non-psychotic offspring by the patterns of communication used by the parents. Doane concluded in a review of the communication deviance literature (1978) that disturbed families were 'marked by a preponderance of parent–child coalitions and a corresponding weak parental coalition, as well as a conflicting marital relationship'. She also suggested that families of delinquents tended to be rather rigidly organized whereas families of schizophrenics tended to be characterized by unstable relationships and competition between parents for the child's support in dealing with marital conflict. Doane *et al.* (1981) attempted to assess the role of family communication in the development of schizophrenic-type disorders prospectively. They measured parental communication deviance and the parents' style of affective communication. Five years later, they found that an index using a combination of both variables statistically predicted the development of schizophrenic-type disorders.

The concept of expressed emotion or EE (Vaughn and Leff, 1976) has proved extremely useful in demonstrating psycho-social factors associated with psychiatric illness. There are in fact five EE scales, which measure criticism, hostility, emotional over-involvement, warmth, and positive comments (of which the first three scales are most important in classifying families as high or low risk). The classification appears to be a potent predictor of relapse rate in schizophrenia in particular. Miklowitz *et al.* (1984) also demonstrated that there was a clear association between observed family processes (in the interaction between the parent and a young schizophrenic offspring) and the measurement of EE in the parent. In particular, high EE parents exhibited more negatively charged emotional verbal behaviour in direct transaction with their offspring than did low EE parents. Some of these high EE parents were distinguished by frequent use of critical comments during the interactions (suggesting a high degree of control) whereas other high EE parents used a more intrusive, invasive style of interaction with the offspring (over-involved parents). Falloon *et al.* (1982) have also shown that family environmental stress increases relapse rate in schizophrenia. Using a combination of behavioural and family therapy approaches, they reduced the relapse rate significantly by intervening with the families of schizophrenics. Leff *et al.* (1982) demonstrated similar effects; although their remediation package was based upon psycho-educational principles rather than upon behavioural and family therapy. Nevertheless, it seems quite clear that social and family factors, whether or not they play any causative role, can be extremely important in determining relapse rates and therefore the success of reintegration into the community for young people after serious mental illness.

There have been a number of criticisms of the EE work:

• although some relatives may be critical, hostile or over-protective when the illness is initially discovered, they may display lower emotional involvement as they adjust to the problem. It could be that the EE measure simply reflects a response to the severity and progression of the illness.

43

- labelling families as high or low EE adds to the danger of blaming the families for the problem or illness.
- though EE predicts relapse in the sense of a recurrence of positive symptoms (e.g. delusions and hallucinations), little is known whether EE in the relative predicts the recurrence of negative symptoms, i.e. lack of normal social behaviour.
- EE refers to one of three alternatives (either high emotional involvement, high criticism, or hostility, or some other combination of these three factors). In clinical practice it generates confusion to refer to high EE as if they are equivalent to each other, since each requires different solutions.

Nevertheless the great achievement of EE work has been to create a focus with which to examine the means of offering support to families who are coping with a psychotic relative. In the future it may well be confirmed that the EE measure is relevant for a number of other problems. Leff and Vaughn wrote extensively about the implications of the EE concept for family work in 1985.

It is also possible to look at evidence from the converse situation. Wynne, Jones and Al-Khayyal (1982) examined the presence of healthy communication patterns and other aspects of family functioning in families who were at risk of severe psychopathology in order to determine what promoted *healthy* functioning in the offspring. Their data suggest that when the parents work together as a pair and communicate clearly in a focused, well structured, flexible and task-appropriate manner their offspring are regarded as academically and socially competent. Hence, there is a growing recognition of the importance of social factors within the psychiatric profession.

A different type of evidence derives from work on social and cultural influences on psychopathology. Some theorists such as Cochrane (1983) have attempted to argue that mental illness is largely a social creation as it can often be viewed as a tactical retreat from a difficult situation. In their classic review of 1974, Dohrenwend and Dohrenwend lamented that the studies up to that date had not settled any of the basic issues about the role of social and cultural issues in psychopathology. They suggested that future research would not do so until it moves from cross-sectional surveys to experimental studies of a prospective nature. Nevertheless, they offered the following conclusions:

- that there probably were cultures that immunized their members against the development of certain types of psychopathology.
- furthermore, that it was likely that some types of psychopathology are differently distributed in contrasting cultural settings.
- in particular, people from different cultural and class backgrounds

express psychological stress in different ways (e.g. more or less somatically).

- there was no evidence for any higher overall level of psychopathology today than in the past.
- certain clear sex differences emerge which appear to be more consistent than social causation theorists have supposed.
- some of the most consistent results reported are to do with an inverse relationship between overall rates of psychopathology and social class, mainly in terms of personality disorder.

More recently Sanua (1985) was more forceful in putting the case for the importance of cultural factors in mental illness. He suggested that there were three reasons why clinical workers often fail to recognize the importance of these factors. First, during training psychiatrists and psychologists have very limited contact with sociologists and other social scientists. Second, cultural explanations for disease are unlikely to be popular since accusing a culture of being disease-enhancing is likely to provoke an extremely hostile response from those in power within that culture, and may lead to overt persecution. Third, grant-giving agencies tend to pursue traditional and primarily organic approaches.

However, despite all these obstacles, it is clear that there is an increasing body of evidence supporting the influence of early attachment patterns upon the subsequent behaviour and mental health of the individual. Patterns of attachments in families are therefore crucial. The network of social relationships is powerful enough to act as a critical factor in determining an individual's recovery from major mental health problems, acts as a powerful protective factor for other emotional problems, and in particular cases can be a causative factor for some mental health problems (but this is very unlikely to be demonstrable for all cases of a particular problem).

Summary

Bowlby's attachment theory gives us a very useful way of understanding patterns of closeness and distance in the development of family relationships and also explains the power of the drive for social relationships as a survival strategy. Another key aspect of family structure appears to be the nature of the power hierarchy and the type of authority used within the family. Communication processes are also highlighted as a key domain. The importance of emotion as a means of expressing basic needs can be seen for individuals (as in grief and mourning processes) and also for the family group as a whole, where emotions can be usefully considered as a crucial form of 'meta-communication'. As such it can be assumed that some of the most important rules by which families operate are those which regulate emotional behaviour. The cultural context, life stages, transitions and events need to be considered. Finally, the perceptions and beliefs of the family members must be considered carefully, since family members construct (multiple) views of reality. Therefore all these issues appear to be important ways of understanding how the family context affects the development of the child.

Another theme to emerge from the literature is simply the importance of family phenomena, because of the profound implications for the individuals within the family. Although attempts to link social relationships and mental health phenomena are fraught with various logical and semantic difficulties, it is clear that the ongoing quality of social and family relationships is a very powerful mediating factor which both protects an individual from and determines an individual's response to a variety of health and other problems. Therefore, there are a number of strands of evidence which suggest that we should always consider family (or social network) and historical factors when assessing the problems of 'an individual', especially a child or young person.

In looking at the literature about human relationships, health care and the family a number of themes emerge which are important for family assessment:

- several authors highlight the need to take a developmental perspective which is exemplified by the family life-cycle and life-stage concepts
- because the distinctions between healthy and dysfunctional families are very complex, and immense diversity exists, others emphasize the need to be pluralistic – to look at the family in a number of different ways using a number of different concepts
- certain themes can be discerned about what kind of distinctions are useful, including family structure, attachments, power, emotional regulation, external context, beliefs, life-cycle transitions and stressful life events.

3

PSYCHOTHERAPY – THE INDIVIDUAL AND THE FAMILY

> Psychotherapy – the treatment of emotional, behavioural, personality and psychiatric disorders based primarily upon verbal or non-verbal communication with the patient, in contrast to treatments utilizing chemical and physical measures.
> Stedman's Medical Dictionary (1976)

There are many definitions of the term psychotherapy, each of which reflects different prejudices. The one above was chosen because it gives a fairly wide definition both of the nature of the problems and of the process within which 'treatment' occurs. If the definition was to be modified to reflect a more broadly based and integrated approach then two changes would be required:

1 the medical emphasis inherent in the expression 'the treatment of' would be replaced with a more general phrase such as 'problem-solving in relation to'
2 the phrase 'and his or her social system' would be inserted after the word 'patient'.

The purpose of this chapter is to provide a context for the ideas in this book by briefly outlining broad trends in psychotherapy over the last fifty years. The concept of the paradigm will be used to summarize and compare some of the basic theories of individual and family psychotherapy. The development of family-based approaches will also be discussed in the light of system theory, and other more recent trends in the literature will be summarized. Finally some of the practical issues involved in working with families will be considered.

Core paradigms for psychotherapy

In 1982 Liddle pointed out some of the problems of an eclectic approach and suggested that all therapists should regularly clarify their theoretical position with respect to the following issues:

• their definition of therapy itself, and of the role of the therapist

- what behaviour is seen as normal and what is seen as dysfunctional (i.e. what theory of pathology is used)
- how the goals of therapy are determined and defined
- how change occurs
- is the therapy to be evaluated, and if so, how?

The following descriptions will make use of Liddle's five key theoretical issues, using them to specify some critical paradigm changes associated with some of the major theoretical contributions to the activity of psychotherapy.

For the purposes of this review we shall regard Freud (see *Complete Works*, 1966) as a starting point. Any interpretation of Freud needs to consider the technical aspects of his theories within his historical context, and consider the enormous impact of his ideas upon Western culture. As a doctor, he viewed psychotherapy analogously to other forms of medical treatment or healing. The role of the analyst was to use the scientific philosophy of the time (observation and deduction) to help the patient understand the roots of their problem in terms of feelings stemming from early childhood experiences and emotional conflicts. It was assumed that in experiential terms we never lose these earlier selves or memories but tend to bury them in the unconscious, sometimes in ways that prevent our own growth. It was assumed that reconnecting the person to their early memories and selves would produce insight, enabling the person to move on in their psychological development. His theories of pathology were developmental and social in their emphasis upon childhood and parental influences; but they were also characterized by an emphasis upon the unconscious (a radical innovation). A more modern experiential interpretation of Freud would stress:

- understanding and accepting the child within ourselves
- as part of this process, also accepting the intensity of our own feelings of need and vulnerability
- similarly, accepting other difficult feelings of pain and rage and other 'irrational' feelings
- realizing how we often keep these difficult feelings secret from our (adult) selves

It is assumed that most psychological problems have their root in some particular early trauma, and by helping the patient to understand and accept their feelings about this trauma the patient will be able to escape the past and move on in their emotional life. Freud relied exclusively on individual case study methods to evaluate his theories, and this has led many later critics to criticize his approach as 'unscientific'. This is in fact an unfair use of hindsight as his theories and methods are clearly within the scientific tradition and philosophy that was generally accepted at the time of his work.

A second major therapeutic tradition with a radically different approach arose from the work of early experimental psychologists who developed theories of learning and conditioning based upon work with animals. Behavioural therapists view psychotherapy as a process of re-learning which is environmentally controlled. The role of the therapist is therefore often to help the person change their environment in such a way as to help the individual learn a more adaptive behaviour pattern. Most behaviour therapists avoid labelling behaviour as pathological, on the grounds that an illness model is an inappropriate way to view learned behaviours. Change occurs in ways that are predictable using learning theory, and the focus of therapy is therefore much more pragmatic and based in the here and now. Several paradigm shifts are of particular significance. First, the focus of how the problem is defined shifts from the individual's history to the individual's current interaction with the environment. Second, the role of the therapist is not as a healer but more of a scientist and teacher, applying psychological principles. Third, the goals and methods of change production focus on changing the current situation directly, rather than producing indirect change achieved through a greater understanding by the person of their own historical context.

A third diverse tradition in psychotherapy (humanism) has its major root in Carl Rogers' client-centred therapy. Rogers (1951) viewed the process of the relationship between therapist and client as the most important consideration in psychotherapy, rather than the particular theories or methods used by the therapist. He suggested that warmth, genuineness and empathy were the essential ingredients which a therapist needed to contribute. His theories have an implicit developmental philosophy of pathology in that it was assumed that the influence of this positive therapeutic relationship would be to help move the client towards personal growth or 'self-actualization'. This is perhaps a long-winded way of saying that the care and love of the therapist within a safe and non-abusive relationship can cause developmental growth in the same way that good parenting does. Clients themselves are deemed to determine the goals of therapy and indeed the clients' view of the whole process is assumed to be of great importance in evaluating the therapy. Since this evaluation is necessarily subjective, Rogers represents a fundamental rejection of the scientific method (which he viewed as an inappropriate model for dealing with human problems). Therefore he represents a humanistic, subjective and existential paradigm in psychotherapy. For those who require more scientific evidence or proof of effectiveness, this seems rather like throwing the baby out with the bath-water. However, the real value of this approach is in emphasizing the critical importance of the therapeutic relationship and the client's own view of the situation.

Public demand for psychotherapy or counselling first arose in the USA where private psychotherapy became relatively fashionable in the first half of the twentieth century among the well-off. Since the Second World War and the advent of the national health service, psychotherapy of varying types has also become available and more widely used in Britain and elsewhere in Europe. Indeed, the current proliferation of the helping professions has led to a veritable industry in which a variety of alternative approaches has developed.

One of the most widely recognized modern approaches is cognitive behavioural therapy which developed from the rational–emotive therapy of Albert Ellis and was subsequently popularized by Beck and others (Beck, 1976). It has come to incorporate the behavioural tradition within a wider approach that focuses upon the ideas and beliefs of individuals as well as their behaviour. The cognitive approach assumes that emotional and other problems arise from unhelpful attitudes and beliefs which are central to the person's world view and which predispose people to suffer problems. A common example is the unconscious belief that if other people do not like you, this means that you are a bad or unworthy person. The therapist's role is to help the person discover, challenge and change these dysfunctional attitudes. Originally popularized by Beck and others in relation to depression in adults, the methods are now used widely for various problems and with all age groups including children and adolescents (see Reinecke, Dattilio and Freeman, 1995). The tradition provides particularly potent methods of psycho-education with young people, who are naturally very receptive to new learning at this life stage.

Family therapy is the other major therapeutic framework, which will be examined in more detail later in this chapter. Nichols and Everett (1986) identify three major sources for the family therapy movement. The first of these was an overt public demand for marital counselling and therapy which began in the USA in the first half of this century. Because of the dominance of the psychoanalytic model in the medical world, which discouraged such unorthodox practices as seeing spouses, most of this work took place in educational settings under the guise of 'counseling' rather than 'therapy'. Nevertheless, this was an extremely significant development since the focus of human problems was for the first time clearly conceptualized as belonging to a relationship between two individuals (a major paradigm shift). The second source of the movement was the pragmatic evolution of family work by those concerned with children's problems. Although child guidance clinics were well established in the USA before the Second World War, where many workers recognized the necessity of involving parents as well as the children, the standard practice was that the children and parents were treated separately, using individual psychotherapy. It was not until the 1940s that the family group itself began to be evaluated. An American psychologist, John Elderkin Bell, is credited with being the first person to work consistently with the whole family as a group following a visit to Bowlby in London during 1951. Ironically enough, it appears that this was due to a misunderstanding. Bowlby emphasized the importance of the family in theoretical ways, but Bell assumed he was also referring to methods of practice. The third source (of more theoretical foundations) was the research into the nature of deviant communication associated with families with severe mental health problems. Bateson (1972) is often cited as the most influential person from this tradition which overtly began to link human problems and behaviour with interpersonal relationships and communication processes. As an anthropologist, Bateson brought a social emphasis which spread rapidly among the clinicians who worked with him on dysfunctional communication between 1952 and 1962. Prior to Bateson few scientific writers had managed to link events in the subjective world with those occurring in the objective world. Bateson was one of the first writers to reach across this dichotomy and link the subjective, humanistic and existential tradition to the objective, scientific and pragmatic tradition. His theories made an explicit link between internal experience (the mind) and the outer world (the ecology or environment). This was indeed a major bridge to build. He has also been credited with being one of the first to link system theory with the family. He was certainly important in popularizing it among therapists. The popularization of general system theory (Von Bertalannfy, 1968) gave an explicit theoretical framework which was taken up eagerly by the family therapy movement to the extent that most books now refer to systemic rather than family therapy (systemic is a better term since it can refer to other social groups).

The family therapy tradition shifted the basic paradigm of how a problem is defined even further from the individual, by suggesting that some of the most important aspects of the problem may lie in the prevailing patterns of relationships and communications within the family or wider social system. With children and adolescents, this is clearly so often the case that family therapy approaches have had a wide impact in child work. The critical paradigm shift is that a proper understanding of the person and their problem is not possible without some knowledge of the family or social context. The role of the therapist varies widely between different schools of family therapy (see later) but all the schools agree about the need to understand the social context of the individual.

Table 3 summarizes the main paradigms of the major traditions. The humanistic tradition is not shown separately, but it has had a very significant effect on the way that therapists of all traditions approach the early stages and process of therapy, and upon how each of the others is used.

Two other notable trends have been towards brief and then integrated approaches. The first was influenced by a strong prevailing North American pragmatism but also grew out of a general concern that long-term analytic psychotherapy created major problems both for clients and for the professionals providing the service. Because it requires so much time, psychoanalysis cannot be viewed as anything other than a luxury treatment.

Table 3 Paradigms for psychotherapy

Therapy school	Behavioural	Cognitive	Psychodynamic	Systemic
Theory of pathology	Problems develop via maladaptive learning process	Symptoms caused/ maintained by maladaptive cognitive habits and schemata (central assumptions)	Problems relate to early development (attachment theory) often with some form of emotional trauma	'No man is an island' problems viewed as part of a social context
Role of therapist	To facilitate an active re-learning process	Help patient to explore meaning of events and correct 'faulty' thinking habits	Provide safe environment to explore inner feelings and how they affect the present	Varies, but often involves active work with spouse/ family/carers
How goals are determined	Normally (but not necessarily) in collaboration with patient	Explicitly collaborative 'research supervisor'	Not directive, but therapist uses 'expert' frame of reference	Normally collaborative but uses various ideas (sometimes covertly) relating to system theory
How change occurs	Re-learning (As *predicted* by learning theory)	New meanings produce different affect and behaviour	Gradual empowerment by development of complex insights into relationships	Intervention aimed at changing critical aspect of system interaction
Method of evaluation	Evaluation of behaviour changes, reported by self/others	Changes in basic schemata (central cognitive assumptions)	Traditionally by case study and indirect supervision, recent developments interesting	Live supervision. Defining and measuring complex systems requires measures on multiple 'levels'

It also encourages dependency upon the analyst; and if provided on a private basis it is financially extremely costly to the client. In a public service context where there are pressures to see large numbers of people there are major ethical problems. Many forms of brief and focal therapy have thus arisen both in the USA and the UK (e.g. Weakland *et al.*, 1974; Bentovim and Kinston, 1978; de Shazer, 1985) in response to these problems. These approaches have been particularly popular within the family therapy tradition but examples can be found in all of the main traditions. Brief therapy explicitly assumes that the therapist should not encourage reliance upon the therapist or develop an intense relationship with a client. He or she is ethically bound to make the intervention short. In order for therapy to be brief it is necessary to develop a clear focus for the work. It is obvious that in order to do this effectively the therapist must make effective assessment and formulation of the problem in terms which the client accepts. Brief focused therapy is therefore normally reliant upon effective assessment ideas and methods.

One very clear example of this stems from the work of the Mental Research Institute (MRI) 'Brief Therapy' group at Palo Alto, California. Some members of the original group produced one of the classic works on communication within family systems in 1967 (Watzlawick *et al.*). A second work dealing with the general nature of how change occurs in individuals, families and social groups then followed (Watzlawick, Weakland and Fisch, 1974) which was both innovative and entertaining. Finally the group produced a book specifically about their therapeutic methods in 1982 (Fisch, Weakland and Segal). They define therapy purely as 'problem-solving' and reject concepts of pathology. They use the principle of circular causality as the foundation of their theory. This is a key idea in systemic therapy which suggests that the traditional way of looking at causes and effects is often unhelpful in human systems as it leads to blaming and scapegoating behaviour. It is more appropriate to assume that all actions are merely part of a repeating cyclical pattern of interactions such as that shown in Figure 1 below:

Figure 1 Example of circular causality

The therapist's role is to intervene in the circular transactional patterns which 'generate' the problem behaviours. The optimal method of intervention is assumed to depend largely upon the person or family's views of the problem, and so the therapist focuses initial efforts upon understanding the person's views about the problem ('patient position') and their expectations of the therapist. These concepts are very useful in understanding motivational aspects of psychotherapy. Then, by making one or two key interventions (often using paradox) the therapist focuses the family member upon a particular task or experience. This is intended to alter the meaning of the problem to the person (or family member) so that they act in a way which breaks the circular causality. The role of the therapist is more contractual than in other strategic models and the aims of therapy tend to be defined by the 'customer' not the therapist. The group also presented supporting empirical evidence based on 97 cases with a variety of problems seen at their centre – and considering that sessions were limited to a maximum of ten the results were impressive (Weakland *et al.*, 1974). However, the nature of their highly specialized setting means that there must be some doubts about the representativeness of the sample. In the terms of system theory, this model emphasizes the problem-maintaining aspects of a system, the subjective views of the individuals within it, and the disruption of patterns of circular causality. There are many other types of brief or focal therapy. For example, the London family studies group developed a form of focal therapy which took its name from the development of a central focal hypothesis about the nature of a child's presenting symptom (Bentovim and Kinston, 1978). It is assumed that this has a particular meaning for other family members which often relates to their own life history. For example a parent may have particular anxiety about a child which is related to trauma they themselves suffered in childhood at the same age. Once understood, this focal hypothesis can help them settle and work more constructively.

However, a more radical approach is advocated by de Shazer (1985) and colleagues, who argue that focusing upon behaviour, thoughts, and feelings associated with the absence of a problem or with solutions to problems generates far more therapeutic change than does a traditional focus upon the problem. While there may be a lot of truth in this argument in some circumstances, the approach means that any attempt at problem assessment is explicitly abandoned in favour of exploring a solution focus. The hidden danger here is that unrecognized health problems will remain unrecognized, with (potentially) extremely serious consequences in health care settings. Although it can be argued that a solution focus will promote coping behaviour with real health problems, the risk of failing to recognize a serious disorder in its early stages is potentially dangerous and ethically dubious if it leads the family to believe that an investigation has been made and no problem found. The approach may be extremely valuable, but it should follow assessment rather than precede it, particularly in health service contexts.

Eclecticism (respect for several different models) has always been popular amongst workers in settings away from academic departments, on the simple logic that

- it is unreasonable to expect one approach to be a cure-all for everything
- given the nature of individual differences it is logical to expect that some different approaches suit different people
- away from academic centres clinicians are more likely to be faced with mixed and unselected populations.

In the past, academics often criticized eclectics for being confused, undisciplined and sloppy in their use of mixed models. However, the new philosophy of science has now made eclecticism academically respectable. In their family therapy text Nichols and Everett (1986) identified a clear trend towards integrating apparently different conceptual models into a coherent combination of approaches. Indeed, their own book is a careful integration of the best of several schools of family therapy. Falloon, Boyd and McGill (1984) have also written about an integrated model encompassing behavioural and family approaches for use with adult schizophrenics and their families; Will and Wrate (1985) have described a family therapy model which blends psychodynamic theory with structural theory and the McMaster model of family therapy (see p. 102); the McMaster model is itself an integration of the behavioural and system approaches. More recently, Norcross and Goldfried (1992) have provided a thorough review of the topic of therapy integration, making important distinctions between types of integration:

- technical eclecticism, or the use of various techniques without being too concerned about the theoretical ideas that go with them
- theoretical integration, in which two or more theories are blended in the hope that the result will be more powerful than any of the original theories alone
- common factors approach, which looks for core ingredients that all effective therapies share.

One of the most important pieces of work giving an integrated and focused model of brief therapy was provided by Budman and Gurman in 1988. The work is the outcome of a deliberate collaboration between a leading individual and group therapist and a prominent marital and family therapist; it represents a condensation of theoretical and practical expertise which is rarely found in one book. The model is termed interpersonal–developmental–existential because it focuses upon basic interpersonal or relationship issues such as attachment or loss. These are viewed against the person's life stage and background (their personal development) in order to clarify the meaning of the distressing experience or existential crisis associated with the problem.

Integrated therapies represent a paradigm shift of great importance. They reflect a growing acceptance that in the real world, the psychotherapist or problem-solver has to be ready to shift his or her own paradigms in order to respond effectively to different needs and problems in different situations.

Therapy with children and their parents

If we consider the use of psychotherapy with children, many approaches can be characterized as variants of the major traditions which have been adapted to suit the particular needs of children. The main adaptation is to use play as a medium for communication, especially with younger children, where the focus was initially on work with the individual child. Thus, Winnicott (1971) represents a Freudian tradition in play therapy; Axline (1969) represents a more client-centred approach to play therapy; while McMahon (1992) gives a more recent and valuable account of child-centred play therapy. Ginsberg (1976) trained parents to use play therapy techniques, representing a pragmatic attempt to work through parents and empower them to help their children.

In fact because the behavioural approach focuses on the environment, behaviour therapists working in family contexts tended to shift their emphasis from the children to working with the parents and families (who were effectively the child's social environment). Forehand and McMahon (1981) carried out a ten-year program of work in the USA, using both normal and clinical samples of three- to eight-year-olds and their mothers. They developed ways of teaching skills to parents during play with young children which they called the parent–child game. Their research showed these skills generalized to the home environment and that (Forehand and Long, 1988) the improved quality of the parent–child interaction and the more positive parental perceptions of the children also survived over this extended time-span. These and other innovative approaches are beginning to be more widely used in response to evidence that children's attachment problems are often visible in early childhood, are also very persistent, but can be helped by early interventions. However, Sanders (1992) concluded that there was little evidence that parent training interventions alone were effective when there were additional family problems such as parental depression, marital or social problems. Since multi-problem families are precisely those who are most difficult to engage in treatment, and whose children are most at risk for long-term problems, then a broader family understanding is required at the assessment stage for these families, and a package of intervention measures which suits the particular family. As a result, early interventions with families at risk in community settings using flexible combinations of accessible counselling services and group approaches are becoming widely used.

There are complex ethical issues that need to be considered in relation to whether to work with the child or through the parents or other family members. On the one hand, empowering parents by helping them to gain skills and confidence may be more beneficial in the long term, more effective in the short term (especially where parents are compliant and motivated) and more efficient in relation to service cost than working directly with a child. This is especially likely to be the case with very young children. Conversely, there are circumstances in which child-centred work is likely to be very important for some problems:

- where the child alone has been traumatized or abused
- where there is significant conflict with carers which cannot be resolved directly
- where there is a particular need for individuation of the child
- where the main problem is a significant attachment disorder in which the child needs an experience of a safe relationship with a skilled therapist before they can begin to make normal attachments.

It is also part of the trend for children's rights that child-centred work should be available as one of the choices that families can be empowered to make for themselves when needed. Nevertheless it should be done in collaboration and partnership with the child's carers, and it can be argued that a systemic understanding of the problem situation gives an overview which enables rational and informed choices about which therapeutic approaches are likely to be successful and which are not (see Chapter 9 for more details). The current legal and ethical frameworks for professional practice emphasize the need to offer a range of services for children with special emotional needs, to help parents make informed choices, and to work in partnership with them. A general overview of work with children and families which is in keeping with these trends and current UK legislation is provided by Herbert (1993). It is this author's belief that clinicians working in the field need to have a working knowledge of a range of approaches so that they can be creative and flexible in their assistance to children and their families, offering help which suits the particular problem and family context, and empowers service users to make informed choices.

The family as a system

Perhaps even more difficult will be the shift in the boundaries of the individual mind. . . . The basic rule of systems theory is that if you want to understand some phenomenon . . . you must understand that phenomenon within the context of all *completed* circuits which are relevant to it. . . . We are accustomed to thinking of the mind as somehow contained within the skin of an organism, but the circuitry is *not* contained within the skin.

(Bateson, 1970)

This section will add some further detail to the context of family work by outlining the paradigms underlying some of the major schools of family therapy. Particular reference will also be made to general system theory because of its central role in most family work.

General system theory (Von Bertalannfy, 1968) as it is applied to families can be summarized as follows. Like all systems families can be thought of as having inherent organization or structure. This structure is usually described in terms of sub-systems (e.g. the parental or marital sub-system, the children or sibling sub-system). How these sub-systems function in themselves and in relation to other parts of the family is obviously crucial. For example, the marital sub-system should:

- meet the adults' emotional and sexual needs
- provide an opportunity for reproduction (and continuation of the life-cycle)
- protect and nurture the children.

Boundaries are another aspect of family organization which differentiate different parts of the system (e.g. between the parental and sibling sub-systems). The nature of the boundaries can be rigid (highly separated sub-systems) or permeable (more flexible roles). The nature of the boundaries affects communication and decision making. For example, a parent would not normally discuss his/her marital sex life with a child (a privacy boundary) or give them major decisions on behalf of the family (power boundary). There are also hierarchies which denote various levels of the family organization (e.g. one parent may dominate all the others in the family). In families, 'hierarchy' is most commonly used to refer to power and authority while 'boundaries' is often used more loosely and may refer either to issues of closeness and distance in personal relationships, to communication patterns, or to power. Obviously the structure of a family, especially the attachment patterns, will have crucial effects upon the growth and development of the children.

Certain concepts are also used to describe events occurring within the system. Since all the parts of the system affect each other, some events in families are perhaps best viewed not in terms of simple cause–effect relationships but rather in terms of circular causality (see p. 53) which suggests that all actions are merely part of a repeating cyclical pattern of interactions. In other words, the child's misbehaviour does not cause the wife's depression or the husband's drinking, but all three are mutually linked in a self-maintaining and repetitive chain of events. To assume that one of these three events is causal is merely to punctuate the cycle at a particular point. (This has the same logic as one superpower blaming the other entirely for the arms race; normally problem patterns develop and intensify over a period of time.) The principle of circular causality suggests, therefore, that individual problems must be viewed in relation to the overall family functioning. In particular, this can avoid the problems of blaming or scapegoating in situations of escalating conflict. Additionally it can sometimes be demonstrated that problems for the individual may be functional for the family system in some way, in which case it is particularly important to understand the overall system functioning. For example, the child's behaviour problem may in fact distract parents from their own irreconcilable differences, provide them with an experience of mutual concern and agreement, and thus help keep the family together.

The internal characteristics of the family system can also be understood both in terms of structure (family organization at a given moment in time) or process (changes in organization occurring over time; which are reflected in the ongoing family events and functioning, but may require historical information in order to fully understand them). For example, it may be clear that a child is isolated in a family, but the process which lies behind this may not be understood until it is revealed that the child is illegitimate. All behaviour within the family system can be viewed as a form of communication with two distinct components: the semantic content of the communication and the relationship aspect of the communication (what is often termed meta-communication). The semantic aspects refer to the meaning of what is communicated (e.g. I want you to tidy your room), whereas the relationship aspect refers to the manner in which the communication is made and the expectations inherent in that manner (e.g. I expect you to obey me).

It is also possible to use terms which describe characteristics of the whole system. Some systems operate as open systems (systems which are responsive to changes in the external environment and will therefore adapt and change themselves to cope with external change) and others as closed systems (which are unresponsive to the environment and tend to utilize a fixed and restricted pattern of responses). An open family system will therefore be flexible and adapt successfully to external life events such as job changes or internal processes of growth in the children, resulting in a psychologically healthy family. A closed family system will tend either to degenerate into a rigid and inappropriate pattern of repetitive responses which takes no account of changing circumstances, or to degenerate into chaos as the internal family organization breaks down completely: either of which may result in presentation to a helping agency.

The principle of non-summativity states that the whole system is greater than the sum of the parts and therefore that the whole family characteristics cannot be inferred from 'summing' the descriptions of the individuals or sub-systems within the family; information about the overall pattern of interactions and relationships within the family, and its interaction with the wider social system, is of critical importance.

Various types of system regulation can also be described. The principle of homeostasis describes how feedback loops normally maintain a steady system. Within families this suggests that there are certain family rules which organize family interactions, maintain a stable system in relation to members' roles, and determine the normal consequences of behaviour. For example there are often unwritten rules about the amount of contact allowed with outsiders. Parents will normally encourage a child to go out if she is tending to isolate herself but encourage her to stay in more if she goes out too regularly. Rules like this may be explicit or implicit. However, at certain times healthy families (open systems) will display morphogenesis which is an ability to respond flexibly to major changes and crises, such as a family member becoming an adult and preparing to leave home. Morphogenesis requires that the system change itself and therefore its organization and rules in order to cope with this change. Finally, the principle of equifinality suggests that the internal organization of the family system can be so rigid, particularly with closed systems, that it often overcomes differing conditions and events to reach a predictable outcome. (This is a very interesting principle in relation to therapy, since it suggests that with closed family systems the therapist probably does not change outcomes but may help the family system to reach an inevitable outcome, such as divorce, more quickly.)

In relation to families, it should be stressed that although system theory has proved to be an extremely useful tool for descriptive purposes, it cannot be claimed to have been evaluated as a predictive theory. Vetere (1987) evaluated the application of general system theory to the family and admitted that 'such jargon often provides a smokescreen for sloppy, ill-disciplined thinking'. She also suggested that system theory has arisen and proliferated as a result of the fragmentation of the scientific community into a plethora of sub-disciplines, resulting in a need for a theory which could link various phenomena at different levels, i.e. individual, social psychological, cultural. She suggested that what family therapists need to do is to clarify and test their conceptual and operational definitions of the terms which they have borrowed from general system theory.

Major schools of family therapy

In the major theoretical exposition of the structural family therapy model, Minuchin (1974) clearly describes the family in system theory terms. He gives a particularly clear account of his theoretical position as a 'developmental structuralist'. Minuchin suggests that psychological problems, whatever their symptomatic form, arise as a direct result of dysfunctional structural relationships in the individual's social (family) system. In addition, the family is viewed developmentally and the concept of the family life cycle is used to illustrate the normal structural changes occurring at various stages of life. Thus he has a clear paradigm regarding the nature of pathology. Minuchin's other therapeutic paradigms are not quite so clear. He falls within the North American pragmatic tradition by offering a definition of therapy only in terms of its purpose: to create a 'workable reality'. Although he does acknowledge that therapy can have an educative function, the therapist generally defines the goals of therapy and the method of reaching them without any necessity for insight or consultation with the clients. The therapist acts to disrupt existing problematic patterns in the family structure, and also through direct intervention produces more adaptive patterns of social interaction, leading to changes in the relationships within the family group. Thus structural therapy is extremely active, directive, and focuses upon an objective view of the present family processes. Several authors have commented that Minuchin's emphasis upon family structure arose as a result of his background of work with chaotic, disorganized (slum) families.

Haley himself summed up his own approach to therapy in 1976 (having acknowledged his debt to Milton Erikson in 1973). He entitled his book *Problem Solving Therapy* although the tradition he represents is more commonly known as the strategic school of family therapy. 'Strategic' refers to the idea that each individual person's problem needs to be approached in a different way, and the critical factors that determine the best way to approach each problem are the way that the person (or family) understands the problem. In this sense strategic therapists shift towards a much more subjective or cognitive paradigm. However, like the structural school, they assume that a high degree of therapist control over the therapeutic process is required. Haley also places an emphasis upon understanding family structure but suggests a particular focus upon one variable that he considers to be particularly relevant to change – the power hierarchy, which is assumed to be the crucial aspect of family organization. He suggests that psychological problems occur when the hierarchical arrangement is unclear or confused. The role of the therapist is somewhat more sophisticated in strategic therapy. Overtly the therapist may accept the patient's view of the problem and indeed this view will often be used constructively to formulate a focused intervention that will force the client to confront his problem in a constructive way. Covertly, however, the therapist may view the problem quite differently from the client. The intervention is designed not to create 'insight' but to create a key change, often a cognitive or attitude change in relation to the problem, which in turn has radical effects upon behaviour. Often the intervention used is paradoxical. While there is no doubt that paradoxical interventions can be extremely powerful, they can be viewed as ethically dubious and should only be used by experienced therapists who have had proper training in their use. Seltzer (1986) provided a comprehensive overview and guidebook to paradoxical strategies in psychotherapy, while Fisher, Anderson and Jones (1981) provide some guidance on indications and contra-indications for use. Most authors agree that using paradoxical strategies effectively requires:

- a reasonable level of therapeutic skill and experience (not a beginner)
- a good understanding of the family as a dynamic system (intervention is well thought through and not impulsive)
- the safety measure of proper supervision or group consultation which helps to think through the likely effects of the intervention
- a therapist style which is comfortable dealing with what may sound absurd or humorous.

A further major tradition that can be identified in family therapy is the developmental/historical tradition whose roots lie in a blending of psychodynamic and system theories. Lieberman (1979) produced one of the clearest and best books in this tradition which he entitled *Transgenerational Family Therapy* (TFT). TFT adopts a very similar human development paradigm to psychodynamic therapy in assuming that the task of therapy is to free individuals and families from the traumatic effects of past events, particularly events occurring in the families of origin of the parents, but the methods of working on this are to develop understanding and insight within the family context, rather than by working with the individual on their own. It is assumed that the childhood traumas fundamentally affect the roles that family members take in relation to each other, affecting partnership roles and parental roles significantly as well as limiting individual psychological growth. Hence, there is a clear 'developmental' theory of pathology which can be clearly linked to the concept of the family life cycle (see p. 12). Lieberman offers a number of innovations which serve to focus the historical work, clarify the tasks involved, and therefore increase the pace of therapy compared to more traditional psychodynamic approaches. For example 'genograms' (family trees) are used in an open, collaborative and empowering way with the parental couple. The therapist uses a large sheet of paper and maps the family history in a conversational way, encouraging a brief but meaningful life story to emerge with potted descriptions of the key people in the parental family of origin. If there are significant traumas in the family of origin these then begin to emerge in ways that can be linked to ongoing patterns in relationships and other current problems. Using the language of the family members helps them to develop these links themselves and this is a very useful technique which can be used with couples in marital work or with children present. Once the sources of trauma are identified, then therapeutic tasks such as writing letters to parental figures can be given in order to clarify unresolved emotional issues. This kind of approach has been particularly popular in Europe where the developmental tradition has remained relatively strong.

Another well-known school of family therapy with a distinct set of paradigms is the 'Milan' group. This approach was developed from 1972 when Palazolli and her colleagues developed a team approach treating families with severe problems, with consultations from Paul Watzlawick. By 1978 Palazolli, Boscolo, Cecchin, and Prata had adopted system theory and its accompanying philosophy as a clear ideological base for their work as they described it at that time in their book *Paradox and Counterparadox*. The Milan group viewed therapy as a process in which the therapist attempted to understand the workings of the family system and particularly the rules that govern the behaviour of the system. They assumed that the problematic behaviours were maintained by an implicit and inherently pathological transactional rule which was a key feature of the family system. By consistently positively connoting the family's behaviour, they avoided a critical or moralizing stance. The 'conductor' of the session (aided by a team of observers) used the principles of hypothesizing, circular questioning and neutrality to elicit and organize information (Palazolli *et al.*, 1980). However, the major goal was to deduce and state the key transactional rule openly as a prescription to the family – but to connote it in positive terms and, paradoxically, to encourage the family to continue operating according to this rule. By making the rule explicit without criticizing the family, it was assumed that even a closed family system will then undergo morphogenesis and change the rule into a more healthy one. The theory of pathology is derived directly from system theory although the methods to produce change were innovative.

The original Milan group therefore suggested that seriously disturbed behaviour is best viewed as a result of dysfunctional rules in the social system of the individual displaying the behaviour. The goals of the therapist were to discover and attempt to change the rules that govern pathological behaviour using a paradoxical injunction. It was assumed that if the system reorganizes its rule system appropriately, the problem behaviours would then disappear. The group attempted to stress the nature of their position as scientific theorists, but like many theoretical innovators the evidence they offered in favour of their theories depended largely on anecdotal reports of individual case studies. The group could also be considered to be radical systemic theorists in their outright rejection of a linear reductionist philosophy. They argued that any attribution of blame to an individual was unscientific, as is the distinction between good and bad behaviour. This somewhat idealistic attitude led to some problems when their model was used to view such problems as chronic child abuse, where it may be impossible to maintain a stance of 'neutrality'. Other writers (e.g. Treacher, 1984) also accused them of being too concerned with technique. However, despite the criticisms they aroused it has become clear that their model and subsequent developments have become profoundly influential in family therapy practice: more in relation to neutrality, circular questioning and hypothesizing than the use of paradox.

In the early 1980s the group began to separate, with Prata and Palazolli pursuing their interests in clinical research while Cecchin and Boscolo devoted themselves more to issues concerning teaching and training; this eventually led to the formation of two 'Milan' groups. Pirotta (1984) compared both teams and suggested that Palazolli's group retained their original emphasis upon the pathological rules within the family system whilst attempting to develop a single sustained intervention: a 'universal' or invariant prescription which consisted of asking parents to leave the home together regularly and secretively. This task appears to have the effect of strengthening intergenerational boundaries; with severely disturbed families (which this group work with) it does appear to have generally helpful effects. This group therefore appears to have retained an emphasis upon the therapist overcoming dysfunctional and homeostatic aspects of the family system. Boscolo and Cecchin's group had become more pre-occupied not only with training students but also with teaching new ways of thinking to the family members. Rather than making one single powerful challenge to the family reality, the latter group therefore adopted a therapeutic approach which can be characterized as continuously understanding and challenging family members' perceptions of reality in order to help them make new connections between perceptions of themselves, their behaviour and inter-relationships. This has in turn resulted in this group viewing families as being in a process of continual evolution and change; so that they emphasize evolution and change within the family system.

Boscolo and Cecchin described this process themselves at the first World Family Therapy congress (1989). They explained that after 1978 they had found that trainees were more interested in their actions, and the types of questions that were asked during the session, than the family system or the final intervention. In addition, they found that when they attempted to repeat prescriptions that had been useful with one family, they often did not work with a different family. This led them to believe that a search for 'universal' strategic prescriptions was a fruitless exercise, and led them to concentrate more upon helping family members to think differently about problems. Trainees also had to adapt their learning to their own particular context, and so there was a shift of emphasis away from understanding the external system characteristics towards understanding the ways that family members understand their family and problems. In effect, this was the beginning of a major paradigm shift which involves focusing upon the subjective perceptions of the problem in relation to the family system held by the family members themselves. New and helpful understandings about themselves are assumed to be empowering and to promote personal growth. This movement was dubbed 'the new paradigm' or the 'social constructivist' position by family therapists and it has become the dominant paradigm in family therapy. At a time when the trend in health care is to acknowledge the consumer's rights and views this is very much in keeping with wider trends. However, the emphasis upon meaning and interpretation is not new outside family therapy and has much in common with cognitive therapy; plus there is an emphasis upon the meaning of relationships and family connections, rather than individual perceptions and beliefs.

One of the most important post-Milan developments has been the work of Karl Tomm (1987b) who has elaborated the idea of circular questioning using the modified terms of 'reflexive questioning' and 'interventive interviewing'. Circular questioning refers to a process of asking a series of questions about the effects of family members' behaviour upon each other in a manner designed both to explore relationships and arouse curiosity. Reflexive questions are defined as 'questions asked with the intent to facilitate self-healing in an individual or family by activating the reflexivity among meanings within pre-existing belief systems that enable family members to generate or generalize constructive patterns of cognition or behavior on their own.' Tomm (1987a) described the three Milan guidelines of circularity, neutrality, and hypothesizing as (respectively) focusing upon the family members' behaviour, upon the family members' understanding, and upon the therapist's understanding. He therefore presents interventive interviewing (using reflexive questions) as a fourth guideline which focuses upon the therapist's behaviour. He describes eight types of reflexive questions:

- future-orientated questions, used to explore goals, plans, anticipations or outcomes, suggest future scenarios, or install hope, e.g. 'How do you imagine things will be in six months if you can make some progress with your problems?'
- observer-perspective questions, used to enhance awareness of self and others or to explore interpersonal perceptions and interactions, e.g. 'What do you think he feels like when you get angry and frustrated . . . and what does he do?'
- unexpected context-change questions, used to help people see things from an entirely different point of view by exploring opposite meanings, introducing a paradox, or linking feared impulses, e.g. 'What stops you killing yourself . . . are there some parts of your behaviour you would like to destroy?'
- embedded-suggestion questions, used to suggest a different interpretation, alternative action, a change of attitude or a hidden motive or volition, e.g. 'When she decides to stop eating, what is it she is on strike about?'

- normative-comparison questions, used to draw a contrast with a social, developmental or cultural norm or to facilitate a sense of belonging for an alienated individual, e.g. 'Do you think that he feels isolated or disconnected from everyone else when he feels suicidal?'
- distinction–clarification questions, used to clarify causal attributions, sequences, perceived motives, or other crucial beliefs and also to introduce uncertainty into these beliefs, e.g. 'When she cries do you think she is upset or is she trying to get her own way?'
- questions introducing hypotheses, used to reveal circular transactions, defence mechanisms, hidden fears, or other complex issues such as a therapeutic impasse, e.g. 'If I realized that I couldn't help you in the normal way because seeing me was only making you feel inadequate, what do you think I should do?'
- process-interruption questions, used to expose ongoing processes in therapy to minimize or reduce the impact of unhelpful processes, e.g. 'Do you think I may have offended your father by the way I have been talking?'

In his discussion of the derivation of this typology, Tomm acknowledges the ideas of Pearce and Cronen (1980), whose theories he draws upon. They pointed out how most of us use (whether consciously or not) a hierarchy of levels of meaning to understand and classify our experiences:

- the actual content of speech or communication, e.g. 'I hate you'
- the action accompanying this speech (meta-communication context), e.g. the tone of voice and emotional expression
- an event or episode of behaviour, e.g. an argument
- characteristics about an individual person inferred from episodes, e.g. aggressiveness
- beliefs about relationships with and between others, e.g. it never works
- beliefs about families, e.g. we are too different from each other
- social and cultural beliefs, e.g. anger is dangerous.

Tomm suggests that one of the essential modes of action of reflexive questioning is to make people compare and correct beliefs at various levels in the hierarchy of meanings. To give an example, if a patient believes that a relationship with someone else does not work (relationship level) how does the patient reconcile this with an action or episode that the therapist points out has been done for them out of a caring motive? Hence it is important in using reflexive questions to pitch questions at various levels of meaning, and to use the questions to expose problem beliefs by linking them with contrary evidence from other levels.

Tomm stresses that the therapist should adopt a facilitative posture and deliberately ask those questions which are likely to open up 'new possibilities for self-healing' by allowing this reflexivity between levels of meaning. The aim is to enable family members to generate new patterns of meaning and behaviour themselves. He clearly falls within the new 'constructivist' post-Milan tradition. Yet there is also a sense in which his work is universally applicable and understandable simply as a classification of interview skills using questioning as the main mode of action. He also has much in common with Carl Rogers in his view of the therapist's role and the manner in which therapy works, although his methods are more active.

One of the most important skills in systemic therapy is known as reframing in which the therapist forcefully uses a new meaning which runs counter to the prevailing belief system. Often language is used in a colourful or creative way to generate alternative and more functional social realities – for example, the therapist may label the aggressive other person as passionate. Reframing can be applied to almost any aspect of a problem. Table 4 shows examples of reframing applied to personality, behaviour, beliefs, causes and outcomes.

Seeing someone as passionate rather than aggressive can obviously result in all sorts of episodes being dealt with in different ways. One of the most effective types of reframing involves the use of metaphor, which is a symbolic representation of the person's belief system that can radically change fixed beliefs (presumably because the metaphor triggers all sorts of possible

Table 4 Types of reframing

INDIVIDUAL CHARACTERISTICS		
withdrawn	v.	thoughtful
weak, fearful	v.	sensitive
easily upset	v.	full of feeling
miserable, sad	v.	sensitive, compassionate
BEHAVIOUR		
seeking attention	v.	'entertaining everyone'
argumentative, aggressive	v.	passionate, fiery
BELIEFS		
always wants to argue	v.	thinks debate is a good thing
needs to control	v.	believes in taking responsibility
CAUSAL FACTORS		
always causing trouble	v.	'the alarm bell'
attention seeking	v.	takes people's minds away from other problems, distracts everyone
OUTCOMES		
makes us argue	v.	brings you together in your concern
puts pressures on us	v.	tests your resolve

new connections and understandings at an unconscious level). Some examples of common therapeutic metaphors are:

- wrapped up in cotton wool
- the family alarm bell
- two boats that have drifted apart
- pouring ice on the anger

Using metaphors like these can cause significant changes in the person's view of themselves, relationships with others, and their problems (Kopp, 1995). The use of metaphors is particularly powerful with children who have traditionally been told stories and fables as part of learning about their cultural traditions and beliefs. Therefore the use of metaphorical stories can be a powerful technique to generate new meanings for a child about their life situation (Crowley and Mills, 1986). For example a child who has had a disrupted early life history can be involved in the creation of a story about the seed of a tree that is initially blown from place to place or moved for other reasons (depending on the actual history) before finding a place to take root, be nurtured, and grow tall. The use of metaphors is common in a variety of therapeutic traditions as adjuncts, and they have a central role as a form of suggestion in some hypnotherapy approaches, such as the work of Milton Erickson. If we consider Pearce and Cronen's hierarchy of meanings, then the power of metaphor partly derives from the ability of symbolism to cause fundamentally different ways of viewing what are otherwise very fixed assumptions at the higher levels of meaning, which then allow changes in the way everything at the level of events is interpreted. Whereas it is easy to retain fixed views in the face of rational arguments or defences against straightforward verbal suggestions, using metaphor creates visual or other symbolic images which are much harder to ignore.

Another clear elaboration of this social constructivist approach can be seen in the work of Michael White and David Epston (1990) which has come to be known as narrative therapy. Narrative therapy assumes that, consciously or unconsciously, we carry central beliefs about ourselves, our history and our world in the form of our life story which becomes accessible in therapy. Narrative therapy therefore assumes that the task of the therapist is to help the person or family reconstruct their life story into a form which is more adaptive, congruent with reality, and has more of a sense of the person as an active participant rather than a passive victim. Therapists of this tradition therefore tend to encourage patients to use creative techniques such as writing poems or stories about key experiences such as bereavement or trauma, sometimes repeatedly, until some kind of readjustment occurs. Resolving these emotional blocks can have dramatic and positive effects. One of the key aims in narrative therapy is to encourage people to let go of meanings imposed by others, particularly in relation to the abuse of power.

These are generally assumed to be unhelpful, so that the aim is to encourage people to make sense of their own lives themselves, and to become more 'self-authored' in their own life story. This is a very modern and existential paradigm which fits well with the concept of empowerment in psychotherapy. In some ways this tradition can be considered as the re-emergence of the individual (and their experience, needs, and motivation) within the family therapy tradition.

Keeney and Ross (1985) contributed an overview of the various family therapy approaches, making several useful distinctions:

- first, that theories may differ in terms of how they define the system, with different emphases upon the individual, the nuclear family, and the extended family
- second, theories differ in terms of how the system is understood, using subjective meanings or objective behaviours or a combination of these embedded within each other in various ways. For example, a developmental perspective examines behaviour within a frame concerned with natural growth and ordered sequences over a long time scale
- a third major distinction concerns how the system is understood in relation to stability and change, and assumptions about flexibility and rigidity, e.g. the difference of emphasis between the two Milan groups
- a fourth distinction concerns the relative emphasis upon behaviour, relationships or meaning within the theory.

Each of these distinctions can be understood as a significant paradigm choice.

Several other authors have compared and contrasted various combinations of these models empirically (e.g. Sluzki, 1983; MacKinnon, 1983) and some discussion of research evidence regarding family therapy will follow in the next section. One problem is that very rapid development of these ideas occurred in the context of a general mushrooming development in the health care industry. Indeed Bloch and Weiss (1981) demonstrated in a survey of training institutions that family therapy training has grown exponentially since its inception in the USA. One of the major reasons for this rate of growth was that family therapy occurs in a variety of institutional and agency settings, i.e. that it is precisely because family therapy did not 'belong to' one particular profession that it has diffused more rapidly among a plethora of professions. The second reason for its popularity would appear to be the fact that it opens up a number of new and exciting perspectives upon individual and mental health problems in relation to the social world. This rapid rate of growth and diversity has led to difficulty in interpreting the results of available research. In their introduction Will and Wrate (1985) also point out that any new form of treatment in the psychotherapy field is associated with an 'evangelical' phase. Such a phase is characterized by claims that new ideas have transcended past mistakes and that the new ideas have almost limitless therapeutic potential. Evangelism of this kind has certainly aroused criticism of family therapists particularly from the social work profession (as Walrond-Skinner noted in 1984). Andolfi (1993) pointed out how family therapists have alienated psychiatrists with omnipotent, unsupported and unrealistic claims about the applicability and efficacy of family therapy.

However, as discussed at the beginning of this chapter, the signs are that the evangelical phase is coming to an end. Some of the most interesting developments in family therapy display the trend towards integrating diverse models of therapy. Stanton (1981) described an integrated structural and strategic approach to family therapy. Perhaps the best-known integrated model is the McMaster model of family therapy described by Epstein and Bishop (1981). The model is a hybrid theory deriving partly from system theory, partly from behavioural approaches, and partly from a large empirical study of normal family functioning. Will and Wrate (1985) describe a further integration of the McMaster model with both structural family therapy and psychodynamic approaches. Nichols and Everett (1986) present a general integrated overview of various family therapy theories in their book, which is a thorough and scholarly overview of the field. They suggest that integration of models may not be easy but is pragmatically necessary in order to prepare trainee therapists to be flexible, so that they can adopt approaches which will suit particular families' needs rather than imposing a single doctrine or model upon everyone.

Some of the most helpful concepts associated with family therapy are:

- understanding human problems in relation to development and the family life cycle
- understanding homeostasis and other aspects of a family system as a possible cause of problems
- the notion of circular causality which helps to understand multiple and complex causal patterns and can provide a way of mapping a focal hypothesis
- understanding that wider social systems can also generate clinical problems (e.g. increased academic pressures in schools leading to a higher rate of exclusion for children with behaviour problems).

Some of the key skills that can be identified in working with families as systems are:

- mapping family systems, including the use of structural diagrams and genograms for family history
- studying sequences of interaction (tracking) in order to understand the family processes

- hypothesizing about links between problems within the family and with the wider system
- creating an appropriate focus or formulation in collaboration with the family by circular and reflexive questioning
- convening and engaging skills, including circular questioning and neutrality
- understanding family members views, and working with them constructively
- other cognitive techniques which are used to generate new meanings, such as reframing, the use of metaphor, and creative writing
- experiential and action-orientated techniques in the session, such as enactment, reseating and sculpting
- the use of therapeutic tasks, including the use of paradox.

In conclusion, the application of system theory to the family has helped to produce a further diversity of models of psychotherapy which focus upon families and relationships. Each model offers some valuable perspectives.

Pragmatic difficulties in family work

This section will briefly consider some of the major pragmatic issues which need to be faced when working with families.

Does it work?

One of the most classic early reviews of marital and family therapy was undertaken by Gurman and Kniskern (1978a). They reviewed over two hundred outcome studies of marital and family therapy at that time and their main conclusions were:

- that the therapeutic efficacy of clearly defined approaches had been established beyond doubt
- that where there were clear marital problems both spouses should be involved in therapy
- that family methods were clearly more effective where family conflict was an integral part of the problem.

Gurman, Kniskern and Pinsof updated this work in 1986 with a comprehensive review of research listing forty-four other reviews published over the preceding fifteen years. On this occasion their conclusions were:

- approximately 71% of child or adult focused problems treated by well defined or eclectic family therapy approaches can be expected to improve

- almost no evidence has been offered on the efficacy of systemic family therapy for schizophrenia
- for alcohol-involved marriages conjoint couples treatment in groups appears to have the best results
- studies of successful marital therapy involving affective and anxiety disorders with adults have relied heavily upon behavioural methods rather than reframing symptoms as systemic functions
- in marital therapy conjoint approaches would appear to be generally superior to individual therapy
- when family therapy methods have been vigorously tested they have been found to be effective
- with regard to the assessment of change, little attention has been given to the study of process in therapy and additionally researchers continue to use inappropriate measures
- there is a need to assess change from multiple perspectives: outcome studies should include an evaluation of system-level variables whose links with the presenting problems should be examined.

Russell, Olson, Sprenkle, and Atilano (1983) emphasized this last point, stating that research linking system functioning with individual symptoms (via an analysis of their functional consequences for the family) is required to improve both methods of treatment and outcome evaluation.

However, other writers have been more critical of family therapy; for example, Maston in 1979 wrote 'there are major short-comings in most of the available data, with only two well controlled studies'. Since her review was concerned with evaluating family therapy as a method of treatment for children, she also complained that there had been little comparison with other forms of psychotherapy for children. Dewitt (1978) perhaps gave a balanced if inconclusive view when he concluded in the *Archives of General Psychiatry* that family therapy appeared to have a similar impact and rate of success to other methods of psychotherapy.

Gale (1979) has pointed out the particular problems of undertaking outcome research in family therapy; for example, whether helping a distressed couple to separate should be construed as a successful outcome or as a deterioration in family therapy. He acknowledges the complexity of the task facing outcome researchers but offers a checklist of questions to be used in considering the methodology of such research. Gale himself is critical of blind enthusiasm, advocates a more rigorous approach, and believes research to be a professional obligation in the sense that a therapist should examine his or her own competence.

Other writers have also stressed this inherent complexity by suggesting that there are major philosophical difficulties in evaluating a system theory philosophy using mechanistic scientific criteria. Schwartzman (1984) has claimed that 'the challenge to a mechanistic view of therapy has been subverted by attempting to evaluate the new theories using methods which rely on mechanistic assumptions'. There is certainly some truth in this argument, but taken too far it might lead us to conclude that family theories and therapies cannot ever be empirically evaluated. This would seem to make no sense, and it might be better to conclude that the evaluation of family theories and therapy may require a different and more complex methodology than that required by individual psychotherapy. In fact, as far back as 1966 Miller and Westman derived some ingenious methods of testing predictions derived from the system theory principle of homeostasis in the families of pre-adolescent boys with reading problems. They predicted that families would resist seeking psychotherapy when it was recommended, that those who did seek it would do so for ulterior motives, that they would misinterpret statements that conflicted with homeostatic maintaining beliefs, and that they would sabotage procedures that threatened equilibrium. These predictions were confirmed.

Other writers (e.g. Minuchin and Fishman 1981) have discussed the educative effects of family psychotherapy when issues concerning developmental changes are openly discussed. The lasting effects of such education can be construed as a third kind of change, which will presumably help people to cope more adaptively with future events. Educational changes are also a different type of change (subjective or cognitive change, as opposed to objective measures such as symptoms). Table 5 shows a means of classifying subjective and objective changes on three levels. The point to note here is that different therapeutic models target different types of change; outcome measures need to take account of this, particularly in comparative studies. As stated, an outcome such as divorce may be viewed as either a positive or negative outcome depending on the therapist's value judgement of the relationship, and it is difficult to be clear whether this is an improvement or a deterioration. However, a change of family membership clearly represents a

Table 5 Types of therapeutic change

	1ST ORDER CHANGE	2ND ORDER CHANGE	3RD ORDER CHANGE
Objective	Symptomatic (behaviour) e.g. reduction of bedwetting	Family structure (internal) e.g. improved parent–child relationship	Family composition e.g. wife leaves home
Subjective	Cognitive change (meaning) e.g. son viewed as upset, not as 'bad'	Attitude change (specific) e.g. realizing other family members care about you	Educative change (non-specific) e.g. teaching parents about the effects of grief in children

drastic reorganization of the family structure which could be added to the table above as a 'fourth order' change (and would certainly be easier to identify than the educative effects of therapy). Hence it may be useful to consider these kinds of distinctions when evaluating therapy outcome, deciding on goals in casework, and selecting measures.

Gurman et al. (1986) also pointed out that in recent times research has shifted from a concentration on eventual outcome to the study of processes within therapy. Many studies (e.g. Alexander, Barton, Schiavo and Parsons, 1976) have illustrated the importance of non-specific factors in therapy. In their study, general relationship skills were the most important variable affecting the outcome of families treated by trainee therapists. Gurman and Kniskern (1978a) reviewed reports of deterioration during marital and family therapy, suggesting that this is associated with therapists who have poor relationship skills, who directly attack loaded issues and family members' defences very early in treatment, who fail to intervene in or interpret intra-family confrontation, and who do little to structure the opening of therapy and support family members. Although historically the methods used to study the behaviour of therapists have been rather poor, Pinsof (1979) has developed an extremely sophisticated coding system for the evaluation of therapists' behaviours.

One further important question relates to whether any particular theories of family therapy are more effective for particular types of problems. Gurman et al. (1986) also gave an 'impressionistic estimate' of how the major schools of marital and family therapy perform with various problems but admitted there was little or no comparative evidence.

Hence the problem of the assessment of outcome is an extremely complex one, which should involve a study of the therapist's behaviour as well as the details of a variety of changes occurring within families. It is notable that in their review of the effectiveness of individual psychotherapy Lambert, Shapiro and Bergin (1986) also concluded that change is multi-dimensional, and that a meaningful conceptual scheme was required to systematize outcome measurement. They also commented upon the trend towards the integration of diverse concepts and techniques. More recently, Lange et al. (1993) reviewed the use of family therapy with schizophrenia, mood and anxiety disorders, eating and conduct disorders, and substance abuse. They concluded that family-oriented approaches were most useful when applied flexibly and in combination with other valid treatment approaches, rather than on their own.

Resistance and other difficulties

The therapist also works within a professional system which can be extremely complicated. In the child services in the UK the number of professions and agencies which can be involved with a single case can be quite extraordinary. The general level of organization between and within agencies is often poor, making the task of therapeutic endeavour with families extremely difficult. Therapists, family and other agencies can become part of a larger and homeostatic system in relation to the problems. The difficulties of working within these larger systems have been well described by Reder (1986). Two of the common difficulties which arise in practice are to do with the motivation for change lying not within the family but rather within a referring agency or professional worker; and a tendency for one agency to be used as a shield by the family in order to protect themselves from intervention by a second agency (e.g. a request for psychological help in order to delay or defer prosecution for school non-attendance).

The original concept of resistance referred to a person's resistance to gaining insight and was often used in relation to a patient objecting to a particular interpretation by a psychoanalyst. More recently the concept has become more associated with the idea of resistance to change (whether this is behavioural or cognitive change). From a system theory perspective, resistance can be viewed as a manifestation of homeostatic feed-back mechanisms and thus as a normal rather than pathological process. In addition, the very nature of therapy which includes the whole family often arouses immediate resistance, since most families who enter therapy will do so in a state in which one particular member of the family is firmly labelled as the problem. Hence, although not all family therapy models require 'insight', the process of therapy will often demand a shift of perspective and an owning of responsibility by other members of the family which is often resisted. Further resistance may stem from fears of the therapist's power, feared consequences of therapy, and other factors such as the idiosyncratic nature of family members' personalities. Other obstacles may arise in connection with family secrets which may be consciously or unconsciously withheld. Indeed, people may give false information for an immense variety of reasons, such as shame, guilt, fear of violence, social conformity or to protect themselves or other family members from disapproval or legal consequences.

Resistance is also not exclusive to the family. For example, Karpel and Strauss (1984) also pointed out that the therapist may suffer certain fears of people much younger or older than himself. In two linked articles Treacher and Carpenter (1982) and Carpenter, Treacher, Jenkins and O'Reilly (1983) provided useful classifications of problems within the family and the therapy systems, respectively, that can lead to therapy getting 'stuck'.

In their book outlining the Milan school of therapy Palazolli *et al.* (1978) make the apparently obvious point that the concepts used by both the therapist and the family are largely determined by the language they use. In advancing this argument, they also point out that most ordinary language is linear and reductionist in its underlying logic and structure.

Only by a process of careful circular questioning, they argue, can this implicit linear logic be replaced by a more systemic understanding. This is an interesting point as it suggests that the family therapist is 'swimming against the tide' not only with the family but also with his own habitual logic.

Ethical and other dilemmas

The rise of consumerism in health care (as opposed to professional led health-care systems) has led to a much greater emphasis upon considering the patient and family viewpoint both in relation to services provided and in respecting the views of family members in a particular case. However there are complex ethical issues involved in reconciling different views of problems.

Vetere and Gale (1987) devoted a chapter to the ethical difficulties involved in the study of the family. They outlined several important issues. First, they discuss the conflicts which arise between clinical and research roles, for example when to intervene and when not to. Second, family groups arouse complex problems in relation to privacy, confidentiality and disclosure; particularly with clients in distress who might reveal things that they would not at other times. Third, the notion of informed consent is very difficult in practice since children (and sometimes spouses) may not be properly consulted by other family members. By the nature of family power hierarchies, conflicts occur frequently when working with family groups, and present the therapist with many challenges in relation to when to intervene and when to stay neutral. Fourth, the fact or even anticipation of observation can produce various changes in behaviour.

The most common ethical dilemmas facing therapists working with families arise from conflicts of interest, including problems of possible child abuse and unsatisfactory marital relationships between parents. Normally a family therapist will view the whole family as 'the client' and will, therefore, tend to avoid splitting or separating family members from each other in evaluating the aims of therapy. However, child abuse is a problem where, if intervention fails, then the child may need to be removed from the family for his or her protection and thus a family perspective becomes an entirely inappropriate way of viewing the problem. Many writers (e.g. Madanes, 1980) have explicitly referred to the danger of blindly retaining a family perspective on therapy in situations of child abuse.

Similarly, a blind adherence to any model can be dangerous in a health care context. Family therapy and social constructivism are powerful models, but where there are behavioural problems arising from unrecognized medical problems such as epilepsy then they can perpetuate a problem rather than solve it. Consumerism suggests we should respect the patient's views, but where these are markedly unrealistic we have a duty of care which suggests we should challenge those views – for example when a parent is minimizing a child's problem because they have a strong wish to be seen as a normal or healthy family.

A second common dilemma occurs where a child is presented as the problem but it appears from a family perspective that the major systemic problem is an unacknowledged deficiency in the marital relationship. On occasions the therapist may well be aware that by making the underlying problem explicit he runs a risk of unbalancing an unstable equilibrium and thus precipitating a family break-up. Other common difficulties for therapists include dealing with crises with inadequate facilities because of the lack of funding of children's services relative to adults (e.g. with no day- or in-patient facilities) and working with problems which are in some sense outside the therapist's experience, for example families from another culture, where values to do with issues such as child management may be radically different. Treacher (1984) makes the point that social class is also an underestimated variable in therapy.

In fact there is an important general issue which relates to the principle of viewing families with problems from a system theory perspective. In order to produce a reorganization of the system (which may be necessary in order to resolve the problems) it can be argued that it is essential to provoke morphogenesis, i.e. provoke a crisis. Several authors have suggested that family therapy can be viewed as crisis induction. In doing so they suggest that a crisis is often necessary for change (e.g. Halpern et al., 1979). Probably the commonest and simplest example of this occurs when problems are not acknowledged by the family members but are apparent to the therapist. Telling the family what you, the 'expert', think is probably the most common way that crises are induced by therapists working with families. As such, families are being presented with an objective view of themselves. When this involves telling people that, for example, their relationship with their child is so poor that the child is likely to be better off with foster parents, or the child has a learning disability, the timing and manner of this presentation is a crucial ethical issue.

Tomm (1989) has also pointed out that there are some much more general ethical issues involved in the choice of therapeutic approach. He uses two bipolar distinctions to categorize different types of therapeutic intervention. The first of these is the difference between interventions using conscious change (insight) and those which utilize methods to achieve change without any conscious awareness. Reflexive questioning is an example of the former, while structural therapy is an example of the latter. The second bipolarity is that between interventions which are designed to increase options and choices (e.g. Rogerian therapy) and those which are designed to reduce options (e.g. hospitalization to prevent violence or suicide). By representing these options as orthogonal dimensions, Tomm generates what he has termed the four 'basic ethical postures' shown in Figure 2.

Tomm makes the point that, in his view, therapists should work to increase options through conscious change (empowerment) where this is possible. He acknowledges that this is not always possible, but makes the point that the unthinking and invariant use of therapeutic methods utilizing the other postures could be viewed as unethical.

Summary

There are many theoretical perspectives and therapeutic methods available both for working with individuals and families, each of which makes certain assumptions about the precise nature of the problems and what the role of the therapist should be in solving them. A brief review of some of the more common types of individual and family therapy has been given, and an overview of system theory as it is applied to the family.

Although there is some evidence that well-defined methods of family therapy are generally effective, there is little clear evidence beyond this as yet (e.g. to suggest what methods are better for particular problems). This is probably because studies of outcome have rarely utilized a multi-dimensional assessment approach, which would be required to assess simple outcomes in relation to more complex aspects of family function.

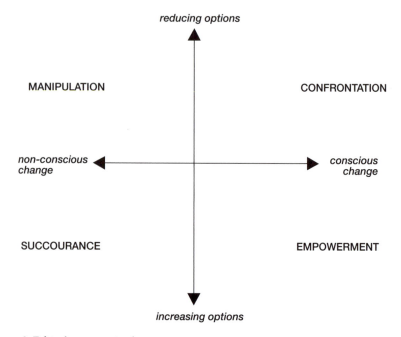

Figure 2 Ethical postures in therapy

Nevertheless it is likely that:

- there are a wide variety of methods available with individuals and families, which can be best understood and described in relation to basic paradigms
- certain key concepts and skills can also be identified
- there is no cure-all; and certain methods will suit certain people and not others
- there is general evidence of the effectiveness of family therapy but not enough knowledge about what is especially effective under what circumstances
- some of the more exciting ideas concern integration of therapies and developing a clearer focus for work
- users have a right to be involved in the choice about the range of options available
- there is some evidence to suggest that flexible combinations of therapy may be more effective
- family situations also present difficult ethical dilemmas for therapists, particularly in relation to confidentiality and privacy
- the complexity and difficulty of assessing and working with family situations should not be taken lightly.

4

DEVELOPMENTS IN FAMILY
ASSESSMENT

Assessment is thus an integral part of intervention, and must
be judged by similar professional and ethical criteria
(Mind Report, 1975)

The historical context

Historically, the study of the family is a relatively recent development
handicapped by a historical divide. The topic was originally ignored by psychologists and left to sociologists. Even today in the UK there is no Family
Division of the BPS and in the USA the Family Division of the APA is a
fairly new body. Those academic psychologists who have become interested
in the family have been very disparaging about the efforts of clinical
researchers. Despite many exhortations for a union of theory, research and
practice, this historical divide is very powerful. Underlying it is also a political struggle between academic scientists and professional practitioners for
control of the discipline of psychology as a whole, best illustrated by the
splitting of the (original) American Psychological Association and the
(newly formed) American Psychological Society. There is no doubt that
there are very important role differences, values and assumptions held by
clinicians and researchers which account for real differences of opinion, but
the dialogue has become hostile and destructive in recent years because of
this political struggle.

Although the field of family therapy is in many ways rich and creative in
ideas, the family therapy movement has never taken assessment seriously. In
their text on family assessment Karpel and Strauss (1984) describe how the
'action orientation' of the early family therapists, particularly the structural-
ists, led to a neglect of the assessment process. This was unfortunate since
the assessment process is critical in formulating the whole shape of an intervention. Indeed in many cases a clearer definition of the problem may be all
that is necessary so that people can go on to deal with the problem themselves. In recent times the social constructivist position has perpetuated this
trend. However valuable this perspective is (and it often is) it can also be
argued that the exclusive use of one theoretical position can be seen as
unethical and unprofessional if it blinds us to other important possibilities.
In health care settings this is especially important.

Three decades ago Lickorish (1968) commented that few well-tried methods were available for the assessment of the family, partly because the study of the family was a relatively recent psychological undertaking. Eleven years later Litman and Venters (1979) gave a methodological overview of research on health care and the family. They concluded that despite interest from behavioural scientists in the role of the family in health and illness, knowledge based upon empirical research had remained rather limited. They emphasized a basic need for measuring instruments to help with research. In fact Strauss (1969) summed up the problem in a comprehensive review of techniques available at that time when he stated 'it is only slightly stretching the point to say that the conceptual status of measurement is not more primitive in the social sciences than in the physical sciences. The key difference lies in the vastly more primitive state of measurement technology in the social sciences.' This was certainly a harsh comment, but at that time was quite accurate. In the last three decades, however, the growing interest of psychologists (albeit in two diverse camps), the development of family therapy in practice and a perceived need to evaluate therapy efficacy have led to a number of developments which are the subject of this chapter.

Assessment and measurement

It is useful at the outset to consider briefly the meanings of such terms as diagnosis, assessment, description and measurement. For the purposes of this work assessment is defined as the process of understanding problems in order to make an intervention which is designed to help solve them. The term diagnosis will be avoided, except when reporting others' work, since it has too many confusing medical connotations. It can be defined as referring more to the final, decision-making, aspects of an assessment. The assessment of families is often mainly descriptive, and clearly the qualities of that description are extremely important. To make a crude distinction, science observes and art creates; but clearly a good assessment relies on good observation and is creative in relation to problem solving. Hence assessment and therapy should involve the strengths of both art and science – they should be creative and rigorous. Although assessment is often descriptive, it can (some would say should) include some kind of measurement. In its crudest sense, measurement refers to the use of some hypothetical or defined standard of comparison, usually with numbers. It might, therefore, be reasonable to assert that a more scientific approach to assessment should incorporate some element of measurement.

Scott Meier (1994) summed up the central problems with all forms of psychological measurement within the assessment process. He begins by giving a clear history of measurement (with its origins in IQ testing) and then describes the development of the split between academics and practitioners. In discussing the origins of this split, he points out how the predictive success of early testing in education and personnel selection led to a neglect of process – of why the tests worked. Yet this is a crucial question. If intelligence is simply a stable capacity to learn, we do not look beyond the issue of selection. But if IQ tests measure culture-specific skills resulting from learning history, we may think about designing intervention programs to enhance those skills. Meier suggests that early measures were too successful and that scale designers still neglect meaning, process and underlying theoretical assumptions about the purpose and function of the measure. There are many other underlying assumptions about what is to be measured that affect the design and use of tests – for example stability versus change, individual differences versus population characteristics, measurement error versus other factors having real effects. Most of the debates in the literature stem from arguments between those who adopt different paradigms and refuse to recognize that other paradigms can be valid for other types of measurement with different purposes. Perhaps the best example is the bitter debate between those who are interested in personality traits and those who are more concerned with how context changes behaviour. Both perspectives can be valid and useful at different times, and neither has a monopoly on truth. Similarly Meier concludes that all measurement devices may be adequate for some purposes but are likely to be invalid for others. Thus the most important principle to grasp about assessment methods is that their value varies widely according to the preconceptions of the designer and their intended purpose. A key difference between the fundamental aims of the researcher and the clinician is that the researcher seeks to establish general laws and rules, while the clinician is more often concerned with understanding the particular idiosyncratic qualities of his clients. Perhaps once it is overtly recognized that different methods are required for different purposes the divide between practitioner and researcher may begin to close.

It is, therefore, useful to sum up some of the preconceptions and functions of clinical assessment with families in the context in which the development of this work occurred. The context was a typical small multi-professional team in a district general hospital. The wide range of (largely unscreened) difficulties focused around children with various problems. This resulted in viewing assessment and therapy as a general problem-solving process. Pragmatically, it became very clear that it was important to understand both the subjective and objective views of a family's problems in order to form a contract for co-operative work which reconciled the two views. Hence the major function of the assessment was to establish whether a contractual arrangement for problem solving could be established with the family (and if it could, what kind of contract was agreed). In order to do this, it was important to listen to and understand the family view(s) of the problem(s) and also how the family members viewed our department. In order to avoid stigmatizing individuals or families it was important to retain a normalizing perspective.

Differences between types or methods of assessment depend on several factors, and different tasks require different technologies. The development of methods of assessment for particular purposes will now be described, considering each in a roughly chronological sequence.

Types of assessment methods

Methods for obtaining information

THE INTERVIEW

In common practice, the interview is used to obtain a purely descriptive form of assessment. However, as early as 1966 Watzlawick had developed a semi-structured interview for families. The imposition of structure within the context of the interview is a critical step which incorporates measurement into what would otherwise be a purely descriptive process. By having a standard procedure, the interviewer comes to define his own standards of comparison after he has used the interview on several occasions. (Responses are then understood as either normal or unusual.) The Camberwell family interview schedule (Brown and Rutter, 1966) provides the classic example of this principle. It was developed to be used with the carers or relatives of patients with severe mental illness particularly where the patient is uncommunicative. The interview facilitates a careful description of the patient's symptoms and behaviour from the relatives' viewpoint plus it often produces great relief for them as they describe their worries and experiences. Most significantly, however, the categorization of carers as low or high expressed emotion is done from this interview.

Towards the mid-1970s a number of other developments began to take place in rapid succession. In the field of adult psychiatry, a number of very elegant structured interviews began to appear which were rapidly acknowledged as extremely useful assessment techniques (e.g. the 'Present State Examination' developed by Wing, Cooper and Sartorius in 1974). These interviews often have forms for observer ratings integrated into the procedure. In child psychiatry Hodges *et al.* (1982) produced a structured interview for use with individual children. In fact there are a number of very good structured interviews (often with associated rating scales) for use with individual children and adolescents (see Harrington, 1993). Although not yet widely used in clinical practice, they provide examples of good practice.

Some well-known training centres for family therapy utilize detailed interview 'proforma' or 'guidelines' (e.g. Bishop, 1987). However there are few widely publicized standardized clinical interviews for families such as that produced by Kinston and Loader (1984; further evaluated in 1986). As these authors point out, many existing interview schedules have not been subject to any formal psychometric evaluation. Even their own study utilized only

17 interviews in evaluating whether the interview was administered in a standardized way, and they ran into a number of other problems. Although they claimed the interviewer 'generally kept to the script', the demands of a clinical situation require some flexibility in order to respond sensitively to a family; this may entail omitting certain items on a script or adding other unscripted items. Hence there is a basic tension between the clinical and scientific purposes of the interview in this context which will invariably reduce the formal reliability of the instrument. In fact their data show that about 40% of the questions were either omitted or changed significantly. However, only 14% of these changes were considered to be inappropriate by an independent observer. As part of their attempts to assess validity, Kinston and Loader also found some degree of concordance between ratings of family functioning based on this interview and ratings based on a task situation, reflecting a moderate degree of concurrent validity. However, what was perhaps more significant is that the researchers ran into particular difficulty when they tried to assess the effects of different interviewers upon the same family. This problem arises from the fact that the interviewer–family relationship will vary in a highly unpredictable manner according to the interactions and transactions generated within this relationship. In particular, the physical appearance of the interviewer and how this is perceived by the family members, and the interviewers' non-verbal actions, cannot be standardized. Training of the interviewers can help to reduce variability of the latter, but there will always be a potentially large reduction of reliability (and thus validity, since reliability puts a ceiling on validity) due to the idiosyncratic qualities of the interviewer in an interview. Efforts to assess test–retest reliability and other aspects of validity were frustrated by poor experimental design. The study illustrates the major problems of interview reliability even when utilizing a structured interview format.

With adequate training, the structured interview in adult psychiatry has been demonstrated to have an acceptable level of reliability and validity (Wing et al., 1974). Although families are certainly likely to generate more unpredictability than individuals, it seems unlikely that this will occur to a degree which makes a systematic and rigorous approach to interviewing invalid – even in a clinical context where the need for sensitivity and flexibility will always make competing demands.

Cox, Rutter and Holbrook (1981) undertook a critical study of interviewing style which supported the use of structured versus non-structured interviews. The former tended to elicit more information without producing any apparent decrease in the amount of emotional behaviour elicited. Furthermore, Brown and Rutter examined the value of the family interview as a research tool as far back as 1966, in a study which also comprised the first development in the technique of assessing expressed emotion. They obtained high levels of inter-rater reliability plus agreement between observed behaviour ratings and global judgements derived from interviews with psychiatric patients and their relatives. They also obtained satisfactory levels of agreement in relation to factual material reported by spouses in separate interviews; with moderate to low agreement in relation to their opinions about relationships. (People tended to be consistent or reliable in their inferences about how their spouses felt, but these inferences were often invalid.) Feelings expressed about the spouse when they were present tended to be similar to when they were absent, with some exceptions. Although these are generally encouraging findings, extensive training was required to produce these results. For children's problems, agreement between the child's report and what the parent reports is low to moderate; children tend to report more affective problems while their parents report more conduct problems (Edelbrock et al., 1986). Hence the differences may reflect important clinical issues which are not 'measurement errors'.

Haynes and Chavez (1983) reviewed the utility of the interview in the assessment of marital distress. They concluded that interviews generally yielded reliable information but that for certain sensitive questions replies could be unreliable. In terms of validity they suggested that the interview adequately discriminated between problem groups and also associated closely with results from other measures such as questionnaires and task performance. However they found that higher levels of validity were found when the spouses were seen separately, as the presence of the spouse particularly affected the replies given to highly sensitive items such as enquiries about the sexual relationship. They interpreted these results as supporting the further development and evaluation of standardized interviews, but also highlighting the need for the use of more than one method of assessment.

Despite enormous problems of reliability, the interview itself remains the most widely used clinical assessment method. It is likely that this arises because the interview provides a context for personal interaction which is considered crucial to the development of a therapeutic relationship. Many authors have pointed out how this must be viewed as the primary task in a helping relationship. Family interviews also provide information about the subjective views and beliefs of individuals and families, and also enable observation of their behaviour by the interviewer. Hence the family interview is likely to remain popular despite a number of problems with respect to variability produced by interviewer characteristics, variations in training, constraints imposed upon the scientific approach by the need for flexibility in a clinical situation, and a lack of disclosure when people feel constrained by the presence of others.

QUESTIONNAIRES

Another common tool for information gathering is the self-report questionnaire. Such instruments originally developed out of a desire to reduce routine repetitive tasks, and became popularized as psychological assessment devices because questionnaire responses could be quantified into totals and sub-totals. This enabled a scientific emphasis to be brought to assessment, since the reliability and validity of the questionnaire scores could be evaluated relatively easily.

However, the design of questionnaires is critical. In particular, in clinical situations it is important that questionnaires are clear, easy to complete, relatively brief, and appear relevant to the family members completing them. From the assessor's point of view, similar characteristics are required in relation to scoring and interpretation. If total scores (or sub-totals) are used then the scale or sub-scale items should be closely related to each other conceptually.

For the assessment of the individual, there is a plethora of questionnaires available. Although there is also a large number of marital questionnaires available, there are few instruments which meet the criteria given above for family work. It is also important to stress that, because of the nature of the self-report questionnaire, this method assesses the individual's view of the family rather than 'the family' itself. This is a major technical problem for scale designers that is often ignored. Where family self-report scales ask for information associated with an outsider's view within a subjective method of assessment, scale validity is inherently compromised, as they confuse one individual's view with whole group phenomena.

Locke and Wallace published one of the earliest marital questionnaires to be used by clinicians in 1959. However, it was not until the 1970s that questionnaires which examined family functioning began to be developed (Pless and Satterwhite, 1973, and Moos and Moos, 1976). Most family questionnaires have been designed by researchers rather than clinicians, and are thus lacking in concepts of clear clinical relevance so that their utility in clinical work, as opposed to academic studies, remains largely unproven. The best of these types of scales is probably Olson's FACES III (Olson, 1986) or the later version of the Family Environment Scale (Moos and Moos 1986). However, Vostanis and Nicholls (1995) reported that this scale showed poor ability to discriminate between well-functioning controls and parents of children with conduct disorder or emotional problems (as opposed to expressed emotion ratings, which did discriminate). They felt that the findings did not support the validity of the scale and advised it should be used with caution by clinicians.

In 1983 Epstein, Baldwin and Bishop published a questionnaire (McMaster Family Assessment Device or MFAD) based upon the McMaster model of family therapy. This would appear to be a significant development since it is one of the first 'family' self-report forms which was purpose-designed by clinical workers around an explicit model of family therapy. Although it is somewhat lengthy and some response choices are ambiguous, it met most of the other criteria for questionnaire design in a standardization using 112 American families. Even so, the MFAD has a low level of discriminative validity, identifying only 67% of non-clinical and 64% of clinical families;

this supports the notion that in many respects there is a wide overlap between these groups. Furthermore Akisker and Stevenson-Hinde (1991) found that the level of agreement between mothers and fathers about their own families within a community sample of intact families was relatively low (correlations ranging from 0.25 to 0.53). Hence there are a number of doubts about the usefulness of family self-reports.

In their guide to methods and measures for family assessment Grotevant and Carlson (1989) identified seventeen self-report measures of whole family function, nine of family stress and coping, and twenty-three measures of parent–child interaction. They assumed that family measures should be comprehensive and complained that only three out of seventeen 'whole family' measures made a comprehensive assessment utilizing constructs of structure, process, affect and orientation to self or world.

In fact the assumption that family questionnaires should be comprehensive is questionable. There is some logic in restricting the content of self-report questionnaires. Self-report methods are likely to be most valid when used to collect information about personal experiences. (Indeed there is evidence to suggest that, because of privacy boundaries, some people will disclose more to a pencil and paper test than to an interviewer, particularly when other family members are present.) From this point of view two developments are significant. The first is the Parenting Stress Index developed by Richard Abidin (1992) available in the UK from NFER-Nelson. This is a self-report questionnaire for parents based upon a clear model of parenting and stress which uses a dimensional analysis to look at child behaviours, temperament, relationship issues between child and parent, and parental supports. It is recommended as a more detailed self-report measure at the parental level. It combines assessment of the child and parent as individuals with information about the parent–child and partner relationship. The Family Grid (developed by Davis and Rushton, 1991, available from NFER-Nelson in the child psychology portfolio: see pages 201–203) is a briefer measure that focuses on the three key areas of self-esteem; satisfaction with partner relationship; and satisfaction with child relationship. It was designed as a clinical instrument which would help give a focus for professionals working in a counselling relationship with parents having problems with their children. It has proved to be effective as a therapeutic tool and as a measure of change in a variety of services dealing with a variety of problems.

Margolin and Fernandez (1983) reviewed self-report questionnaires and outlined some of their chief uses:

- a valuable perspective on the perceived intensity and details of problems
- helping to plan an intervention by specifying target problems more clearly
- enabling normative comparisons for specific problems
- a cost-effective way of collecting information or screening for problems

- a safe medium for disclosing information which might not be readily disclosed in an interview.

Hence although questionnaires can only provide subjective information, and appear impersonal, they have several important uses (in addition to being much easier to evaluate psychometrically than the interview).

NATURALISTIC OBSERVATION

The ethological approach to the study of animal behaviour developed out of a reaction to the artificiality of laboratory experimental work. Similarly, it can be claimed that the behaviour of families in a clinic situation is likely to be rather different from their behaviour in their natural environment or home. (Indeed, the environment that the family lives in is itself an important feature of the situation which should be included in a comprehensive assessment of a family and its problems.)

However, the difficulties of using a purely ethological approach in a clinical context are immense. First, the ethical constraints in human research require that observations are made overtly and with consent, giving rise to problems of privacy versus subject reactivity (see the factors mentioned by Vetere and Gale in 1987). Second, properly conducted naturalistic observation is a very time-consuming procedure because of the need to repeat observations over an extensive time period. The time constraints on most public service personnel preclude spending such a large amount of time to collect information about particular families. Although community approaches are current policy, time pressures on most child and family services lead to the majority of the work being clinic-based as a matter of 'efficiency' (seeing more people by reducing travelling time). Third, even if these other conditions can be overcome, the situation whereby a family either seeks or is referred for help carries certain 'demand characteristics' which are likely to prevent behaviour from being 'natural'. (For example, a family actively seeking help may deliberately exaggerate any problem behaviours; while other families who are embarrassed or have been encouraged to attend by another agency will be likely to inhibit displays of problem behaviours.) These problems, inherent in any referral to a clinical service, result in naturalistic observation being little used, despite the obvious attractiveness of observing the family system in its natural context. In the terms of generalizability theory (Cronbach, Rajaratnam and Gleser 1963) it seems axiomatic that naturalistically generated observations of behaviour should be much more generalizable since the behaviour observed is presumably more typical, and therefore more likely to be repeated in other contexts.

Hence as a method of collecting information, naturalistic observation can perhaps be considered as the ideal method to provide objective information about family behaviour. However the demand characteristics and time constraints inherent in a clinical service make this method difficult to use in clinical practice. The reader is referred to Vetere and Gale (1987) for further information.

One of the major problems with naturalistic observation is that in order to observe behaviour which is important and relevant, much time is wasted observing other behaviours which are not. In practice, therefore, the imposition of structure within an interview situation can be taken so far as to include a directive for the family to perform a particular task which is designed to reveal important behaviours. Family tasks are an interesting variant of the structured interview because they reveal a different type of information. Family tasks are designed to reveal ongoing patterns of behaviour or 'family processes' rather than a family's verbal understanding of the problems. This purpose arises from the fact that a family may not be willing or able to give an accurate description of the problems that would be seen by an observer. In family therapy terms, the family task is a standardized 'enactment'. Note, however, that while an interview may reveal verbal understanding and processes, a task will usually only yield process information.

Particular tasks are specifically designed to highlight particular aspects of behaviour, such as the degree of co-operation in approaching a task that requires concerted action. Clearly all tasks involve demands of an explicit nature and the level of compliance to this demand by the various individuals involved will be influenced by the general demand characteristics of the situation. Hence the probability of the observations being generalizable is likely to be lower than for naturalistic observations, but the method is a briefer and more efficient way of collecting data about observed behaviour and relationship processes.

Another problem concerns the complexity of the observed processes. Task approaches have proved more popular with individuals or with dyadic tasks in parenting skills or marital therapy. These behavioural tasks are inherently easier to structure and analyse than a task which involves an unspecified number of family members.

In marital work Keck and Sporakowski (1982) asserted that it was essential to have information about observed behaviours and interactions as well as self-reports. They categorized tasks into three main types – problem solving, decision making, and conflict resolution, giving examples of each.

Tasks for parents and children allow an objective assessment of parenting behaviour or parenting style. The 'Parent/Child Game' developed by Forehand and McMahon (1981) uses play as a medium for training parenting skills. The authors carried out a ten-year programme of investigation in the United States, using both a non-clinic and clinic sample of a total of 140 three- to eight-year-olds and their mothers. As a result of the training given to the mothers, using the Parent/Child Game, there was a significant increase in their differential use of contingent rewards, clear commands and time out in response to their children's behaviour. A decrease in non-compliant behaviour by the children was also shown to have occurred at a significant level. Follow-up at six and twelve months also demonstrated that the newly acquired parenting behaviours had generalized to the home environment and been maintained over the follow-up interval. More recent data (Forehand and Long, 1988) have established these trends over the much longer follow-up period of 8–10 years. In addition the authors have shown that the improvement quality of the parent/child interaction and the more positive parental perceptions of the children also survived over this extended time-span. Eyberg and Robinson (1981) developed three specific tasks within the same situation to examine the quality of parent–child interaction. They utilize a playroom situation under three conditions: child-directed play, parent-directed play, and child tidies up. This allows for the consideration of both care and control within the relationship. It certainly seems possible to establish a reasonable degree of validity and reliability for task approaches if there is a purpose-designed means of classifying and scoring the behaviours observed (see the section on coding systems). For example, Eyberg and Robinson validated the clinical utility of their procedure in 1982 by showing that changes observed in their task correlated with general improvements in behaviour problems and family functioning for disturbed pre-school children. The methods do demand time and resources but they appear valid, reliable and clinically potent.

Whilst marital tasks (also dyadic) have also been shown to have adequate psychometric properties (Filsinger, 1983) it is not so clear that a task involving whole family groups can be proved to be as reliable and valid given that the potential for random effects is likely to increase with the size of the group. Gilbert and Christensen (1985) pointed out that most studies of task approaches tend to demonstrate low cross-situation generalizability with respect to family interactions. However, Kinston and Loader (1988) recently developed a set of six (or seven, in the revised version) tasks into a standardized package known as the 'Family Task Interview'. They stress that in their view the task is a context for research, not a measurement instrument, which is intended to produce clinically relevant behaviour. Although the tasks do seem to be relevant, the means of scoring the task relied mainly upon the use of a general family behaviour rating scale rather than a purpose-designed scoring system for each task. Nevertheless they claimed to demonstrate adequate levels of test–retest reliability, and of concurrent and discriminative validity in a study using 300 British families with mixed clinical and normal samples. This work offers some promise and clearly might be improved by using more specific measures of task behaviours. On the other hand, there is no doubt that objective assessment of family transactional behaviour is conceptually complex and likely to be very expensive.

Projective tests can be considered a variant in which the task is deliberately less structured often with very free or flexible response formats so that the respondent is assumed to project hidden or unconscious aspects of themselves into their responses. For children, this can illuminate needs, preoccupations, attachment styles and conflicts. There is no doubt that with younger children projective techniques such as free play, drawing and role play are widely used as forms of assessment since they may be the only way that meaningful communication can be established. As an example, Figure 3 shows a drawing produced by an adopted girl struggling with an attachment disorder stemming from difficult early childhood experiences.

The drawing most powerfully and eloquently explains her feelings of isolation and difficulty connecting with her (very caring) adoptive parents. Another useful and more specific projective technique is the 'make a world'

Figure 3 Drawing by child with attachment disorder

(Lowenfeld 1979) which entails creating a miniature world in a sand tray. The Bene–Anthony Family Relations Test (Bene, 1978) is a particularly useful semi-projective task which is adapted to the developmental level of the child. The child constructs their family using a set of figures and then posts messages about important feelings, phrased in children's language, to the figures. When used conversationally it can be a superb way of getting to know and understand the child's world. However the manual is outdated and weak; and there is little or no comparative data. This is in fact the main problem with most projective methods – sometimes the results are spectacularly clear, as with the drawing illustrated. However, much of the time an inexperienced practitioner may have little idea how significant or unusual the results are.

Methods for recording and organizing information

OBSERVER RATING SCALES

Clinicians working with families tended initially to opt for a checklist of areas of family functioning – which might be considered to be a crude and purely descriptive form of observer rating scale. For example, in 1971 Kadushin produced an instrument of this type which attempted to integrate systematically concepts from a variety of theories and studies. As such it was an interesting instrument which gave a wide variety of perspectives upon family life but lacked a central theme.

Observer rating scales have tended to be popular with clinicians because they usually provide a brief and efficient record form which summarizes the important aspects of the 'thing observed' (in this case, the family). Once one is familiar with a rating scale, they can be completed extremely quickly. Provided that the content of the scale matches the theoretical perspective of the observer, they are genuinely labour-saving. They also have the attraction of introducing a crude type of measurement into the situation. More sophisticated scales also provide inbuilt guidelines for summarizing the information and guiding the clinician through the decision-making process of the assessment. Their disadvantages are that, because the judgements required tend to relate to a small range of specific issues, rating scales tend to provide a 'narrow focus'. They also rely heavily upon the skill of the observer as well as the clarity of definition of the terms used. Even relatively simple rating scales require a period of practice and training for the user to familiarize themselves with the particular concepts and terms used in the scales. In essence, although they can be claimed to be an 'objective' method of assessment they are liable to profound subjective distortions by the user. Reliability, which may be poor initially, drops when it is not assessed (Reid, 1970). Nevertheless, procedures for evaluating reliability and validity of rating scales are well established, and so their deficiencies can at least be put to the test.

Lewis *et al.* (1976) utilized ratings of global family health and pathology in their study of psychological health in families. They found that when ranking heterogeneous groups of families inter-rater reliability was high, but that this reliability dropped when attempts were made to rank within a homogenous group of families. Hence the distinctions that can be made using rating scales with families are likely to be crude at best.

Despite this inherent problem, the rating scale has continued to be one of the most popular types of instruments among clinical workers. The 'McMaster model' of family functioning and therapy (Epstein and Bishop, 1981) is based upon six dimensions of family functioning (problem solving, communication, roles, affective responsiveness, affective involvement and behaviour control). To accompany the model of therapy, there are various assessment forms, including descriptive rating scales for each dimension.

In Britain, the London Family Studies group produced a succession of instruments culminating in the 'Family Health Scales' (Kinston, Loader and Miller, 1987). The aim was to develop a global measure of the effectiveness of family functioning or 'family health'. Various family systems concepts are used as observer rating scales which give a method for structuring and organizing a detailed description of a family's structure and function in a way which is likely to be clinically useful. There are six main scales (affective status, communication, boundaries, alliances, adaptability and stability, and family competence) and twenty-six sub-scales. Each sub-scale has a seven-point rating scale with defined anchor points for ratings 1,3, 5 and 7 which represent breakdown of functioning, significant dysfunction, adequate function, and optimal function. The instrument certainly has adequate reliability but efforts to demonstrate validity had mixed results. These scales are most suitable for clinicians or researchers who have further training in systemic practice who require a comprehensive assessment of the family system.

Another clinically derived alternative would be the Beavers Interactional Scales (Beavers and Hampson, 1990). These consist of two observer rating scales related to family competence and family style. The scales have been developed over a twenty-five year clinical treatment, training and research program by the Timberlawn group including W. Robert Beavers from whom the scales take their name. The Family Competence scale is intended to assess a global quality of competence, or how well the family performs its necessary developmental tasks: providing support and nurturance, establishing effective generational boundaries and leadership, promoting growth and individuation of the offspring, negotiating effectively, and communicating effectively. The Family Style scales refer more to the systemic characteristics of the family system as a whole. These scales are directly related to the more theoretical aspects of the Beavers model of family functioning, which characterizes family systems as either centripetal (inward looking and internalizing in their beliefs, values, views and actions) or centrifugal (outward looking with tenuous boundaries, tending to look outside the family for key values, separate more readily, and act more as individuals). The Competence scale offers a shorter alternative to the Family Health scales for those interested in assessing the global characteristics of the family from a systemic point of view. The Family Style scale is one of the best examples of a more theoretical (as opposed to functional) approach to overall family characteristics. Like the FHS, these scales will be of particular interest to practitioners and trainers in systemic therapy.

Carlson and Grotevant (1987) give an excellent summary of the major issues for rating scale designers. In relation to the choice of scale dimensions they recommend that dimensions should be clearly defined; should reflect stable, enduring and observable constructs; that the behaviour to be observed is likely to occur in the context used; that the construct is single rather than mixed; and that there is an adequate standard of reference with an adequate number of discrimination points. They go on to review eight scales for family assessment, concluding that in general their psychometric quality is mixed (particularly in relation to the choice and characteristics of dimensions used) and that they concentrate too much on whole family characteristics and not enough on the parts. Nevertheless they conclude that the rating scale, although 'replete with methodological challenges' is still likely to be a method of choice for the practitioner because it is cost-effective, non-intrusive, gives a perspective on severity, and helps to focus interventions.

In summary despite their popularity rating scales have distinct problems with reliability and validity – hence they are unlikely to provide anything other than crude distinctions on global measures. In addition, the concepts and points used within the scales need to be carefully defined, and preferably the ratings should be completed using information obtained from a standard procedure. If these conditions are met rating scales of individual and dyadic behaviour can usually be shown to be reliable and valid. In respect of family ratings, there is not enough evidence to draw the same conclusion – but good clinical scales also offer a practical method for organizing complex patterns of information.

BEHAVIOUR CODING SYSTEMS

Behaviour coding systems are the main method for organizing information derived from an 'objective' analysis of a sample of behaviour, usually obtained from a task or naturalistic observation. They have an intrinsic scientific appeal and face validity, since they provide a more powerful level of measurement of observed behavioural events. However, coding systems rely on very precise linguistic definitions of behaviours and clear criteria for quantifying them. If the definitions and criteria are clear, they can provide potentially very powerful methods of measurement in respect of observed behaviours and processes. Their major disadvantage is that most methods require very thorough training of the scorers and the process of accurately coding behaviour is also very time-consuming.

Coding systems were first used by social psychologists examining inter-personal behaviour in groups (e.g. Borgatta, 1962). These methods were also used with a great deal of early success by some of the workers investigating communication processes in the families of schizophrenics around this time. Singer and Wynne (1963) showed that coding of communications could discriminate relatives of psychotics from relatives of non-psychotics.

However, this early work did not lead to great interest in coding systems and it was the popularization of behavioural therapy which led to them being more widely used. Patterson, Cobb and Ray (1973) developed a coding system which was used to identify problems and monitor therapeutic progress with the families of delinquent boys. However, this coding system was complex and time-consuming to use, as it uses naturalistic observations to gather the data. In fact Eyberg and Robinson (1981) derived their coding system, which is much simpler and easier to use, from the Patterson system. Unlike the Patterson system, this coding method is designed for use in a specific clinical setting (a playroom) and for younger age children. The behavioural definitions and concepts used are clear and relevant to important aspects of parent–child interaction, and the system is used in conjunction with the standardized task procedure mentioned earlier. The system shows good discriminative and other validity (Aragona and Eyberg, 1981; Robinson and Eyberg, 1981) and has also been shown to be sensitive to changes occurring during therapy (Eyberg and Robinson, 1982). This coding system appears to be unusually brief and efficient to use compared with others.

In child work they have been mainly used with parent–child interaction, although other workers have developed equally useful systems for use with marital problems. Filsinger (1983) reviewed a collection of assessment methods which included several coding systems for marital work. Most demonstrated adequate reliability given proper training plus good discriminative validity, as well as being able to document changes occurring during interventions. He also listed several factors which are important in the selection or design of behaviour coding systems. First, the codes can refer to various levels of behaviour, i.e. from global, interpretative codes such as 'friendliness' to very specific microbehaviours such as 'shaking hands'. Second, codes can focus upon various aspects of relationships depending upon the preconceptions and purposes of the user – in other words, the type of behaviours being coded such as 'parent–child inter-actions'. Third, the time and energy available and required for particular systems has to be considered. This is largely a function of the number of codes and the particular methods of data collection (naturalistic observation, interview or task) and its organization. Dowdney et al. (1984) distinguished between methods of organizing data which only rely upon frequency counts (and whether this is by event sampling, momentary time sampling or interval time sampling) and those which also utilize time sequencing (sometimes utilizing a 'key' event to begin a sequence recording). Clearly the more complicated these methods are, the greater the time required for the collection and analysis of data. (Sequencing is a particularly interesting strategy as it gives direct access to process information, but the data produced are much more complex to interpret.) Fourth, Filsinger pointed out that in addition to time constraints the purpose of the assessment also determined the level of information required, the context of the assessment, and the nature of the data collection methods (e.g. if one was interested in assessing repetitive patterns of marital interaction, it would clearly be essential to use sequencing strategies). These factors are not only critical in the design of coding systems but they also limit the generalizability of the findings derived from their use. For example, Stuart (1980) commented in a text on marital work that the interpretation of codes may appear straightforward, but cites examples where investigations found confusing results. For example, 'laugh' may be coded as a positive event but occurs frequently in conflict as a cynical expression; conversely 'disagreement' can be classified as a negative event but has been found to occur more in non-distressed couples (who are more open in their conflict resolution).

Generally speaking, it has certainly been demonstrated with both parent–child and marital coding systems that adequate levels of reliability and validity can be obtained. Usually, however, this is at a great cost in terms of time and effort – the system reported by Dowdney et al. above required three months' training for the coders.

However, efforts to code behaviours relating to whole family transactions (rather than dyadic interactions between two family members) have been less successful. Grotevant and Carlson (1987) reviewed family interaction coding systems (primarily of verbal interactions) developed since 1970. They describe only thirteen systems, many of which were not formally published. They concluded that few of the scales had very much in common owing to differences in theoretical orientation, underlying assumptions, and constructs used. Although reliability was usually adequate, evidence for the validity of most of the systems was poor. They also noted a trend towards 'macroratings' rather than the coding of microbehaviours. (In fact, a rating scale can be considered to be a coding system which is based upon a single, lengthy time sample; the distinction between rating scales and coding systems is not absolute.) It seems likely that the complexity of whole family phenomena makes it more difficult to establish valid and relevant behavioural codes, whereas for individual behaviours and dyadic interactions this is easier. Whatever the reason, evidence for the applicability of dyadic coding systems is much more convincing than for coding with families.

Family coding seems only to be practical when it focuses upon particular aspects of behaviour. Stratton *et al.* (1986) have produced a coding system based upon attribution theory which examines the views and causal beliefs of individuals within families regarding their problems. This is therefore an unusual coding system in that it codes beliefs expressed by family members during discussions rather than behavioural events. This method therefore assesses subjective and cognitive characteristics of both the individual and the family, and may lead to a greater understanding of how family rules and beliefs determine behaviour. Another important development concerns the concept of expressed emotion which can be considered as a hybrid of rating and coding system. Berkowitz (1987) showed that the EE coding method could be applied reliably to family members observed during initial (unstructured) family interviews.

DIAGRAMMATIC METHODS

Finally, mention should be made of diagrammatic methods of summarizing and organizing information about families. In particular, Minuchin (1974) developed a useful shorthand for representing family structure in a simple diagram. Other authors such as Lieberman (1979) utilize genograms or 'family trees' in order to summarize important relationships and issues within families. Whilst no efforts seem to have been made to collect any psychometric data on such issues as reliability, these diagrams are certainly widely used by clinicians to summarize important features of the family, generate hypotheses about underlying or unconscious problems, and determine therapeutic strategies.

General trends and theoretical considerations

The developments in these methods need to be understood in relation to the general background of family work. In what is effectively a new and evolving field, there has been a rapid growth in the availability and impact of technology (audio and video recording facilities) as well as the new theoretical approaches described earlier. The application of system type theories has created a quiet but massive revolution in child and family work by giving a conceptual framework with which to understand the family as a whole, and the relationships of the parts of the family to the whole, rather than simply understanding 'individuals'. Since nearly all psychotherapy had previously been conceptualized in terms of its impact upon 'the individual', this new framework has aroused several interesting issues in relation to assessment.

One of the problems of rapid growth has been a tendency to proliferate new ideas and methods rather than consolidate and integrate what is already known. Fisher reviewed the existing literature back in 1976 and extracted five key 'dimensions of family assessment'. In simple terms, these were the 'common threads' that ran through all the various methods of assessment he reviewed, in terms of the types of phenomena which were thought to be important in clinical work with families. The dimensions were structural descriptors; controls and sanctions; emotions and needs; cultural aspects; and developmental aspects.

The issue of how to classify is another extremely important issue. Medical classification schemes are usually categorical because of the historical success of illness categories derived from bacteriological infections and other discrete causes. However, they are unlikely to be much use in a situation of multiple causes. In a further important review in 1977, Fisher looked at previous attempts to 'classify' families and concluded that the notion of family 'types' or 'categories' was simply not supported by empirical evidence. He argued that it would be far better to use 'dimensional' analyses which were purpose-designed for broad types of problems (e.g. child-focused problems). Within child psychiatry, a growing awareness of the importance of psycho-social factors had already led to the abandonment of exclusively 'categorical' diagnosis in favour of a multi-axial diagnostic system (e.g. Rutter, Shaffer and Shepherd, 1975). Hence the use of simplistic categories can be challenged on two main grounds. First, it can be argued that there is a finite limit to the descriptive meanings that can be packed into one label or descriptor. Hence assessment using categories is likely to result in stereotyping and other confusion and misconceptions (e.g. with depression and its sub-types). Second, there are also empirical arguments as to whether such 'clusters' or 'syndromes' exist – which Fisher discusses in relation to families, and concludes that they do not.

In 1976 Cromwell, Olson and Fournier reviewed marital and family assessment methods and pointed out that different methods of assessment provide different types of information (see Table 6).

Keeney and Cromwell elaborated these ideas in 1977 in an important article entitled 'Towards systemic diagnosis'. The latter term was defined as 'a way of knowing a given problematic situation through evaluating various system levels and their interplay'. This theoretical approach acknowledges that

Table 6 Assessment methods

		Type of data	
		Subjective	Objective
REPORTER'S FRAME	Insider	Self-report methods	Behaviour self-reports
OF REFERENCE	Outsider	Observer subjective reports	Behavioural methods

(From Cromwell, Olson and Fournier, 1976)

different diagnostic procedures provide different types of information. The information yielded can be classified by what level of system is assessed. Critical to the notion of systemic diagnosis is that different system levels can be assessed and evaluated within the context of a multisystem perspective:

> information is drawn from various system levels by tools and techniques which are appropriately matched to the particular system level(s) of interest and the therapist's 'need to know'. Then the collected bits and pieces of information can be interpreted as a whole, i.e. from a general systems perspective. This multi-level systemic approach enables the therapist to obtain a more holistic picture of the problematic situation.
>
> (Keeney and Cromwell, 1977)

In other words, they argued that one should not only evaluate the system as a whole, but also the interplay of the various individuals and sub-systems within the family, in order to obtain a more holistic picture of the situation.

However, perhaps the best clarification of this approach was that of Cromwell and Peterson who proposed the notion of 'multisystem–multimethod' (MSMM) assessment in 1983. This elaborated the notion of 'systemic diagnosis' by proposing that it was not only important to evaluate the parts and their relationship to the whole ('multisystem') but it was also important to utilize different methods of assessment since they yield very different types of information. 'Multimethod' assessment can be illustrated by Table 7, which shows a further classification of various types of assessment methods in more concrete terms.

MSMM is defined as relying upon four key principles:

1   the use of strategies to understand wholeness, hierarchy and parts of the system
2   the use of formal assessment methods as clinical aids
3   the correct matching of assessment methods to the information required
4   the need to develop links between research, theory and practice.

Table 7 Multimethod assessment

	Family perspective	*Observer perspective*
Cognitive understanding	Questionnaires	Family rating scales
Behaviour processes	Interview	Observation, tasks + coding systems

One of the major arguments for multimethod assessment is that if we rely on only one of these assessment methods, we are likely to have problems since an observer's view of a family often differs from their own (various) views of themselves, and what they say they do may not be confirmed by observations of their actual behaviour. Nevertheless, families are inter-dependent. Examination of the meaning underlying disagreements is highly likely to yield information which is clinically relevant. (There is also a difficult ethical question involved in this issue, which hinges upon whether the subjective or objective perspective is 'more correct' than the other. When does a clinical worker have a right or duty to impose his or her view on the family? Three issues appear to be important:

- the confidence of the clinician in her view
- the potential risks of not challenging the family view
- the contractual issues involved in the relationship, i.e. seeking permission to confront.)

As a further illustration of the need for MSMM assessment, let us take the observer's standpoint and assume on this occasion that his perspective is more valid. Table 8 then shows how the changes required in therapy vary according to whether the family and the observer agree about whether the problems exist. In practice there are often differing views within a family, so that the table is an over-simplification, but this distinction has important implications in certain situations (e.g. parents who complain about behaviours which are an integral part of normal development).

Without considering both kinds of views, the nature of these changes cannot be defined in this way. Hence the use of multiple methods of assessment can clarify important issues in assessment with relation to therapy.

The MSMM notion has aroused some controversy and the debate about it has been a very rich one. Reiss (1983) in particular made some

Table 8 Type of change required

		Subjective problems i.e. acknowledged by family	
		YES	NO
Objective problems i.e. observed by outsider	YES	Behaviour change	Perceptual and behaviour change
	NO	Perceptual change	No change

important comments. Though he applauded Cromwell's and Peterson's efforts to introduce formal methods of assessment into family work, he criticized the MSMM concept as confusing, deceptive and misleading. In particular he attacked the notion of systemic levels (or 'hierarchies') pointing out that without clarification or understanding of the relationships and processes between different 'levels' there was a danger of being seduced by a false sense of sophistication. Reiss was fair to criticize a lack of clarity in the specification of relationships between various systemic levels. However, it seemed unfair to criticize on the grounds of empirical data being required, since an application of the MSMM approach would provide what has so far been lacking in this respect. Reiss also criticizes the concept of multimethod assessment, advocating a much sparser approach in which clinicians select out particular tests of relevance rather than using a 'test battery' *in toto*. He suggests that MSMM is likely to lead to an over-reliance on testing by the clinician, and feared that it may have negative effects on certain families. This is a sensible point which any clinician would accept but it relates to sensible practice rather than any fundamental rejection of the idea. In their reply Peterson and Cromwell (1983) emphasized that their aim was to recognize and explore the interdependence between parts of the system (i.e. individuals, marital dyad, family).

Meanwhile in other fields of psychotherapy there is support for some of the principles underlying this approach. Achenbach (1986) recommended the use of a 'developmentally-normed, multidimensional and multisituational' classification of psychopathology.

The practical work in this book (see Part II) was initially heavily influenced by the idea of MSMM assessment. The Darlington Family Assessment System (DFAS) in its original form consisted of an integrated package of assessment methods developed at the Marion Family Centre in Darlington between 1983 and 1993. It used a deliberately pluralistic framework to understand the family (and individuals within it) using core concepts from the literature as problem dimensions. A semi-structured family interview showed how the framework could be used in practice and a matching rating scale was also provided. As time has gone by, my personal view is that the most valuable aspects of the system have been the conceptual framework and the act of focusing on the process of the assessment. Because the conceptual framework is designed around widely acknowledged concepts it is easy to use in conjunction with other established assessment methods; so that the system can be used at the centre of a very flexible initial assessment. One of the aims was to develop an efficient and pragmatic assessment which could be used for both clinical and training purposes – so that I have come to see the system in total as a set of elaborated clinical guidelines (see p. 245). The main uses of the system therefore are:

- as the basis of a comprehensive child and family assessment, screening and consultation package for child services dealing with a wide variety of problems
- as a training device at basic or immediate post-qualification stage to encourage the understanding of the family background in relation to the problem and therefore to develop formulation skills
- to encourage the development of family interviewing skills

The DFAS has a developmental–eclectic theory as a central theme which has been developed to suit the majority of mainstream clinical practitioners. It is explicitly pluralistic in evaluating both individual and family system characteristics. It was developed to fit in with mainstream clinical practice, and to be used with other assessment methods in a flexible way. Because it was developed in a small clinical service the empirical support for it is weak using academic criteria, but it was always intended as a practitioner's tool and was not designed for use as a research instrument.

There are three other models of clinical family assessment which have produced a range of assessment and training devices. The London Family Studies Group (Kinston, Loader, Bentovim and colleagues) is similar in being a practitioner-based group but the difference is that their conceptual frame stems more from the family therapy field. This group produced the family interview mentioned earlier, the 'Family Health Scales' (Kinston, Loader and Miller, 1987) and the 'Family Task Interview' (Kinston and Loader, 1988). All these instruments have been loosely designed around the model of focal family therapy (Bentovim and Kinston, 1978) and they are intended primarily as devices to aid training in this model, as well as for research purposes. Perhaps because of different emphases within the group, however, the three instruments tend to have been published separately, without very clear links being made to the focal model. Therefore although this can be considered as an MSMM package, it is not widely known, nor has it been applied, as such.

In Canada and the USA, the McMaster group (Epstein and Bishop, 1981) have produced a coherent MSMM system based upon their model of family therapy. This system is explicitly intended as a training model, places clear emphasis upon the assessment process, and incorporates an interview schedule, rating scales and a self-report questionnaire. It has an explicit systems-behavioural base as a central theme, and the model is extensively explained in a number of publications. However, one major problem is that its systems-behavioural ideology may reduce its appeal to practitioners with different orientations; this also leads to a neglect of assessment of family members as individuals. In practice, some users complain that the model also requires an unwieldy amount of detail which makes it difficult to use in a busy public service setting. As an assessment 'package' it lacks a task and a behaviour coding system (although given the nature of the McMaster theory these should not be difficult to produce). While the London group have tended to publish their methods separately as research devices, the McMaster group have been preoccupied with presenting their system as a therapeutic method rather than as a method for assessment. Thus this method has also not been publicized or widely used as an assessment package.

A third clinically derived model is the Beavers and Hampson model which was mentioned in relation to rating scales. Using this assessment framework allows families to be categorized into one of nine groups according to family system properties, and interventions suitable for each group are described. This model has self-report and rating scales, one of which is completed in relation to a brief family task. It has been used over a long period as a training device which is aimed at systemic therapists who wish to bring some clear rationale and organization to their choice of technique with particular families. It therefore tends to focus rather too much on system properties at the expense of other perspectives.

Therefore, it is difficult to comment on the wider applicability of such packages, and the advantages and problems of using them, except indirectly. Some evidence on the actual relationships between assessment results using different methods is already available. For a variety of problems, it has been shown that methods using different perspectives often have quite low agreement. For example, the correlation between self-reports and observer ratings of depression only accounts for about one third of the variance (Bailey and Coppen, 1976). Margolin (1978) found little or no correspondence between global ratings of marital satisfaction and observer ratings of positive and negative communication skills. Griest and Wells (1983) pointed out the low concordance rate between parents' perceptions of behaviour and observed deviant behaviour in children. Oliveri and Reiss (1984) found no significant association between similar concepts assessed using a family self-report scale and family task. Walker, Thompson and Lindsay (1984) found little generalizability of results obtained from rating a number of aspects of family relationships based upon either an interview or direct observation of task behaviour.

Although this lack of agreement using different methods of assessment may appear discouraging, an examination of the meaning underlying the disagreement confirms that investigation using different methods is likely to yield information which is clinically relevant. For example, in the case of children's behaviour problems the use of a questionnaire completed by parents and an objective assessment of behaviour could yield four alternatives using the scheme used in Table 8, which could be interpreted as:

1   the problem exists in reality and co-operation is likely
2   the problem exists but the parent has no insight and is unlikely to co-operate

3   the parent has unrealistic expectations of the child's behaviour, which is
    in fact normal for his age
4   there is no actual (or perceived) problem.

Each of these four situations are clearly qualitatively different. Since it
appears that different methods often produce discrepant results, the use of
multiple methods of assessment is therefore likely to clarify important clinical issues. However this will also mean that traditional scientific methods of
assessing reliability and validity within the package will yield 'poor' results.
This is a crucial point to bear in mind when evaluating empirical studies.

It seems likely that the major difficulty with MSMM assessment is
pragmatic: how can such a complex approach to assessment remain brief
and efficient?

An article by Bentovim (1989) illustrates this potential complexity. He
contributed a means of analysing different methods of family assessment by
providing a classification of seven levels of descriptions that can be made in
relation to families. (This is an application of a more general model of
enquiry described by Kinston in 1988.) In order to provide more of a
hierarchy, the order of the levels presented has been modified slightly:

Level 1: items of interaction   These are observable events or interactions
which must be interpreted in their context but are nevertheless relatively
clear and unambiguous behaviours, such as shouting.

Level 2: episodes of family life such as an argument.   These are built up from
Level 1 patterns and refer to a broader time span of interaction between
family members. As such, they constitute a subjective judgement by the
assessor about family events.

Level 3: concepts or dimensions of interaction   These are necessary to organize
and make sense of Level 2 information – concepts such as boundaries, power
and communication. As such they should be logical, comprehensive and
consistent with Levels 1 and 2, and form a means of giving a higher order
interpretation.

Level 4: type formulations   These are an even higher order interpretation of
information ultimately derived from Level 1, such as the classification of
families as 'chaotic' or 'enmeshed' owing to the perception of a known
pattern by the assessor in Level 3 descriptions.

Level 5: patterns of subjective meaning   This refers to a different domain – the
meanings and interpretations made by family members, such as the father's
fear of separation from his wife. Although this can be inferred from patterns
of Level 1 or 2, obviously it may also be accessed directly.

Level 6: holistic views This refers to attempts to integrate information from the other levels to produce an overall explanation or hypothesis which connects various levels such as the observed family patterns of interaction, certain life events and their meaning to family members. An example of such a view would be a 'focal hypothesis' that a family's difficulties resulted from unacknowledged grief which prevented the parent from letting the children separate.

Level 7: predictions of outcome This level focuses upon characteristics which are thought to be useful in predicting response to therapy, based on research or experience. An example would be characterizing families as either open or closed systems. This level of description can be derived in various ways: from observed interactions, type formulations, interaction with the assessor, or indeed from subjective attitudes expressed by family members.

Bentovim suggests that it is useful when evaluating an assessment device to consider how many of these levels are encompassed within the device, and what emphasis is placed upon each level. A comprehensive assessment should include aspects of assessment on each of the levels. This is a somewhat daunting standard to aspire to.

In fact, the current state of the art is rarely so comprehensive. As a conclusion to their guide to methods and measures for family assessment Grotevant and Carlson (1989) identified several major problems:

- a lack of theoretical consensus adding to a proliferation of different measures
- poor links between theory and measurement in practice
- a lack of empirical support for many measures
- most research measures are not yet adequate for use by practitioners
- measures also need to assess various levels of the family.

Academic-generated developments can be accepted as scientific – but often do not seem relevant to practitioners who continue to regard them as irrelevant to practice. Practitioner developments, on the other hand, arise from innovations in practice settings which will often be regarded as unscientific or without proper scientific proof by academics and leading researchers. Often this is because the practitioner does not have access to the resources needed to prove the work is useful, and the divide persists. It is easy to add to this list of difficulties. Most of the family relationship concepts are inferred from group behaviour which are likely to be very difficult to define and measure compared to aspects of individual behaviour. Traditional scientific methods of assessing reliability and validity within complex assessment packages are likely to yield 'poor' results because of the process of comparing data from different system sources or different methods.

The result of all this is that at present family and relationship measures tend to be either scientifically respectable or clinically useful but rarely both. Because this book is primarily for practitioners the instruments considered in detail have been chosen for their clinical and training utility. They may have potential as research methods, but this is often unproven.

L'Abate and Bagarozzi (1992) provided another sourcebook on marital and family evaluation which criticized both researchers and clinicians but at least acknowledged the differences in roles and value systems between them which underlie the divide. They conclude that any instrument used for diagnostic assessment with families should have its roots in a theory of family development across the life cycle – and be multi-dimensional.

Recent trends

In the UK the profession of clinical psychology was the subject of an independent review as part of a government-led report. This delineated one core professional skill as the ability to utilize and integrate psychological theories and methods derived from several perspectives in a way that meets the particular needs of the situation concerned (Manpower Advisory Group, 1990). In relation to children and families, this can mean using a variety of assessment methods and therapeutic models (behavioural, cognitive, psychodynamic and systemic) in creative ways which meet the particular needs of the child and family.

This model of professional activity connects very strongly with the trend towards psychotherapy integration mentioned in Chapter 3. Some assessment devices are explicitly derived from a single therapeutic model, while others are derived from several models which may be integrated in a new way to form a new model. Assessment is clearly linked to the specification of problems or theory of pathology. A model of assessment which relates to this integrative function cannot be all-inclusive, but will have to focus on core concepts which are widely accepted – the 'common language' of well-informed practitioners. Otherwise assessments may be valid but not useful, since usefulness is partly a function of whether the user is familiar with and sympathetic to the therapeutic frame(s) of reference used in the design of the assessment method.

Many writers (e.g. Wynne, McDaniel and Weber 1986) also refer to the concept of 'family consultation' (as opposed to therapy) in which the point is made that in many cases assessment is *all* that is required. At the time of first contact many families are not looking for therapy. Most will prefer a clearer definition of the problem which may be all that is required for the family members to deal with problems themselves. The 'reflecting team' approach in family therapy can also be considered a variant of this kind of clinical consultation. Other families do need more intensive help, but may need time to consider choices before committing themselves. Giving an assessment back to the family in a collaborative, contractual, and empowering way is crucial. The use of appropriate assessment methods, combined with a written report to the family (as in Street, Downey and Brazier, 1991) can be an extremely effective way of undertaking this task in a manner which makes appropriate use of professional skills.

This also overtly recognizes the issue of patients' rights and is thus in line with a proper recognition of the consumer's view by services. It also recognizes that assessment of any kind is an interactive process with the patient or client and their family. While we assess them, they are quite rightly assessing us to see if they want to risk letting us get involved with their problem (see Mace, 1995). The overt discussion of problem definition and options for further work brings this interaction to a clear focus, and this can include a consideration of how the interaction between assessor and family has gone so far.

Lastly, the growing importance of clinical guidelines in health care must be considered. This is part of a drive to ensure that practice does not lag behind research and that practitioners use methods which are known to be effective. The assessment process is a crucial one which should give a rational basis for deciding what treatment choices are likely to be effective in a particular case. Therefore clinical guidelines for the assessment of child and family problems are central to the delivery of effective services for children. Furthermore, it can be argued that clinical guidelines provide the bridge between science and practitioners by setting out guidelines which are based upon the literature and evidence. This book is an attempt to provide that bridge.

Summary: concluding principles for child and family assessment

The first two chapters argued a case for working with families and then outlined some of the difficulties of doing so. This chapter has examined the current state of the art of family assessment, reviewing each method of assessment in turn. It is apparent that there is a relative paucity of systematic family assessment methods available.

It is easy to be critical, but more constructive to acknowledge that child and family assessment is a relatively recent activity handicapped by gaps in the knowledge base and splits among and between the various groups concerned. The following principles for good practice have been updated and revised from those defined in an earlier review (Wilkinson, 1987):

- adopting a broadly based approach, i.e. one which allows holistic analysis but does not neglect examination of the child and other individuals and their relationship to the family system

- having a central theme such as a coherent framework to examine child and family functioning
- using a common language of widely recognized and validated concepts to construct this framework
- in doing so, adopting a pluralistic approach using the best principles from various theoretical perspectives
- paying particular attention to the process of assessment in an empowering, interactive and contractual manner
- using both subjective and objective views within the assessment process, and carefully comparing these views
- where appropriate, using methods with proven clinical utility such as structured interviews, questionnaires, observation, and tests as initial assessments, to clarify specific issues and organize information
- carefully matching the choice of assessment method to the situation, so that methods are appropriate for the purpose, acceptable to the clients, efficient and effective
- being aware that although different methods based on different viewpoints often give different results, this can illuminate important issues
- adopting an open and contractual approach to assessment wherever this is possible, which includes giving the assessment back to the family in a professional manner.

Part II

FAMILY ASSESSMENT IN PRACTICE

This part of the book describes the practical issues involved in child and family assessment using the principles outlined in the first part of the book. This is the result of over fifteen years' work as a major clinical, training and research interest. The research project resulted in the development of a conceptual framework and the piloting of a package of integrated assessment methods, and evaluating its use as a training device. It is now possible also to reflect on many years of applying the ideas and methods and teaching them to trainees in several professions. Although the particular package was developed in a child-focused health context, it is possible that the methods could be adapted and modified for use in other contexts.

In order to present the assessment system as a set of practical and adaptable procedures each chapter in this section presents a different aspect of the system. The presentation is intended to emphasize practical explanation and discussion whilst also highlighting the principles which have guided the development of the assessment approach:

- Chapter 5 outlines the framework of ideas used to conceptualize family problems. The framework uses four perspectives upon the family with a set of problem dimensions for each perspective. This helps to develop links between problems so that causal effects between individual and relationship difficulties can be perceived more easily. The developmental perspective is used to gain an overview which gives an understanding of the history and origin of problems as well as the broad pattern.
- Chapter 6 examines the topic of preparation for family assessment. This is complex because family members often have different views and the first part of the chapter examines ways to understand and work with patient views and motivations. Ethical dilemmas include dealing with privacy boundaries and conflicts of interest, welfare versus confidentiality, and dealing with unrealistic expectations. The wider system also has

to be considered, and principles for convening family members are summarized. It is argued that an initial interview understanding patient and family views which prepares for a contractual assessment (utilizing formal assessment methods as the practitioner thinks appropriate) has a number of practical and ethical advantages. Effectively, this preliminary client-centred interview can be used to select more specific assessments if required. Finally, practical policies and procedures for preparation of families are specified.

- Chapter 7 discusses the application of a family interview schedule and an accompanying rating scale which can be used to obtain a broader, comprehensive view of the child and family. This broader view is important because the level of public awareness about children's mental health problems is low, leading to a high rate of unrecognized problems; plus in health contexts there is an implicit professional duty to screen for health problems. The interview has three key principles: the use of normalizing statements, which facilitate disclosure, prior to the probe questions; an emphasis on seeking permission to make enquiries; and a sequential progression into more sensitive areas.

- Chapter 8 begins by describing the use of the original Darlington Family Assessment System package and the lessons that were learned for clinical practice from its use. The advantages and disadvantages of formal assessments are summarized. The second part of the chapter considers the issue of communication with children as a special topic and gives a summary of the main principles for effective communication. Finally the use of other more specific procedures is considered and useful methods for clinical practice recommended. A selective and informed use of these methods can form the basis for a skilled and professional approach to assessment with children and families.

- Finally, Chapter 9 examines the central issue of how information gained from the assessment is used to determine a therapeutic strategy. Six stages are proposed as a framework for choosing a therapeutic strategy. Each stage is considered in turn, with examples and guidelines for the practitioner. Giving an assessment back to the family in a collaborative, contractual, and empowering way is also very important. The use of a written report, using plain English and avoiding jargon, to follow up verbal discussions is recommended.

5

A FRAMEWORK FOR FAMILY
ASSESSMENT

This chapter summarizes the framework of ideas upon which the DFAS is based.

The structure of the assessment system

The first and most important step in the development of the Darlington Family Assessment System (DFAS) was the decision to construct a 'checklist' based upon holistic analysis of the family (Keeney and Cromwell, 1977). Four key perspectives upon the family (or 'systemic levels') which seemed most appropriate for child-centred problems were used to construct the checklist. These were the child perspective, the parental perspective, the parent–child perspective (parenting style) and the whole family perspective (what is often termed family dynamics, transactions or processes). In this way the characteristics of the children, the parents, the parenting style and the family group as a whole can be examined in turn. Subsequently this checklist was developed into a formal rating scale by choosing a set of 'problem dimensions' for each systemic level. For each perspective, the task was to choose a set of dimensions which would:

- provide clear and meaningful distinctions between different types of problems on each systemic level
- enable a clear understanding of complex problems through the use of descriptors of key aspects of the family system
- be based upon widely accepted and validated concepts, phrased in simple terms, avoiding jargon
- provide a brief but reasonably comprehensive set of descriptors for each perspective.

The list of dimensions used in the rating scale, which forms a basis for the whole assessment system, is shown in Table 9.

The importance of some of these dimensions is self-evident, since most of the concepts are widely accepted and validated by other literature

Table 9 Conceptual framework for DFAS

Child-centred problems:
- child health (physical)
- child development (including self-care, communication, independence)
- emotional disturbance (mood disturbances and their effects)
- relationships (within and outside family)
- conduct (behaviour towards others)
- negative life events* (bereavements, separations or other trauma)

Parent-centred problems:
- parental health (physical)
- parental health (psychological)
- marital partnership
- parenting history (parents' experiences of being parented)
- parents' social support (social support available)

Parent-child interaction:
- care (including over-involvement)
- control (including over-control)

Whole family functioning:
- closeness and distance (attachment patterns in the family)
- power hierarchies
- emotional atmosphere + rules (family affective patterns)
- contextual stresses* (living conditions, poverty, stigma)
- summary of family development (in relation to problems and life cycle)

---

* Additions to the original framework

(see Part I of this book). However, for the benefit of less experienced practitioners some comments will now be made in respect of each of the dimensions. More experienced practitioners may find most of this chapter rather basic, but some commentary is required.

The child problem dimensions

The selection of the six dimensions chosen for the analysis of the child perspective is supported by the work of Hoghughi, Dobson, Lyons, Muckley and Swainston (1980), who used a very similar analysis for a problem-orientated assessment of children in residential care.

Child physical health

All physical health problems require some psychological adjustment on the part of the child and his or her family, and thus physical health problems can readily contribute to psychological problems if the required adjustments are not forthcoming. In particular, child health problems commonly create a great deal of anxiety in both the child (depending upon the impact of the problem and developmental level of the child) and the parents, and can thus affect family function in diverse ways. One of the commonest problems is an over-protectiveness generated in one or both parents by this anxiety.

As examples of health problems, consider epilepsy, asthma, eczema, diabetes and any form of sensory loss or disability. In assessing the severity of a particular health problem, consider such factors as level of discomfort, pain or embarrassment, need for long-term medication, independence of others versus need for supervision, 'visibility' of the problem, effects upon communication with others, and threat to life. Regarding this last area, do not undervalue problems such as epilepsy where normal activities and behaviours such as swimming become potentially life-threatening. For adolescents, consider also any possible effects (of health problems) upon peer and sexual relationships.

Child development

This is such a central concept in child work that its inclusion is mandatory. In its broad sense, health and development can be considered to subsume the other dimensions used; but in order to make some meaningful distinctions about the total pattern of health and development this dimension is limited to certain functional areas, i.e. physical growth, motor skills, speech and language, intellect and education, self-care skills (especially toileting) and independent functioning (i.e. being allowed to go places and do things unsupervised).

The key to rating this problem is a sound knowledge of what is age-appropriate for children in each of these areas, and of what is a significant delay and what is not. Those who are uncertain are referred to any standard text on child development. It is surprising how often developmental problems are not detected, particularly learning difficulties of various kinds. These often result in serious and secondary emotional problems caused by the child being labelled as difficult or lazy. This is particularly frequent where there is a mixed or specific learning disability so that the child is competent in some tasks but fails or gives up with others. Problems of attention deficit (with or without hyperactivity) can be best understood in this way as a neuro-developmental disorder with particular impact on learning and social skills (see Barkley, 1990). It is very important to recognize problems as early as possible since the sufferer who is not recognized can become scapegoated, isolated socially, and go on to develop multiple secondary problems.

Child emotional disturbance

Disturbed emotional behaviour is often a key feature of children's problems but one which can also be unrecognized by parents and/or teachers. In order to clarify the distinction between this and other problem dimensions it is emphasized that any indications of emotional disturbance must be clearly observable by the clinician, or reported by a reliable informant.

Types of emotional disturbance which are subsumed under this problem dimension include anxiety and depression, fears and phobias, tics, stammers, temper tantrums, obsessional and compulsive behaviour. Anxiety and depression deserve some particular comment. There is often an overlap between the two and mixed states are common. Since children do not often have a sophisticated vocabulary regarding their feelings, they often cannot verbalize their feelings and behavioural signs are especially important. In pre-school children, mood disturbances are often characterized by hyperactivity, apathy or psychosomatic complaints. Other signs to look out for in children are unaccountable tearfulness, irritability, outbursts of temper; poor concentration, complaints of boredom, lack of interest and loss of pleasure in activities; constant fidgeting, lack of spontaneity, slumped or tense posture, motor slowness, under- or over-activity; headaches, recurrent abdominal pain, preoccupation with sickness and death, sleep difficulties; a persistently fearful or sad expression; ideas of guilt, failure or worthlessness; self-destructive behaviour such as self-mutilation, drink or drug abuse. It is always useful to ask others who know the child well about these areas. In doing so, it is useful to ask what the child does rather than how he feels (i.e. 'when you praise him, does he behave as if he believes you?' rather than 'does he feel worthless?'), since many adults have a strange belief that children do not have a deep experience of emotion. In fact it is likely that some children have more intense emotional experiences, since they have not yet fully developed language and other modes of intellectual experience which can function as a defence against affect. For an excellent brief review of depression in childhood see the manual of the Children's Depression Scale (Lang and Tisher, 1978).

Another crucial point to remember when rating this dimension is that what is inappropriate emotional behaviour at one age may be quite normal at others. For example, in younger pre-school children certain phobias and temper tantrums are quite normal. An appreciation of age-appropriate emotional development is required, plus an appreciation of how emotional problems present in children (e.g. see Rutter, Taylor and Hersov, 1994).

Child relationships

Human beings are primarily social animals whose lives revolve heavily around mutual activities rather than solitary ones. The tasks of child development can be seen as ultimately helping the child to make mutually satisfying social relationships. The family can be seen as preparing the child for this, so that he or she can ultimately set up a new family unit with his chosen partner. If relationships are not satisfactory within the family (particularly early in life) then this can disrupt the person's ability to form relationships outside the family. If the child does not learn to make satisfying relationships with his peers, he will obviously be prone to loneliness, anxiety and depression although this may not actually manifest itself until adult life.

The assessment of this problem dimension is also difficult because, like mood disturbance, it can sometimes be denied to be a problem by the child, parents and even teachers – even when to an observer it patently is a problem. It is therefore advisable to watch out for other evidence (e.g. a persistent inability to communicate spontaneously, in the absence of mood disturbance; solitary activities, hesitancy when asked about 'special friends', complaints about intense sibling rivalry by parents, complaints of bullying or 'oddness', etc.). To assess the child's abilities directly (i.e. by observation of his behaviour in a group), it helps to have some understanding of the concept of 'social skills' and its application to children (e.g. see Spence, 1980). Where there are marked problems with social relationships it is important to consider whether some autistic features are present as in Asperger's syndrome (see Aarons and Gittens, 1987 for methods of assessment).

Social skills develop, and thus what is appropriate at one age may be inappropriate later. For example, toddlers rarely indulge in co-operative play and generally interact in quite an egocentric way. This may lead to some verbal or physical conflict but they also have a remarkable mutual tolerance for each other's behaviour. It is important to remember that the interaction with siblings and peers has a special place in the social, cognitive and moral development of children. There is growing evidence that troubled sibling and peer relationships are associated with difficult adjustment in later life (Dunn and McGuire, 1992).

Child behaviour and conduct disorder

Behaviour problem is a term used loosely to refer to difficulties in the child's behaviour which may be occasional, situation-specific, and not necessarily a result of emotional problems or social problems. It is useful to start by considering the child's natural temperament in relation to patterns of behaviour and how to manage it. Temperament can be considered as the earliest, innate, genetically influenced aspects of the child's personality which are then moderated by experience and by family and cultural rules (Prior, 1992). Recent advances in personality theory (see Widiger and Costa, 1994) have led to the recognition of five main factors:

- introversion v. extroversion (sociability)
- emotional stability v. emotional reactivity
- compliance v. stubbornness
- conscientiousness v. self control
- curiosity v. need for stability.

This may be particularly important where parents use methods of control which do not suit the child's temperament.

Conduct disorder generally refers to more serious problems in children who primarily cause distress in others rather than experiencing it themselves. They express their disturbance in anger rather than experiencing anxiety or depression, and as a result are unlikely to respond to individual work unless the conduct problem is secondary to, or mixed with, anxiety or depression. It can be effective to work with parents with the younger age range, but once they get beyond parental control, it is often impossible to reverse the developmental process and support for families becomes largely a matter of damage limitation. Severe conduct problems are often associated with family breakdown; these youngsters need care and containment and cause major headaches for social service agencies, often drifting into drug use and crime.

Conduct problems can be associated with disturbed attachments and relationship problems but not necessarily so. Indeed, some conduct problems are 'socialized', i.e. they occur only in the context of a social group to which the child belongs (e.g. the delinquent gang). 'Socialized' problems can sometimes be less worrying in the sense that they may not reflect such a difficult personal problem (if the child forms reasonable relationships within the peer group). However, socialized conduct problems can be much harder to change because of peer group pressures for conformity.

The kind of problems to which we refer under this dimension include persistent aggressive acts, destructive behaviour, bullying, stealing, lying, manipulative behaviour, indecency and promiscuity, drink and drug abuse, and fire-raising. When judging the seriousness of the conduct problem, it is important to use some external criteria such as legality, risk to health or life, and the opinions of others outside the family since some parents become excessively concerned about misconduct, particularly in adolescents. It is therefore important to gain some concrete information about the frequency and seriousness of the acts, for example parents who complain bitterly about 'stealing' may, in fact, be referring to the child taking food from the family larder when he is hungry. Again, different problems are manifested at different ages and some appreciation of what is age-appropriate conduct is needed.

Negative life events

This dimension reminds us to think carefully about the history and types of life events which are known to cause major problems for the developing child or adolescent. This includes separations from parents or other family members or carers, other bereavements and losses, traumatic effects of being a victim of violence or accidents (or witnessing it) and the impact of child neglect or maltreatment.

The parental problem dimensions

Parents might be considered as the heart and engine room of the family system. In assessing the function and dysfunction of the parenting system we have used five problem dimensions, covering the physical and psychological function of the parents as individuals; the quality of the parents' inter-relationship (or the lack of it in the case of a single parent); the models for parenting acquired by the parents in their own childhood, and the way that the parents relate to the wider community outside of the family, since this provides a model for the way that the children will relate to their peers. The parental dimensions therefore provide a similar means of specifying the pattern of problems for the parents.

Parents – physical health

In a similar way that child health problems create anxiety in the parent, parental health problems can create anxiety in the child. Indeed, the physical health of the parents also affects the whole family functioning in a variety of other ways (economic, social, etc.). When assessing the severity of a health problem, the factors listed under child health should be considered – with an additional emphasis on any potential effects of the illness upon sexual behaviour or fertility.

Parents – psychological health

A separate section has been provided for parents' psychological health because of the special effects that problems in this area can have. Depression is recognized as very disruptive to the normal bonding processes of parents with their infants, whose development can be affected in a variety of ways. Other examples are the bewildering effect of adult psychosis upon a child or the many possible effects of having a parent who abuses alcohol. Therefore under this section any form of formal psychiatric illness should be considered (e.g. schizophrenia, manic depression, etc.) in addition to chronic neurotic behaviours, long-standing personality problems, drink and drug abuse, or recent bereavements.

Assessing the severity of these kinds of problems is not easy. As a general guideline, consider the impact of the problem upon the ability to meet the children's physical and emotional needs. More specifically, consider the impact of the problem upon ability to look after the child's physical welfare and upon the following psychological functions: communication, both expressive and receptive, verbal and non-verbal, and in particular the expression of affect; honesty or dishonesty; flexibility or rigidity; ability to accept criticism or help; general ability to make and retain social relationships.

In addition, readers who are uncertain of the kind of questions to ask in order to elicit formal psychiatric disorders are recommended to look at the questions used in interviews such as the Present State Examination (Wing, Cooper and Sartorius, 1974) or any other structured interview for adult psychiatric and psychological problems. Although primarily designed as an aid to diagnosis, simply perusing the content and format of the interview provides extremely useful guidelines for any professional about the way to phrase questions about psychotic and other severely disturbed behaviour.

Marital partnership

In our culture parenting tasks are, in the normal ideal terms of that society, shared to a greater or lesser extent by two parents. However, the exact nature of this sharing varies to a very wide extent between families – as do the habits and customs of child-rearing. Hence couples may start a family with widely differing expectations of their respective parenting roles and how they expect their partners to treat their children. These different expectations directly affect the parenting functions; the couple's ability to resolve these differences will be determined by the strength of their own relationship. Conversely, problems in the marital relationship will often affect the parenting functions in a family. Commonly, underlying tension or hostility will prevent parents reaching agreement about decisions regarding the children. This can lead to children manipulating one parent against another. In severe cases children become weapons in the battle between two warring parents. Hence the tasks facing the parenting partnership can be stressed directly (by differing role expectations of parents) or indirectly (by any other problems in the marital relationship).

Some of the commonest types of marital problems include conflicts over power and dominance, problems in the expression or acceptance of affection or sexuality, conflicts over roles and responsibilities, past liaisons and identifications, and problems where a partner is chosen because they represent 'lost' aspects of the person's own personality (Dicks, 1968). Dominian (1981) has broadly suggested that there are three important areas which couples need to consider in marriage – their socio-cultural background, their conscious desires from their partner, and their unconscious needs derived from their own family dynamics. He suggests that a mismatch in one area can be overcome, but if two or three of these areas are mismatched the marriage is likely to falter. Marriages contracted when either or both partners are under stress are particularly at risk.

Non-verbal interactions and behaviours are of critical importance in assessing whether there is a marital problem and also whether or not to proceed in discussing it. Farley and Patterson (1979) suggested that the following six signs (particularly the first two) were very important when interviewing a couple:

- spouse does not visibly attend to partner's comments
- no expression of humour
- imbalance in the amount of conversation
- lack of agreement
- no positive physical contact
- lack of compromise.

Additionally open conflict, a tendency to sit apart, hints about previous separations and absences, threats of sanctions to the partner, and persistent use of 'he' or 'she' rather than forenames, can be potent indicators of marital problems.

There are many texts on how to identify and help distressed marriages (e.g. Ables and Brandsma, 1977). However, in families who present with child-focused problems the marital problems can often be hidden from the clinician, either deliberately or unconsciously. The degree to which this can occur is surprising – a sense of loyalty to a partner can make a spouse paint a picture of a happy marriage when in reality there may be quite bitter and violent conflict. Sometimes the deception is quite deliberate, for example where the parents fear a child may be removed into care, and at other times it may be simply a result of social embarrassment. Sometimes partners continue with an appalling relationship 'for the sake of the children'. In some cases their self-sacrifice may be justified, in others the children may suffer more in the long run. Assessing and helping troubled marriages is fraught with ethical and moral dilemmas. It is important to examine one's own views and attitudes and ensure they do not prevent the practitioner from helping clients to find their own solutions to the problems.

Since this dimension refers explicitly to parents 'partnership' functions in a family, the special problems of single parents on other dimensions need to be considered. In common-sense terms a single parent who has been left by his or her partner has a double load to bear as he or she now has to fulfil the roles that previously were shared, as well as coping with his or her own feelings about the lack of or loss of a partner. The results of marital breakup and those of loss through bereavement are often similar. For single parents these problems should be considered carefully, whilst remembering that many single parents cope well.

Where a single parent marries or re-marries a new partner, there are many adjustments to make in the relationships and lifestyle of the family. Problems presented within the context of a step-family unit need to be examined within the context of the tasks involved in re-marriage. The tasks of re-marriage and subsequent stages of family life in a step-family situation are fundamentally much more complex and difficult than in a 'primary' family unit (see Visher and Visher, 1980). In step-families issues in the parent's own relationship can easily become confused with problems involving the children; indeed to some extent this is to be expected. Greater care should therefore be exercised in clarifying and defining the problems rather than making any premature judgements.

Parenting history

It has long been acknowledged in child work that the influence of the parent's own childhood is often very powerful, since we all learn how to behave as parents from our own parents. Hence difficulties are commonly encountered where one or both parents have lost parents in childhood, been brought up in institutional care, or suffered a form of child abuse. However, some parents seem to overcome even these severe kinds of difficulty. Research on adult attachments suggests that those that overcome such events appear to have fully accepted and learned from their negative experiences, and do not minimize or deny them. Conversely, those who report such experiences but state that 'It never really affected me' or 'It never did me any harm' appear to be most at risk of behaving in a similar way towards their own children. Intelligence and literacy also play a part as mediating factors which can assist learning of more appropriate parenting behaviour in later life.

It is therefore very important to discover whether a parent has suffered some form of abuse in childhood and ask how they consider it has affected them, both as a child and as a parent. Physical abuse appears to be disclosed most readily; emotional abuse is much harder to define and detect, particularly retrospectively; and sexual abuse is least readily disclosed, for obvious reasons.

Since descriptions of emotional abuse can vary widely, some criteria are helpful. Bowlby (1977) lists seven types of 'pathogenic parenting' (or emotional abuse) which he suggests can lead to problems in adulthood. Therefore when listening to accounts of the parent's childhood history the practitioner should be alert for any of the following:

- one or both parents being persistently unresponsive to the child's care-eliciting behaviour and/or actively disparaging and rejecting
- discontinuities of parenting, occurring more or less frequently, including periods in hospital or institution

- persistent threats by parents not to love a child, used as a means of controlling him
- threats by parents to abandon the family, used either as a method of disciplining the child or as a way of coercing a spouse
- threats by one parent either to desert or even to kill the other or else to commit suicide (each of them commoner than might be supposed)
- inducing a child to feel guilty by claiming that his or her behaviour is or will be responsible for the parent's illness or death
- a parent exerting pressure on a child to act as a care-giver to the parent. Children treated in this way are likely to become over-conscientious and guilt ridden as well as anxious.

The account of the parent's history should also give general information about the nature of the parent's relationships with their own parents. The parent's own childhood bonding experiences can be seen as crucial mediators of what each parent will expect or desire (they may strongly wish their children not to repeat their own experiences) as the appropriate balance of closeness and distance in their relationships with their children and sometimes with each other. This expectation may not be acknowledged or discussed. Needs for closeness which were unfulfilled in childhood may be particularly strong but unacknowledged and may lead to a reversal of parent–child roles. Additionally, unmet needs for approval within the parent may lead to unhealthy drives for 'success' and 'achievement' in work settings or in roles as parents.

Parents' social support

As well as providing models for methods of parenting, parents also provide models for the social relationships of their children. If the parents have a very restricted social life they may also become dependent upon their children, and they will be more vulnerable to stresses of all kinds. Therefore this problem dimension refers to a variety of possible problems in the way that the parents relate to the community outside the family, particularly repetitive and problematic interactions between the family and the environment, which are partially due to the attitudes or behaviour of the parents. This can occur in conjunction with contextual stress, or simply be a result of parental behaviour only. In either case this can aggravate other problems within the family by limiting access to social support or prevent the family from gaining access to formal support systems in the wider community.

The parent–child interaction (parenting style) dimensions

Some observations of parent–child interaction are essential for a proper assessment of these dimensions. The two parent–child dimensions chosen have been widely used to summarize critical aspects of parenting behaviours and style (e.g. Schaefer, 1959; Parker, Tuckling and Brown, 1979). They can also be used to generate a useful typology of parenting styles by representing the two dimensions as orthogonal to each other, as in Table 10.

Some of the concepts used in assessing parenting skills are self-evident, e.g.:

- do the parents play with their child(ren)?
- do they have age-appropriate expectations of the child's behaviour?
- do they treat the child as a person or as an object?
- do they attempt to understand and empathize?
- do they listen to the child?
- do they follow through with commands or instructions if the child does not comply?
- can they cope with emotional outbursts without losing control?

An understanding of behavioural approaches to child management is a useful guide to assessing parenting skills, e.g.:

- are the methods of control entirely punitive or do the parents use rewards as reinforcers?
- do they deliberately attempt to teach skills to the child?
- do they specify commands clearly, or use abstract instructions?

The type and quality of attachment should be considered in the light of this information.

Care

This is an extremely important problem dimension although sometimes a very difficult one to assess initially when many parents appear rejecting because of their level of distress. Severe problems on this dimension have clear implications for children in terms of making it likely that the child may

Table 10 Typology of parenting styles

High care (over-involved)	Overindulgence ('spoilt')	Enmeshed	Over-protection
Balanced care	Affectionate anarchy	Ideal?	Benign dictatorship
Low care	Neglected	Disengaged ('distant')	Affectionless constraint
	Low control	Moderate control	High control

need to be found alternative living arrangements on a temporary or permanent basis.

'Overt rejection' refers to explicitly rejecting statements or actions by a parent. For example, persistent threats to the child that they will be 'put in a home' as a sanction for undesired behaviours; an excessively punitive attitude or an explicit scapegoating process; or a clear statement by the parent that they wish the child to be removed from the parental home, for whatever reason.

'Covert' or hidden rejection is more difficult to assess. In this case the parent steadfastly asserts his or her care for the child but their actions reveal a lack of care. Commonly, 'covert rejection' may be characterized by, for example, the child being ignored in all sorts of ways; being left out of family life; or not having other needs for affection and care fulfilled. Hence it is particularly important to observe the parent–child interaction and consider whether normal healthy expressions of affection are absent – such as touching, smiling, praise, warmth in tone of voice, body posture and facial expression.

In some cases, it is extremely difficult to assess whether the problem is a lack of care, a lack of parenting skills, or both, particularly in cases of child abuse. Historical factors can give important clues. Particularly, what was the parent's own history and how is this perceived (see under Parenting history); under what circumstances was the child conceived – was the child really wanted? With whom is the child identified? Was a child wanted of the opposite sex? Was the child wanted at all?

A further important distinction to make is that between perceived care (by the parent) and care which is expressed in behaviour. Often it is clear that a parent genuinely feels that they care for a child but they seem to be incapable of acting in a caring way towards the child (often because of egocentricity, impulsivity, or other personal problems). Some parents seem unable to distinguish the child's needs from their own. The crucial criterion when judging this problem should be care in action. In this context Bowlby's (1977) seven types of childhood experiences – mentioned on pp. 120–21 – should be considered.

Most lay people tend to conceive of problems of care as to do exclusively with rejection, but some of the most difficult problems occur where a parent is emotionally over-involved with the child. In fact, a parent who is over-involved with a child to the extent that they treat the child as an intimate associate puts a great deal of subtle emotional pressure on the child. Phrases like '(s)he's everything to us' or 'really special to me' can indicate problems in this way. Often the child is used as a substitute for a lost parent, sibling, or partner. Because of the parent's reliance upon the child to meet the parent's emotional needs – and the child's natural loyalty – problems of individuation or separation will occur. Over-involvement may prevent a child from relating normally to peers, developing a normal sense of independence or otherwise 'growing up'. School refusal is a common result, but some children may also be at risk of incest. Later in adolescence intense loyalty conflicts can occur as the effects begin to be perceived, so problems may be manifested in a variety of unusual or bizarre behaviours which the adolescent subconsciously chooses as a means of shocking and distancing the parent.

Finally, it is important not to forget to assess the physical care given, i.e. adequate food, warmth, and shelter – for which a home visit is essential at some stage if this is in doubt.

Control

Problems of parental control over children are extremely common among families who present for help. These problems can be roughly divided into under-control and over-control.

Under-control is usually characterized by complaints that the child is unmanageable, disobedient, or hyperactive. Generally, it can result from a number of factors (see Abidin's model of parenting stress). Where there is a lack of parenting skill this may be secondary to low mood, and is often characterized by hesitancy, lack of assertiveness and firmness with the child, a tolerance for unsociable behaviour (e.g. allowing cruelty to others without punishment), a tendency to always ask the child rather than use commands, and to allow the child to make choices and decisions which he is not really capable of dealing with. These problems can usually be observed by asking the parent to undertake some particular tasks in play with their child and observing the results. Where under-control is accompanied by a lack of care or parenting skill the parents may be unconcerned – though others outside the family will be concerned at what they perceive as neglect. Other parents may be very caring, but simply do not provide any firm guidelines and expectations for the child, or are afraid to be firm for fear of damaging the child. In these circumstances under-control is associated with simple over-indulgence or 'spoiling'.

Similarly, a dictatorial approach is characterized by high control but the level of care may be quite good. Extremely restrictive codes of behaviour, a lack of choice, inability to allow the child to make decisions, intolerance for spontaneous and playful behaviour, rigid adherence to rules, and a tendency to invade the child's privacy may be displayed. Sometimes this generates a great deal of ill-feeling in the child as they get older but others may accept this as normal behaviour until late adolescence when a crisis is likely to result.

Over-protection often has more of a benign appearance but can be equally damaging. The child is often smothered with affection, restricted, and isolated for reasons which may be plausible to the parent but are unconvincing to an outsider who examines them carefully and rationally.

Often the child's anxieties or discomforts are given as a justification for the over-protective acts as if it were essential that a child should be protected from discomfort at all costs. (In fact, if anxiety is avoided it persists – the only way to conquer anxiety is to confront it.) This problem is often associated with family social isolation or child health problems and school refusal or phobias may result.

Finally, inconsistency can also be considered as a problem under this dimension (if there is a great deal of variation in the management approach, this can be very confusing to the child).

N.B. In reality this typology is something of an over-simplification. Many practitioners would suggest that covert rejection can manifest itself as problems of control (over-protection). In addition, neither is a simple bipolar dimension, for example rejection may be overt or covert, and control may be physical or verbal. However, it is still a useful framework.

The family level problem dimensions

The dimensions chosen for the whole family analysis are specifically derived from Fisher's review (1976) of the topic and modified according to other themes from the literature reviewed in Part I of this book. The interesting point about these family level dimensions is that they provide a framework for understanding the problems of individuals and families from a general developmental perspective. As such the dimensions have integrating themes which are social and developmental in nature. The most important dimension (which integrates all the others into a coherent overview of the family) is the concept of family development. As applied to a particular case, this essentially means understanding the family in relation to the life cycle of the family and its members (see Chapter 2). Therefore particular efforts will be made to illustrate the links between each of the family level dimensions in the following descriptions of them.

The first two dimensions (closeness and distance, power hierarchies) are clearly 'structural' descriptors of family functioning which provide a clear description of current 'here and now' family functioning. In order to gain a clear understanding of family structure it is important to build up a clear picture of how each family member relates to all the others in the family. The least reliable way of doing this is to rely on what family members say about their relationships. Often they will have an idealized view of themselves and will fail to recognize difficulties. The most reliable way is to observe family interactions carefully. Who speaks first; who speaks to whom; who is the leader; who is the spokesperson; who speaks on behalf of others; and who speaks about others rather than to them? Where do people position themselves relative to each other, in terms of proximity and orientation; what is their body posture relative to each other; how much eye contact, smiling and touching occurs? In discussions, what is the sequence of communications; who tends to support or contradict who; are there any other patterns? In discussing problem situations, note the details of what occurred.

Three of these concepts (power; closeness and distance; and family development) are widely established ideas in the family literature, another relates to external stresses, whereas the remaining dimension may not be so familiar to some readers (emotional atmosphere and rules). Therefore the concept of emotional rules will be outlined in greater detail than the others.

In looking at the family it is important to understand the overall pattern in order to assess how a family might break up and how likely this is. The use of diagrams is extremely useful to summarize family structure, as Minuchin (1974) has illustrated.

Closeness and distance

First, what are the patterns of closeness and distance within the family? Are there significant degrees of under- or over-involvements in the family? Minuchin refers to generalized closeness within a family as 'enmeshment' and generalized distance as 'disengagement'. However there are often patterns of extreme closeness and extreme distance within the same family. This dimension is closely related to attachment theory in which the balance between physical and psychological closeness (for security) versus distance (for autonomy) are clearly discussed. In infants and children the process of bonding and the resulting attachment behaviours are considered to be crucial to proper psycho-social development. Early learning experiences are assumed to affect the way later relationships are made, so that attachment problems experienced in early life may continue to cause problems in achieving intimacy or autonomy in later life. In particular, low amounts of closeness are likely to produce a child who is disengaged from his attachment figures. This results in a person who fails to develop a sense of inner security when alone, but also finds closeness uncomfortable so that they find other relationships difficult. A child who is 'enmeshed' may be under great pressure to adopt the parents' attitudes and beliefs and may have great difficulty in developing independence and autonomy in later life.

For adults it is assumed that healthy adult social relationships are also characterized by a balance between psychological closeness and distance.

Power hierarchies

The second family problem dimension (power hierarchies) refers to issues of dominance, leadership, decision making and responsibility. Clearly these are major issues within any social group and the importance of this dimension for the family and the individual is self-evident. As with closeness and distance in social relationships, it is assumed that the nature and types of power hierarchies that a person experiences early in life will clearly influence their relationships later in life. In particular, the patterns observed in parental figures are likely to influence individuals through role-modelling when they become adults or parents themselves.

It is assumed that healthy power systems are characterized by clear but (preferably) ability-related allocation of power and responsibility. In most healthy families, most of the power and responsibility is vested in the marital dyad (sometimes termed the executive system in this context). The responsibility and decision making for various aspects of family life is normally divided up between the couple according to their interest and skills.

Unhealthy power systems are characterized by one of the following:

- unclear allocation of power which leads to disputes about responsibility and decisions. Commonly the issue of personal dominance may not be resolved by a couple, leading to continuous disputes about minor decisions. Conversely some couples with strong unmet needs to be parented will fight to avoid power and each complains that the other does not pull their weight
- the allocation of power to individuals who lack the ability to take appropriate decisions or actions. For example a child can sometimes become dominant in a family where they are simply not capable of handling such responsibility
- rigid and inflexible concentration of power which is characterized by a family dictator, a stifling of autonomy in other members, and a pecking order often resulting in scapegoating of the weakest member.

When applied to the current family situation, these first two dimensional descriptors of the family (closeness and distance, power hierarchies) provide ways to understand the structure of the family system.

Emotional atmosphere and rules

There are a number of sources within the literature that point to the importance of emotional behaviour, which will be briefly summarized in order to give some background to the concept of emotional rules.

The first source arises from various traditions of psychotherapy. Freud introduced the notion of the unconscious and described mechanisms by which material was prevented from becoming conscious – defence processes. Of these, the major process was the repression of threatening thoughts and associated feelings or emotions, particularly sexual feelings. Freud also suggested that the repression of certain emotions led to specific psychological disorders, for example that repression of anger contributes to depression. Other schools of psychotherapy have adopted radically different methods to those of Freud but nearly all use the emotions as a central concept within their theories. For instance, Rogers (1951) suggested that individuals who live in very emotionally deprived conditions, or who only receive 'positive regard' under very rigid conditions, may develop various maladaptive self-concepts. They may be forced to view potentially positive situations as negative (such as that sex is bad or unpleasant) in order to maintain their parents' positive regard. Ellis (1962) argued that thinking and emoting were intrinsically linked. The exact form of thinking (the person's interpretation) determined the emotions that a person experienced. He also argued that many people have irrational ideas or beliefs as a result of early learning which produce inappropriate emotions. These beliefs could distort the perception of both negative and positive events.

In recent years an integrated cognitive–behavioural approach has been produced by Beck (1976). This model expands and elaborates upon Ellis's ideas. In particular Beck proposes that people have important schemata (rules which govern the interpretation of their experiences) which are fundamental in shaping the way that people experience the world and respond to events. These schemata are rarely accessible to consciousness. In people vulnerable to depression or anxiety the form of the schemata is likely to generate streams of automatic negative thoughts in stressful situations. For example, a typical anxiety-generating schema would be 'If I am not a perfectionist this means I am irresponsible'. This places the person in the dilemma of either driving themselves to exhaustion or of labelling themselves in a very negative way, thus generating intense anxiety when the person comes under stress. Beck emphasizes that many patients are not initially aware of the content of their negative thoughts (which he therefore terms 'automatic'), let alone their schemata, which operate at a pre-conscious level.

In general, various schools of psychotherapy seem to find some common ground in agreeing that:

- emotions have a central role within the production and maintenance of psychological disturbance
- as a result of their family and life experiences, people learn a set of rules and beliefs which determines their perceptions and experience and thus regulates their behaviour in various situations.

Other ideas concerning the importance of emotions stem from developmental psychology and from the sociology of the family. The building of social relationships or attachments is a crucial process in child development which involves important emotional behaviours. Infants require affection in order to develop normally, and they will rapidly engage in emotional or 'proximity seeking' behaviour (crying) in order to gain attention, physical comfort and protection. The primary function of the family group for an individual is that of socialization – the development of normal social and emotional relationships by providing models of behaviour. Furthermore,

Jackson (1965) asserted that within families rules are essential to provide organization; without rules families would be chaotic. (In the terms of system theory, rules usually help to maintain stable systems.) Ford (1983) proposed that many psychological and psychiatric problems could be explained by a lack of clarity of social rules which therefore leads to uncertainty, anxiety and the manifestation of symptoms. Satir, Stachowiack and Tachsman (1975) also suggested that in healthy family systems, members are more aware of the family rules which are also more flexible. In unhealthy family systems the rules tend to be implicit, fixed and non-negotiable even when they are brought into the open. Finally, Fleck (1980) argued that a variety of disorders have their origins in family dysfunction and that affective disorders were particularly likely to result from inappropriate emotional expression within the family. Hence emotional behaviour is a crucial part of developmental processes, and family rules play a vital role in family functioning.

Further evidence comes from the literature on health care and psychiatric illness which was reviewed in Chapter 2. This suggests that maladaptive emotional behaviour may result in physical or psychosomatic illness. Conversely, Brown and Harris (1978) demonstrated the overwhelming importance of a confiding relationship (which in effect means the opportunity to reveal our most private thoughts and emotions) in protecting women from vulnerability to depression, and Caplan (1981) concluded that social support was crucial in enabling individuals to overcome stress. He concluded that 'empirical researchers confirm that exposure to high stress by individuals receiving adequate support does not increase the risk of mental and physical illness'. Other literature suggests that social support in the form of confiding relationships can insulate individuals against the most negative effects of physical and mental health conditions. The concept perhaps most relevant to emotional behaviour has been the concept of expressed emotion or EE (Vaughn and Leff, 1976) which appears to be an aspect of family functioning that affects the course of psychiatric illness (see Chapter 2).

A final but most important source is the literature about human communication processes that emerged from the application of system theory to human communication (Watzlawick, Beavin and Jackson, 1967). All behaviour can be viewed as a form of communication with two distinct components: the semantic content of the communication and the relationship aspect of the communication (what is often termed metacommunication). The semantic aspects refer to the meaning of what is communicated (e.g. I want you to tidy your room) whereas the relationship aspect refers to the manner in which the communication is made and the expectations inherent in that manner (e.g. I expect you to obey me). Watzlawick et al. pointed out, among other things, that a relationship communication will usually have far more powerful effects upon behaviour than any semantic content. Any significant level of emotional expression is, in itself, a very powerful relationship or meta-communication.

It follows from the above that all social behaviours (and communications) are subject to certain implicit and explicit rules. Given the importance of emotional phenomena, it is therefore assumed that all individuals have internalized certain rules about emotional behaviour as part of their social repertoire. These rules are critical psychological phenomena for two reasons. First, emotional experiences are central aspects of our life experiences as individuals, if not the central aspects of our internal experience. As discussed, nearly every theory of individual psychotherapy has given a central role to emotional experiences, which appear to function as a means of sensing and expressing our basic needs and drives. Obviously if we ignore or lose sight of our basic needs and drives we will end up deep in trouble! During our development as individuals certain emotional responses are necessary in order to cope effectively with life events, for example sadness in bereavement, excitement in sexual relationships. It is therefore also assumed that a psychologically healthy person can be defined as someone who can accept and tolerate the experience of, and to some extent comfortably express, a range of emotions. Second, it has been argued that in respect of social relationships the impact of a person's emotional behaviour (including all the powerful influences of non-verbal communications) normally has a greater influence upon others than does the semantic content of what that person says. Therefore the range of emotional behaviour which is available to a particular individual (which is determined by their particular rules) will determine the forms of social interactions and relationships available to that person. A restricted range of emotional behaviour will limit the kinds of social relationship available to a person. Hence these rules determine not only how we cope with life events, but also how we 'meta-communicate' and form social relationships.

To illustrate the concept of emotional rules a typology of six basic emotions has been constructed which is shown in Table 11A.

This table relates each of six emotions to the type of situation in which it is experienced by an individual, and defines the effect of the relationship communication associated with that emotion. If we further assume that each individual has a set of internal rules or schemata concerning emotional behaviour, then for each of these emotions examples of healthy and unhealthy rules can be generated. The table gives two examples of rules associated with each emotion: one which encourages emotional expression and one which discourages it.

It is possible also to consider some of the links between emotional behaviour and the other concepts used. As individuals and families pass through the life cycle they will experience life-cycle transitions and other unplanned life events. For individuals, the difficulty experienced with a particular transition or life event will be partially determined by emotional rules likely to be activated by that event. For example, the rules about the expression of love and affection will be most important in marriage

130

Table 11A Typology of emotions

Emotion	Type of situation	Primitive communication to others	Prohibitive rules (unhealthy)	Sensible rules (healthy)
Being frightened, anxious	Thinking about something in the future which is viewed as unpleasant	'Protect me' 'Help me deal with what will happen'	Fear is a sign of weakness	Fear is natural and often alerts us to real dangers
Excitement	Thinking about something in the future which is viewed as pleasant	'Be happy with me' 'Let's have fun together'	Excitement is a sign of immaturity and babyhood	Excitement is a way of sharing pleasant expectations
Sadness	Response to loss of something	'Comfort me' 'Look after me while I am unhappy'	Sadness is a sign of madness	Feeling sad shows that we care about what happens
Happiness	Response to gaining something	'Share this with me' 'Enjoy this with me'	Happiness is a sign of stupidity and foolishness	Expressing our happiness allows us to share it with others
Anger	Response to frustration or pain	'Listen to me' 'Take notice of me'	Anger is very dangerous and must not be allowed	Anger tells us and others that things are important to us
Love, sexuality	Response to pleasure	'Be close to me' 'Be my friend or lover'	Pleasure and sex are signs of laziness and wickedness	Sharing pleasure, closeness and affection are vital to our psychological health

formation, particularly if a person has very inhibited expression. Some of the most difficult people to work with are those who report that they find it difficult to show any emotion openly. Sometimes a problem may occur more because of a mismatch of rules. A person who rarely expresses anger may find their spouse is very expressive, and may misinterpret this as meaning that their spouse does not care for them. For families, the ongoing structure of the family will also help determine how they cope with life events as a group. If one child is particularly close to a parent who deserts the family, that child is likely to have more problems adjusting to this loss. If the child has also internalized emotional rules inhibiting the expression of his or her grief about the loss of the parent, the difficulty will be compounded.

Emotional atmosphere refers to the general emotional tone within the family. It is assumed that this is very significant although care must be taken to check whether the tone is typical or not. Often emotional atmosphere or tone results from an immediate stress upon the family. If no stress (such as a recent bereavement) is obvious to account for the emotional tone, the atmosphere may result from chronic unresolved conflict and/or a chronic difficulty in emotional expression. The latter may result from a shared and unhealthy emotional rule in the family. (For example, what has been termed the 'pseudo-mutual' family displays a tension associated with an implicit rule 'Anger is a bad thing and must not be allowed'.) A particularly disturbing or striking emotional tone, when the family members are all present, can often be a clear indication that there is some rule about this emotion which is part of the problem.

Table 11B elaborates upon these ideas by showing how these rules can produce different emotional atmospheres within families, and how these rules can interact with life events of various kinds to cause problems.

Obviously, other innate temperamental factors also influence emotional expression. How much our emotional rules are 'temperamental' and how much they are learned in childhood is a debatable point, likely to be variable and interactional. Clearly they are also subject to developmental changes (since what is expected of a child normally differs from what is expected of an adult). Each parent is likely to have some different rules, although it is possible that similarities of emotional expression may, unconsciously, make adults attractive to each other. Therefore it is assumed that family members will sometimes, but not always, share rules. The type of family system will also influence the amount of pressure to share and conform to these rules. Some empirical work supporting the validity of this concept was described in Wilkinson, 1993.

Contextual stress

This dimension considers stresses upon the family system resulting from its interaction with wider social systems. This can include social ostracism,

Table 11B Typology of emotions

Emotion	Type of situation	Interpersonal communication	Example of prohibitive family rule	Typical result of prohibition in individual	Family atmosphere indications	Types of life events which may cause difficulty
Fear	Anticipation of negatively construed life event	'Protect me' 'Save me from harm' 'Be like a parent to me'	Fear is a sign of weakness	Psychosomatic problems. Avoidance and phobic behaviour.	Brittle, pseudo-bravery. Tense non-verbal behaviour. Denial of fear and anxiety. Hysterical laughter and giggling possible.	Early stages of separations from growing children. Chronic illnesses. Fears of any negative events repeating themselves.
Excitement	Anticipation of positively construed life event	'Let's have fun' 'Be happy' 'Behave like a child'	Excitement is a sign of immaturity and babyhood	Sexual problems, prohibition of play activity	Victorian stiffness and formality. Indications of sexual prudery. Hysterical flirtatiousness possible.	Marriage and sexual relationships. Social events.
Sadness	Response to loss	'Make it up to me' 'Give me love' 'Treat me like a child' 'Comfort me'	Sadness is a sign of madness	Behavioural signs of depression with smiling 'mask'	Smiling exterior with strong undercurrent of black humour. Atmosphere of tension and hopelessness.	Bereavement, miscarriages. Later stages of separation from growing children. Desertion and divorce.

Table 11B Continued

Emotion	Type of situation	Interpersonal communication	Example of prohibitive family rule	Typical result of prohibition in individual	Family atmosphere indications	Types of life events which may cause difficulty
Happiness	Response to gain	'Share this with me' 'Relax and enjoy this' 'Be like a child with me'	Happiness is a sign of stupidity and foolishness	Seriousness. Social problems – difficulty in attaining intimacy.	Flat, pessimistic atmosphere with frequent complaining and criticism. Inert lifeless feelings.	Marriage. Childbirth. Partner's successes.
Anger	Response to pain or frustration	'Be frightened of me' 'Do as I wish' 'Listen to me'	Anger is dangerous and must not be allowed	Overt anxiety and depression	Pseudo-mutual atmosphere: antagonism not expressed verbally but displayed in non-verbal behaviour. Stiff, tense posture – and snarling smiles.	Marital conflict. Bereavements. Infidelity.
Love, Sexuality	Response to pleasure	'Be close to me' 'Let's stay together' 'Be my friend or lover'	Love and pleasure are signs of wickedness and laziness	Social and sexual problems – difficulty in attaining intimacy	Overwhelming expressions of anger and hostility but in semi-joking fashion. Feelings of 'abrasive affection'.	Marriage. Childbirth. Comforting and consoling others.

scapegoating and conflict due to social class or other sub-cultural differences; political, cultural and religious differences, including racism; unemployment, deprivation and other work-related problems such as a parent working away from home.

Family development

This family problem dimension of family development is used to integrate the other dimensions within the developmental perspective of the family life cycle. As individuals and families develop, they pass through transition points in the life cycle and they also experience various unplanned life events. At each of these points the family as a whole must develop in the sense that the family system as a whole must adapt to the change and modify the overall family functioning to meet the demands of the situation. Normally structural changes (to do with power hierarchies and closeness and distance) in the family will be required to do this. In addition, certain emotional responses are required from the individual in order to adapt to particular life events (e.g. grief in bereavement, love in marriage formation). At crucial developmental times such as marriage formation, the matching of emotional rules and the expectations of relationship structure (i.e. power and closeness and distance) will be critical for the way that the couple relate to each other.

Hence the other whole family dimensions give us a clear way of understanding the nature of the changes and adaptations that people make, or fail to make, at important points of individual and family development. Conversely, the family life-cycle concept provides a means of integrating and linking diverse aspects of individual and family function within a developmental framework in order to understand the sequence of events. This is the fourth principle of the assessment theory.

To illustrate this, the summary of the family life-cycle concept in Chapter 2 was constructed in such a way that it describes the changes required at each life-cycle stage in the terms of three other family dimensions (closeness and distance, power hierarchies, and emotional rules).

The links between these dimensions are also illustrated in Table 11B which listed for each of six emotions referred to earlier:

1   the essential type of situation that elicits the emotion
2   what the emotion 'meta-communicates' interpersonally
3   an example of a prohibitive family rule
4   hypothesized results of the prohibition in an individual
5   hypothesized results of the prohibition in families
6   types of life events or transitions with which it is hypothesized a particular emotional prohibition might cause particular difficulty.

In general therefore the family analysis used can be summarized as a developmental model which stresses the interactive nature of family functioning, life-cycle transitions and life events, and the idiosyncratic emotional qualities of the individual and family. A typical example of a family problem which develops rapidly into a crisis because difficulties from all dimensions have combined together is shown in Figure 4.

During the piloting period it was also discovered that the notion of overall family development can be used to generate some useful distinctions between the severity of different families' problems. This entailed some necessary overgeneralization which results from the distinction between individuals and families – sometimes some people in the family have suffered developmental problems, and others have not. For instance, one spouse may have had a difficult childhood and a broken marriage, but the other has not. Although families do change and develop, they are comprised of individuals some of whom will have a history prior to the family formation. Nevertheless certain kinds of 'milder' problems could be identified which were very typical of unresolved transition points in the life cycle, and others were clearly caused by bereavements, separations or other traumatic life events. With recent onset, there often appeared to be a pattern of fairly specific problems and a fairly rapid response to therapy. Other problems could be identified which were typical of mid-range severity, where some important aspects of the problem could be traced back to a previous stage of the current family (often marriage formation). Here there was often a pattern of a greater number of problems acknowledged

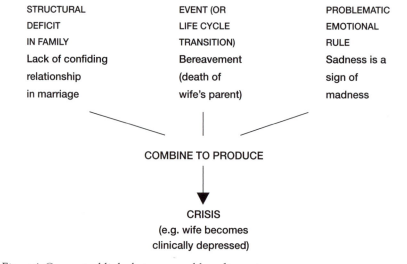

Figure 4 Conceptual links between problem dimensions

but still a good number of healthy functioning dimensions of family life. Therapy took more time, but if a reasonable contract was achieved it proceeded fairly smoothly. Finally, there was a third group of problems of greater severity where important problem aspects originated from earlier family systems. These 'transgenerational' problems were exemplified by work with families where the parents were victims of child abuse or suffered an unresolved loss of parent(s) in their own childhood, suggestive of severe problems in early attachment processes. Here the pattern was often of global problems and also a slow, partial and uncertain response to therapy.

These distinctions are best illustrated using some case examples from our study. The first two cases illustrate the mild level of severity:

CASE 1 : FAMILY DEVELOPMENT RATING A (MILD)

This was a case of depression in an adolescent boy, referred by a pediatrician after a psychosomatic presentation. Assessment revealed that the boy's natural father had left the family several years before. Although the step-father was clearly integrating himself well into the new family unit, it was felt that the boy had not resolved his feelings of loss with regard to his father and he was also under too much pressure in relation to his school work. Otherwise, however, the family appeared to be functioning well. The case was managed as a delayed grief reaction and treatment was offered on a family basis to discuss these issues openly. No other problems emerged during therapy. After five sessions measurable symptomatic improvements occurred, confirmed by changes in the boy's socialization patterns, which were maintained at follow-up (when an improvement in the wife's marital satisfaction was also noted) and confirmed according to telephone contact eighteen months later.

CASE 2 : FAMILY DEVELOPMENT RATING A (MILD)

This was a problem of an aggressive conduct disorder in a young child, referred by community health. Assessment revealed a very bright child, a severe sibling rivalry problem between the identified parient (IP) and a younger sister, and an overburdened mother of four children who was tending to reinforce the behaviour problems with attention. Otherwise the family seemed stable and the two older children were clearly doing very well. A treatment offer combining behavioural management sessions with structured play sessions for the IP together with his sister was accepted. During therapy it became clear that the father was rather peripheral and special efforts were made to involve him in all decision making about the work involved. Twelve sessions (six of each approach) produced measurable change in the child's behaviour and some possible minor change in parental roles although this was not detectable on the measures used. This change was maintained at follow-up and confirmed eighteen months later.

The next two cases illustrate cases of intermediate severity:

CASE 3 : FAMILY DEVELOPMENT RATING C (INTERMEDIATE)

An adolescent girl approaching school-leaving age with learning difficulties was referred simultaneously by the social services and the GP after a family crisis in which she was threatened with ejection from the family for persistent stealing. The assessment revealed that the girl had a long-term developmental problem, and that the family was also still adjusting to the father's 're-entry' after he had returned from working abroad. The father appeared ambivalent in his attitude to the girl and a younger sibling commented that his sister was never punished. The problem was conceptualized as a lack of adjustment to the girl's handicap by the family. On further investigation, she turned out to have highly specialized cognitive difficulties with a pattern of functional abilities ranging from moderate handicap to a high level of ability. The treatment offered (which was initially accepted) focused upon developing clear and realistic expectations for her behaviour, and used a combination of individual, parental and family sessions. The ramifications of the development problems were complex, particularly for a bright younger sibling who was treated as if she were the elder, and so 23 sessions were held – in addition to a spell in an adolescent unit in an adjacent health district. Eventually it became clear that the parents were withholding information about their personal problems. Efforts to discuss these problems with them led to the family discontinuing therapy. At this point it was felt appropriate by everyone involved that the girl should go to a special residential college (which she did) as a constructive type of change for the family. Symptomatic improvements were maintained at follow-up and confirmed according to telephone contact after nine months.

CASE 4 : FAMILY DEVELOPMENT RATING C (INTERMEDIATE)

This severe conduct disorder in a young child was referred through the GP at a point of crisis which necessitated the boy's admission to a pediatric ward for fear that his mother might harm him. The mother was noted to be 'neurotic' and she had been treated unsuccessfully by the adult psychiatric services. Family assessment revealed young parents with severe marital problems associated with chronic gynaecological and hormonal problems. After eight sessions which focused upon both the personal and parental aspects of their marital relationship, measurable symptomatic and structural improvements occurred which were maintained at formal follow-up. Beyond some examination of the mother's childhood and family history, no other significant factors emerged in therapy. Informal follow-up fourteen months later revealed a recurrence of the child's symptomatic behaviour which appeared to be a response to the arrival of a new baby; the couple reported that they were both still happy with their own relationship, particularly since her gynaecological difficulties had been resolved. Hence although the symptomatic improvement was not maintained, the change in family structure apparently was. Observations during additional sessions appeared to confirm their reports.

Finally, the following two cases illustrate the most difficult types of problems:

CASE 5 : FAMILY DEVELOPMENT RATING E (SEVERE)

This family was referred in conjunction with enuresis of the youngest of three children. However, assessment revealed a chronic and potentially violent marital conflict, with one partner (the wife) controlling the other and preventing a separation by implicit threats of suicide. In addition, each parent had suffered loss and deprivation in childhood. The therapy therefore focused initially upon the marital problems and subsequently upon aspects of the mother's own personal development (she had never known her father and had been totally dominated by her mother). Offers to involve the husband in therapy were not accepted by him. After a total of seventeen sessions the mother improved symptomatically and she reported improvements in the family structure.

The father remained unhappy with his role, and did not feel that anything had changed – although his score on one questionnaire did show an improvement. He did not leave the family despite his wife eventually telling him to go if he wanted to. Subsequent contact after the follow-up confirmed that although improved in other respects, the father's commitment to the family remained ambiguous; he continued to complain about his wife and perhaps remained mainly because of the children. This can therefore be regarded as a partial improvement. A letter written to the referrer immediately after the assessment predicted that 'the family may prefer to remain symptomatic rather than risk confronting the difficult issue of separation'.

CASE 6 : FAMILY DEVELOPMENT RATING E (SEVERE)

This case presented as a conduct disorder, including offences of theft, in an adolescent of school leaving age. Family assessment revealed a boy with poor socialization and a single parent who had been multiply abused in childhood, and further abused by the boy's father before their divorce. The relationship between the boy and his mother seemed to be a mixture of dependency and hostility. Treatment consisting of individual and family sessions were offered. After conventional approaches made little headway, a paradoxical approach was used which sympathetically predicted that separation was inevitable for the boy and his mother. This appeared to succeed dramatically with measurable improvements reported in symptoms and family functioning, and the family requested discharge (after nine sessions). Unfortunately it was revealed at follow-up that this change was a transitory effect; perhaps even a manoeuvre to escape therapy. A home visit at follow-up (after no response was made to an appointment) revealed that the boy had committed a further serious burglary and was now serving a long sentence in youth custody; a clear deterioration. In systemic terms, it is probable that this was his escape route from the family situation.

To summarize, reference to the normal life cycle can clarify many issues – particularly in relation to the expected and actual family structure. Given some understanding of the family's emotional rules, and some historical information, key points at which particular problems arose can often be identified.

In addition, the concept of family development appears to offer a useful way of assessing problem severity in particular. As such, this dimension is a global descriptor of 'family psychological health'. (Family development can be considered to be an integrating 'meta-dimension' and thus one would expect that a significant problem on this dimension is likely to be accompanied by significant problems on several other problem dimensions.) The use of the family development concept provides a useful way of assessing the severity of the problem, by comparing the actual difficulties in the family to those expected at the appropriate stage of the normal family life cycle.

The theoretical framework underlying the assessment system

The first important point about the overall framework is that it is clearly eclectic since the problem dimensions can be seen to have a number of theoretical roots (e.g. medical, developmental, behavioural, cognitive, dynamic, and systemic approaches). Because of this the assessment approach should be of interest and value to the majority of mainstream practitioners who tend to be eclectic in their approach. The first important principle arising from the use of different perspectives is that it becomes possible to link problems at different levels in the family using the perspective of time; for example that father's health problem predates the child's behaviour problem, and perhaps has caused changes in his parenting style. Therefore it becomes possible to generate rich hypotheses about the onset of problems and the connections between individual and relationship difficulties using a developmental perspective.

Because the family needs to be described in terms of its characteristics as a system, the concepts of power hierarchies and closeness and distance in personal relationships are used to summarize current family functioning. Therefore a second principle of the assessment system is that structural descriptors are used to gain an understanding of the current family system.

As described above the third family dimension is derived from a number of theoretical sources. Emotional atmosphere refers to the overall emotional tone within the family group which is readily observable. From this emotional atmosphere (and from the behaviour and statements of individuals) it is often possible to infer hypotheses about the individual family members and their idiosyncratic rules of emotional behaviour. Since these rules not only shape our social behaviour and relationships but also determine our manner of responding to and coping with life events and transitions, this concept clarifies some important aspects of individual differences and responses to problems. Therefore a third principle of the assessment theory is that emotional behaviour is used as a means of clarifying important responses and coping styles of the family members.

The family life-cycle concept provides a means of integrating and linking diverse aspects of individual and family function within a developmental framework since this entails the use of a sequential perspective. This is the fourth principle of the assessment theory.

The fifth principle of the assessment theory is that the use of the family development concept provides a useful way of assessing the severity of the problem, by comparing the actual difficulties in the family to those expected at the appropriate stage of the normal family life cycle.

Summary

The dimensional framework underlying the assessment system has been described. It is contended that this theoretical framework provides a useful means of describing families and offers a way of generating hypotheses to link individual and relationship phenomena in problem-solving therapy. The principles upon which the framework rests can be summarized as:

- the systematic use of a set of descriptors for each of four systemic levels of family organization; the children as individuals, the adults as individuals and as a parenting system; the style of parenting; and the family as a whole
- the use of (mainly) widely recognized and validated concepts as problem dimensions
- the use of these problem dimensions enables causal links (linear and circular) to be perceived more readily between problems in different parts of the family system
- structural descriptors are used to gain an understanding of the current family system
- emotional behaviour is used a means of clarifying idiosyncratic qualities of the family and the individuals within it
- the family development (life cycle) concept provides a means of integrating and linking diverse aspects of individual and family function within a general developmental framework
- the family development concept provides a useful way of assessing the severity of the problem, by comparing the actual difficulties in the family to those expected at the appropriate stage of the normal family life cycle.

6

BEGINNING THE ASSESSMENT

Working with children and their family groups rather than 'individuals' creates a number of additional difficulties. The first arises from the fact that families are not simple conglomerate entities that can be treated as if everyone in the family has the same characteristic beliefs, attitudes, experiences and behaviours. Families consist of a number of individuals, each of whom may have radical differences from the others in certain ways. They may, for example, have radically different expectations about who is involved in the problem and who should come to the appointment. Over the last twenty years, there has been a marked increase in the numbers of fathers who attend with their children, but there are still wide variations between families about this. In practice, when a family is deemed to have a problem it is crucial to understand who in the family is defined as part of the problem (and by whom) in order to be clear about motivation for change. Although this sounds simple, in practice it is not, particularly when the role of other child agencies involved is considered. Child development involves health, education, and social factors. Some problems require the involvement of several agencies to resolve effectively and others can at least partially result from an unsatisfactory relationship between the family and one of these agencies. Another issue for child and family workers concerns the strength of privacy boundaries within such a natural social group like the family, leading to problems to do with the disclosure and confidentiality of information, particularly where there is a conflict of interest between family members.

These difficulties cause major problems for the practice and process of assessment. This chapter will therefore consider issues relevant to the process of planning and preparing for effective assessments.

Understanding the views of family members

It is important to understand how each of the family members understands the problem(s) rather than assuming that everyone views the situation in the same way. In this context, two of the simplest but most important concepts to arise from the literature on strategic therapy have been the concepts of 'patient position' and 'customerhood' described by Fisch *et al.* in their classic work on brief therapy (1982). These concepts produce a very useful way of understanding patient views and working with motivational issues.

In the initial stages of 'engaging' or 'forming an alliance' with people, it is very important to understand very clearly their view(s) of the problem. If this is not done, it is very easy to say or do something which will upset or annoy them and may put them off accepting advice or help. 'Patient position' refers to the person's views about the problem and can be summarized as:

1   Whether a particular person is defined as part of 'the problem'
2   Whether they are a 'customer', i.e. whether any changes are desired, how strong this desire is, and the exact nature of the changes desired
3   If not, the degree of sympathy with which they view the person who is labelled as the problem – e.g. as sick (sympathetic) or bad (unsympathetic)
4   Whether the person is optimistic or pessimistic about the possibility of change
5   If so, whether they accept this role willingly or reject it
6   Key self-concepts with which the person tends to identify themselves, e.g. 'caring mother', 'working man' or 'honest and straightforward'.

Using the concept of customerhood (dimension 4 of 'patient position') helps to clarify the degree of effort and co-operation that can be expected of each person in the family; the other aspects of 'patient position' are particularly useful for deriving a therapeutic or assessment contract, as the offer of help can be framed in that person's own concepts and language. Clearly where views differ radically, it may be important to offer different contracts to different members of the family.

As a general rule, it is assumed that it is usually better to accept the person's views at first contact with them, even if it is obvious that you do not agree with them. The principle involved here is that people will usually only accept a view that challenges their own after they have developed a working relationship with the other person. The main exceptions to this are:

- when their view is so unrealistic that it would be unprofessional not to be clear that one's own position is different, e.g. demanding access to confidential information
- when someone is deliberately provocative, often as a means of finding out what sort of person you are.

General rules about confidentiality need to be made clear at the outset. In the latter situation it is sensible to make some comment about this process, for example:

144

'I can understand that is what you think, but it is part of my job to stay undecided about that.'

'You would really like to know my own personal views on that, I can tell, but that isn't the point. If you want me to help you, you have to let me make my own mind up.'

It is wrong to collude with something that is against professional ethics, but in general such confrontation can often be deferred. If not, the risks of opting out have to be balanced against the risks of apparent collusion. It is commonly assumed that even if the therapist confidently disagrees with the family members' view, it is part of the professional task to move towards some kind of compromise later as part of the therapy or counselling process. Therefore, it is more often a case of accepting unusual views now, but noting that it will be important to work towards clarification or change at a later date.

By showing that he/she understands their view, the therapist will be able to negotiate a therapy contract much more easily. A contract in this sense means an explicit agreement about what the work is about: what are the problems and how can the therapist and clients go about solving them? Contracts are extremely important; otherwise the time spent together is likely to be wasted, if they are working to entirely different agendas. Each dimension of 'patient position' will now be considered in turn, showing how it can affect the process of reaching a therapy contract.

DIMENSION 1: THE 'IDENTIFIED PATIENT'

Often where there are health problems of whatever cause one person is labelled as 'it' (the ill or mad or bad one) and often the problems are assumed to 'belong' to this person. A closer look at situations, however, often reveals that this is a vast oversimplification. For example, a wife who is depressed may be identified as the patient (until we find that her husband beats her). Also, children are often identified as 'unmanageable' by a parent (but we may discover that in other situations they behave perfectly well).

Nevertheless, it is important to be clear to what degree people identify themselves as part of the problem, or as a 'bystander'. If this person is identified, how do they feel about this themselves? Some people feel angry if they are labelled as the problem, whereas others accept this role willingly and in a psychological way sacrifice themselves for the sake of the other family members.

A typical example of difficulty with this dimension could occur where a therapist is asked to see an adolescent boy and after an assessment interview with the family asks him if he would like some help with his problems. The boy indignantly says he has no problems, it is his parents who are far too strict and 'they are the ones that need to see a shrink, not me'.

DIMENSION 2: CUSTOMERHOOD

People may not be identified as 'the problem' but it is just as important to check how much they are affected by the problem. The concept of customerhood is defined as the degree to which the person desires changes. This is a particularly important dimension since issues of motivation are crucial in any form of problem-solving therapy. The concept of 'customerhood' is an extremely useful one to help understand and thus enhance motivation. Customerhood can be loosely defined in this context as a desire for change of some kind (as yet often undefined; the type of change required or desired may vary). If there is no customerhood available in any of the family members it can be argued that it is best not even to begin since work will certainly fail without it, and failure may prevent them seeking help again at a future time when they otherwise would be more motivated. If they seem to have a serious problem but cannot or will not acknowledge this, some kind of crisis will be required to create customerhood. Sometimes a potential therapist needs to 'manufacture' a crisis via the assessment to 'create' customerhood by spelling out just how bad things will become if no action is taken. Sometimes it is useful to involve the referrer directly in this process, particularly if it is important to clarify communications, opinions or roles. (In terms of process, often the referrer unwittingly takes on the role of worrying about the problem of the person or family and he/she may need help to pass this role back to where it belongs.)

The degree of customerhood varies enormously in individuals – and in a family situation there are often some family members who are good customers with a clear desire for change, and others who may not be customers at all. In general it is useful to distinguish between three levels of customerhood:

1   Non-customers, e.g. 'No I don't think we have a problem.'
    'I'm not really bothered about it.'
    'I can put up with it.'
    'I only came because the doctor told me to.'
2   Clear customers, e.g. 'Yes, I asked to see a specialist.'
    'I can't stand this any more.'
    'I really want to get this sorted out.'
3   Unclear customers who are simply ambivalent or who may have hidden
    agendas, e.g.   'Yes I suppose so . . .'
    'If you say so but . . .'

If the customerhood is unclear, it is essential to clarify it or one may unwittingly begin working at cross-purposes if the person has a hidden agenda (see p. 148). As a general rule, it is more effective to work with people who have the clearest customerhood as they will be most likely to co-operate and put real effort into the mutual process of problem-solving which constitutes therapy. (Families present particular difficulties since some members may desire change while others resist it. Hence it is preferable to have some idea about the degree and type of customerhood for all family members, as much as possible.)

Establishing customerhood can be done in various ways. It is useful at the outset of therapy (and continuously throughout) to begin a session with a general probe, e.g. 'I would like to know what each of you would like to get out of this meeting today?' This usually elicits 'customer statements' which may be of two basic types. The first type is positive customer statements, e.g.:

'I want to be able to make friends.'
'I would like to get along better with my son.'
'I need to be able to control his behaviour better.'

These sorts of statements specify clear goals and should be treated as 'music to the therapist's ears'.

The second type is negative customer statements, e.g.:

'I do not want him to wet the bed.'
'I am sick of her moaning.'
'I have had enough of his cheek.'

These are also important, but require some clarification of the actual goals. It is therefore particularly helpful to get the person to restate them in positive terms and clarify the goal. The therapist will need to ask questions such as:

'Would it be OK if you knew he was trying, even if he failed?'
'What would satisfy you, if she only moaned once a week?'
'Can you be more clear about what is acceptable?'

in order to provoke a restatement of goals for change in positive terms.

Another technique is to encourage customerhood by long-circuiting. When customer statements occur, the therapist should reinforce them by sitting upright, looking interested and enthusiastic, nodding, and making enthusiastic comments. Furthermore, the therapist should also 'long-circuit' the conversation at this point by encouraging the person to repeat and clarify their ideas:

'Tell me more (about this) . . . '
'Can you be more precise . . . ?'
'I do not quite understand this properly, can you explain it?'
'What exactly do you want?'

By getting the person to repeat and clarify their ideas about aims and goals, the therapist helps to increase the motivation for action. If the goals are not clear it is helpful in itself to clarify them. A further technique is to ask what change would make the person feel they were getting somewhere:

> 'What is the smallest improvement that would have to happen to make you think you were getting somewhere?'

(Getting the person to define their minimum goal for change can help the therapist to see if they are being realistic about the situation or not.)

Often a lack of clarity about customerhood is due to fears or doubts about the negative consequences of coming, or some kind of implicit expectation or 'hidden agenda'. Fears or doubts can often be elicited with questions:

> 'How did you feel about coming today . . . ?'
> 'Have you ever seen anyone like me before . . . ?'
> 'Did you have any doubts about coming?'

'Hidden agendas' are more complex issues where there is as an important but covert reason for attending which may not surface in an initial interview unless a therapist is extremely careful and/or lucky. Some examples of hidden agendas are:

- I really just want my child medicating so that he does not bother me and I can get on with my work
- I really came along because I want to be rehoused and I thought a letter from your department would help
- I really want you to stop my ex-wife having access to our child
- I am not really worried about my child's behaviour but I want to talk to someone because my husband is having an affair, although he does not know that I know.

Sometimes a direct appeal can clarify these situations, for example 'Mr X, I am a bit confused about all this. What is the one most important thing you would really like from me?'

Often patience is required if the agenda is very personal and a strong degree of trust and confidence in the therapist needs to be established before a secret is shared. Some such agendas may never surface, but hints may be given as clues which have to be watched for closely.

At the end of a session it is useful to check by summarizing and paraphrasing what you understand about the person's customerhood, and then to ask them if you have understood them properly. It can save a lot of wasted time to be quite explicit:

> 'How important is this to you?'
> 'How many times would you be prepared to come to the department to sort this out?'

A typical example of difficulty with customerhood would be where a therapist assumes that parents are very upset by an older child's enuresis but after some erratic attendance sessions the parents tell him that this is normal behaviour in their family.

DIMENSION 3: IDENTIFIED PATIENT SEEN AS 'BAD' OR 'MAD'

This dimension largely depends on the degree of sympathy the person feels towards the identified patient. Lack of sympathy leads to the IP being seen as 'bad' whereas a very oversympathetic person may label someone as 'mad' or 'sick' because 'they would not normally do that sort of thing'.

A typical difficulty on this dimension would be where a parent is told by a therapist that their child is clearly 'in need of help'. The parent angrily retorts that he needs a good hiding.

DIMENSION 4: OPTIMISM V. PESSIMISM

This is largely dependent on mood state and how long the problem has existed. It is important to match the person on this dimension as a pessimistic person will not respect an optimistic therapist, and vice versa. With pessimistic people, it is useful to ask if they think therapy could make things worse; and to ask them if they have anything to lose by trying therapy. It is equally important to discover whether a person has a wildly optimistic view as they may expect instant 'cures'. This can be a common problem with parents of children with learning difficulty who cannot accept that the disability cannot be removed.

A typical difficulty would be where a therapist meets a problem she has dealt with successfully before and tells the parent that she is sure he can help. Unfortunately, the parent is very depressed and pessimistic and thinks the counsellor is either very naïve or a fool. Consequently, the parent does not turn up for their appointments.

DIMENSION 5: PASSIVITY V. CONTROL

Some patients approach therapy with a very passive attitude and expect the therapist to solve all the problems (the 'magic wand' expectation). Others can be extremely controlling and may repeatedly try to dominate the therapist in various ways, for example by out-talking the therapist, by dictating unreasonable conditions about the therapy, or by always giving the impression they know more than the therapist. The therapist must be careful to take the right approach by ensuring that passive patients are given time and encouragement to become more active, and that controlling patients are allowed to feel that they have control over what goes on without disrupting the therapy. A typical difficulty might occur where a counsellor persistently asks a passive patient to choose between several different options at the end of the first meeting. The patient feels the counsellor should be the expert and make the decision and thus decides the counsellor is incompetent.

DIMENSION 6: SELF-IMAGE

All of us have certain concepts and images of ourselves which we hold dear and which form a foundation of our self-identity, for example 'a working class man'; 'determination'; 'honesty'; 'friendliness'; 'cheerfulness'.

If someone else identifies our own self-image quickly, we feel that they are an understanding, sensitive person who has come to know 'the real me' very quickly. Therapists can therefore enlist people's cooperation much more readily by identifying and appealing to these essential characteristics of a person's self-image:

'I can see you work hard and I would ask you to work hard with me on this.'
'I can see you are a very determined person and I think this will help.'
'I can see you are very honest and so I will be honest with you.'
'You are clearly a person who values friendliness, and that is important in therapy.'
'A cheerful person like you will find this work easier than most.'

A typical difficulty arising from this dimension might occur where an adult patient clearly identifies themselves as being moral and religious, but seems to have a sexual problem. The therapist offers to help with the sexual problem rather too soon, without understanding how the patient's religious views affect their sex life, and is seen by the patient as 'encouraging sin'.

Some other useful questions for establishing the person's view of the problem are listed below:

How did you come to see me?
Whose idea was it?
How do you feel about it?
Do you think you have any problems?
What do you think is the problem?
What else is a problem in your opinion?
How much does it bother you?
How do you feel towards X?
Does it seem impossible to find a solution?
How hopeful are you of sorting this out?

(Issues of passivity versus control can be judged from what the person does, and self-image deduced from how they talk about themselves.)

Putting the six dimensions together to summarize a person's view of the problem and gain a person's co-operation

By using all these six dimensions carefully, a message which reflects the person's view of the problem can be constructed which maximizes the chance of gaining their co-operation. In effect, the concept of patient position helps to construct the form of a contract for assessment or therapy by paraphrasing and summarizing the patient position:

> Mrs X, I can see that even though you are a very dedicated and careful mother you are having problems with your son which are upsetting you a great deal. I can see you are not very optimistic, and quite reluctant because it was not your idea to come, but I do not think you have anything to lose by having, say, four more sessions to discuss his problems with me. Do you? Could it make things worse? (Discuss) You probably want to think more about this yourself, so perhaps you should think it over during the weekend and let me know.

Working with the wider system

A number of writers have taken these ideas about problem definition further and applied them to the wider network of professional systems that children and families interact with. This is particularly appropriate where there may appear to be a clear problem but the family themselves are not motivated for change. Often the referring agency may be the real 'customer' here (i.e. they are the ones that desire change, sometimes because they feel trapped in a situation with poor outcome). For example, social services may feel very concerned about the welfare of a child, but do not think there are grounds to enforce statutory action by removing a child. They may then indirectly coerce the family to attend a clinic which appears to be the only constructive alternative. In these circumstances the most appropriate or 'therapeutic' action may be not to attempt therapy in the normal sense as it may be doomed to failure if there is no commitment in the family. However, an assessment or consultation process which clarifies the nature of the crisis or longer-term outcome facing the family and the other agency may be more likely to result in some constructive change. This could entail network meetings with the referring professional and others, jointly or separately with the family, as well as the use of normal assessment procedures, and a written report explicitly discussed with the family. It is also important to clarify the professional role in this kind of consultation, as it has critical implications for the issue of confidentiality. If this is a normal referral for health services, the professional acts for the child and family who have the same right to confidentiality as anyone else.

If there is an explicit request for a professional opinion from another agency, then first there should be a clear contract relating to this work, and second the family should understand the purpose of the work and the role of the assessor.

Another common scenario occurs where a referral to a third party is made as a result of overt conflict between a family and another system, for example between school and parents, each of whom may then try to recruit the therapist as an ally in the conflict. This has become increasingly common in recent years in the UK because of government policies which have put pressures on schools to raise academic standards (via league tables for schools) and have also had a secondary effect of indirectly encouraging schools to get rid of troubled and troublesome pupils. It is estimated that the number of school exclusions has increased dramatically (Hyams-Parish, 1995). Associated with this is a large increase of children presenting with emotional distress with at least a partial root in their school experiences. Once again, simply to attempt 'therapy' with the child would be inappropriate if the child is a victim of school pressures or a conflict between home and school. More useful roles would be: to involve supportive educational professionals; to act as a mediator to encourage direct and constructive talks between the parents and the school; to act as an advocate for the child's point of view; to explain the effects of any health problems upon the child's behaviour in school. Halpern, Canale, Gant and Bellamy (1979) give a clear and useful account of how to solve problems using the wider system.

General principles for convening family members

As a general principle it is wiser to accept whoever comes to the first interview(s) and work with them, whilst making enquiries about whether absent members wanted to come, and what their attitude would be if invited. It is, after all, rather patronizing and discourteous to assume that the family has not thought about this. It also respects people's rights to choose. However, there is a competing problem that assessment may not be possible, let alone effective, unless the right conditions are achieved. The most important aspect of these conditions is simply 'Who comes?' There will be times when the results of an absence of a key family member makes assessment or therapy difficult and sometimes this needs to be confronted.

The practical problem of convening and engaging unwilling family members is a key pragmatic issue in the assessment process which can sometimes be tackled using the concept of patient position. By carefully questioning other family members, the absent person's views can be understood and a message sent in a way which is more likely to get a positive response. It is usually possible to get someone to attend once, or agree to come occasionally. The degree of persuasion used to try to convene people for the assessment interview depends upon the likely importance of the person, and the risk of aborting the contact. Natural parents, common-law spouses, step-parents and foster-parents in the main household should be included unless there are very good reasons for not doing so. Separated parents may wish to both attend, but separately, and this should be respected. How much per-suasion is needed depends on the circumstances; but the message should be conveyed that normal procedure is that parents do attend. Siblings are sometimes very important for some problems, and the message conveyed should include this, but in general they are not as essential in the first inter-view as parents. Hence the attitude to their attendance is more that it would help, and we prefer it, but that we accept it may not always seem appropriate to others. In general, be flexible; given time, reluctant members often appear. For example, one case with a reluctant father required a series of pre-liminary interviews with other family members and careful use of other professionals to convene the father. He did not attend many interviews, but the short contact we did make provided enough leverage to make headway with the others despite his absence. This (very common) problem can be understood as the natural reluctance of (some) family members to broaden the focus from the identified patient, even implicitly for assessment pur-poses, for fear of having to accept blame and/or responsibility. If this fear is so strong that someone refuses to attend, the issue is clearly important. Nevertheless it may be possible to construct an approach that will benefit the other people involved, and this should always be considered. Even if the absent member is the identified problem it may be possible to coach another family member to act as a therapist or to effect behaviour change using behavioural or strategic interventions.

Generally at this stage of initial contact problems are often viewed as 'belonging' to an individual and efforts to involve other family members will sometimes meet with confusion and hostility. In many cases great care needs to be taken to surmount this and a number of authors have written exten-sively on this topic (e.g. Carpenter and Treacher, 1983; Margules and Havens, 1981; Stanton and Todd, 1981). Stanton and Todd listed a number of principles for convening and engaging other family members successfully, which have been condensed and summarized below:

- the therapist decides whom to include in assessment and treatment
- agency policy should encourage family members to attend the intake interview as a routine part of the assessment procedure
- do not expect the patient to convene other family members
- contact other family members directly rather than through the identified patient or others
- obtain permission to contact significant others during the intake inter-view if they have not attended it, and do so using the telephone rather than a letter where possible

- contact patients, and other family members, as soon as possible after referral
- encourage early referrals
- view family recruitment as crisis inducing
- use treatment rationales that are non-judgemental; do not blame the family. Similarly, present the rationale for assessment attendance simply as 'helping the therapist to understand'
- emphasize help for the identified patient, not 'for the family'
- present rationales for attendance clearly so that family members who do not participate are effectively indicating that they wish the patient to remain symptomatic
- tailor goals for therapy to suit the patient and family members
- the therapist should try to ensure that any other professionals involved with the patient and family inform him of their actions
- role confusion should be prevented
- the therapist has to invest effort, flexibility and skill in recruiting family members
- the agency in which the therapist works should have a clear policy that encourages proper assessment utilizing relatives' views.

In some cases, however, it may become clear that the particular person plays such a crucial role in the problem that it is best to be honest and state that effective therapy is impossible without the involvement of that person.

The role of the practitioner

Problems of confidentiality and disclosure

After all these principles are followed other problems may arise which relate to the issues of confidentiality and disclosure. Even if family members do attend, they may do so under duress. Secrets such as family violence may increase resistance to attend or result in false impressions being deliberately conveyed. Since children and spouses often present problems within a context of general family or marital stress it is likely that this scenario is much more common than many therapists assume. Privacy boundaries also cause dilemmas for the therapist. Where a clear conflict of interest occurs (e.g. in child maltreatment) it may not be possible to observe the normally accepted customs of confidentiality. In many cases where the child functions as a family scapegoat it may be very difficult to decide whether this constitutes 'child abuse' or not, creating a further dilemma if change is not forthcoming.

One of the main points made in the Mind Report (1975) on the assessment of children and their families is that assessment is a form of intervention into people's lives which necessarily entails having some power over them. Particularly when assessing children's problems, the welfare of the child makes a necessity for accurate information from other members of the family whereas the right to privacy is a fundamental civil right. This conflict underlies a number of difficult ethical conflicts. How much should therapists actively encourage disclosures of private information, such as by questioning children about their parents? Under what conditions should such information be fed back to the parents? (It is clear that a child also has a right to confidentiality.) In a public service agency (as opposed to a research one, or a child protection agency) the types of situations encountered vary enormously; many families will neither expect to be assessed about personal issues nor be willing to undergo this.

The major practical strategy that can be implemented to deal with these difficulties is to make the whole assessment process a contractual one. As a general principle, one of the golden rules for successful therapy is to have a continuous negotiation with the client(s) about what is going on to obtain feedback about their view(s) of the problem, their views of the therapist and his or her actions, and what is helping and what is not. The same rule applies to assessment. In particular the reasons for the assessment, the goals of the assessment, an explanation of what is involved, and the limits of confidentiality should be discussed explicitly with the family beforehand. Indeed, the ethical issues in themselves provide a number of good reasons for having a more formalized and standardized assessment process which can be clearly discussed and negotiated with families.

In addition to these ethical reasons, there is pragmatic evidence to suppose that this makes for more effective professional practice. Day and Reznikoff (1980) demonstrated the importance of addressing clients' expectations in a study which showed that the most powerful factor influencing non-attendance was the appropriateness of expectations regarding therapy. Churven (1978) produced a dramatic rise in attendance rates as a by-product of some research in which families were consulted very carefully about their expectations prior to their attendance at the clinic.

Crisis intervention is an exception to this rule. In certain (crisis) situations such a careful approach to assessment is not feasible, and one must work more rapidly. Nevertheless the principle of the therapeutic contract should still be adhered to, in the sense that even in a crisis it is important for the therapist to explain his actions (unless there are good reasons for not doing so) and to consult the family members where choices are available, albeit more rapidly.

Retaining flexibility

A second general issue during assessment concerns the role of the practitioner and the degree of control and responsibility assumed during the assessment process. As discussed earlier, different theories of psychotherapy implicitly assume different roles for the therapist. In this respect a further concept discussed by Fisch *et al.* which is of great importance is that of 'therapist maneuverability'. They suggest that therapists will need to adjust the nature of their role and must be prepared to take a flexible approach if they are to deal effectively with a broad range of problems. This idea can be applied to the therapist's role in a number of ways, such as level of formality, supportiveness, degree of control, and to what degree the therapist commits himself to a particular type of intervention. Some clients prefer a therapist who is friendly and informal whereas others find such behaviour 'unprofessional' and much prefer a therapist to be formal. Bearing in mind these general preferences, there will be times when a therapist needs to be supportive and sympathetic with a client whereas at other times they may need to be formal and authoritative with the same client; they should be careful not to appear to commit themselves irrevocably to one of these roles. Similarly there are times when a directive approach may be required with a person or family, and other times when it is important to be non-directive. As a general rule during the assessment stage it is desirable for the therapist to adopt an open and collaborative attitude to the family and leave the responsibility for choices with the family, whilst retaining an option to take control if this appears necessary. (Occasions will arise where the therapist may need to assume greater control, such as by insisting that an adolescent's friend who appears to wish to intrude on a session is not allowed to.) Similarly, it is dangerous for a therapist to tell the client(s) that he or she is committed to a particular style or type of therapy, since this may lead the client to believe that no other options are available if initial difficulties are encountered using the therapist's preferred approach.

In certain situations the client(s) may try to lay down conditions which will limit the practitioner's role in some way. For example, one parent may refuse access to the other. It is important to clearly establish the reasons for the request, especially if there is any real danger, and not to make quick decisions based on rigid interpretations of rules. Such a request should be considered carefully in the light of professional practice guidelines, legal status, and the risks specified. Generally a respectful but cautious response is appropriate: for example 'I normally respect privacy where I feel this is appropriate, but if you told me about something really dangerous to yourself or your child I would be in a difficult position. I might have to do something, but I would discuss it with you first. To a certain extent you will have to trust my judgement if you want my help.'

Practitioners also need to begin to see how patients and parents respond to various ideas and interventions. An extremely useful tactic to help practitioners avoid committing themselves to a particular viewpoint is to use conditional or hypothetical statements and questions, such as 'If I said that you were being very strict about this what would you think?' This enables the therapist to check the person's reaction to a statement without actually endorsing it. If this provokes an unhelpful reaction, the therapist can then manoeuvre out of trouble by saying something that acknowledges this was not a correct approach and demonstrates some empathy, for example 'I had a feeling you would say that . . . would that feel as if I was criticizing you?'

Giving the child a voice

Since therapists are invariably adults, there is also a clear danger that assessment will focus too much upon the adults' point of view. In terms of parental responsibility for younger children it can be argued that it should do so; but clearly it would be incomplete if the children's views were ignored. It is likely that the most common error made by trainees working with families is to focus upon the adult perspective and thus to fail to understand the child's position. The second most common error is the converse; to become so sympathetic to the child that the parent is blamed for all the difficulties amid a desire to 'rescue' the child. Many writers have discussed means of involving children in the process of assessment and some basic skills are discussed in Chapter 8. For a more detailed account of methods for working with younger children see McMahon (1992).

Personal reactions and supervision

As all dynamic therapists would emphasize, a therapist will also need to evaluate his or her own personal qualities, and experiences of family life, so that personal reactions do not overshadow other issues. Walsh (1982) made this point in a common-sense way when she suggested that therapists need to guard against imposing their own values or fantasies of health and normality, derived from our childhood experiences, upon others. As in any form of therapy, access to proper supervision is the essential means of dealing with these kinds of difficulties.

The 'puzzle' contract

The actual process of defining the problem can be very complex, particularly where there is conflict within the family. In these circumstances it is often advisable for the initial contract with the patient and his or her family to be explicitly related to assessment only – or to be somewhat vague, in order to safeguard against activating resistance whose nature is not yet clear to the therapist. Making a clear distinction between assessment and therapy for the clients' benefit has a number of advantages. The clients have time to get to know the therapist before committing themselves – and vice versa. Irrational fears and unrealistic expectations can be dealt with, and the usual result is that most terminations tend to be negotiated rather than come about by drop-out or failure. Another major advantage, as will be discussed in Chapter 9, is that a therapeutic approach can be chosen which is more likely to benefit this particular family situation.

Starting with the wider view and using the motivation available

In using an approach which centres upon individual and family development, this necessitates taking a broader look at the problems first, and then focusing upon certain key problems which have been assessed as likely to give maximum leverage in therapy. In order to get this broader view, it helps to begin the assessment with as many family members involved as possible. After we have listened to their points of view, and observed the processes ongoing in the family relationships, then we can select out the key people to work with – but not before. Clearly there are many occasions when family members will not attend or participate and at that point choices will have to be made as to whether an effective therapeutic intervention is possible. Views vary on this issue but this author has found that if there is some clear customerhood it is usually worth persisting with those family members who have it, even if the problems have to be tackled indirectly.

Some useful policies and procedures

Many clinical families do not all come along together willingly, precisely because they are experiencing some problems in family relationships. Careful preparation during the referral process pays dividends. The following procedures are useful.

REFERRER CONTACTS

Particularly if the referral letter is unclear, contact the referrer by telephone to:

- clarify any ambiguities, missing information, and potential problems, particularly regarding the family's attitude to referral
- assess how well (s)he knows the family and whether (s)he is still working with any of them. If (s)he intends to carry on seeing them, some discussion about demarcation of roles will be very useful. (In some cases it may be necessary to refuse the referral if these issues cannot be resolved.)
- enquire if (s)he knows whether any other agencies are involved and what is known about their involvement
- if the referral seems appropriate, proceed to the next stage.

BRAINSTORMING AND HYPOTHESIZING

Where teams of workers are available, it is often productive to consider each referral (briefly) during a team meeting, which is effectively used as a 'brain-storming' session to generate a few preliminary hypotheses – the nature of which will depend upon the detail given in the referral, but should include:

- the degree of urgency of the case
- possible underlying causes and hypotheses
- important information needed to clarify the assessment
- important features to look for, and useful strategies for dealing with this kind of problem.

CONTRACT TO APPROACH FAMILY

Contact the family preferably by telephone to arrange the first contact at a time when (both) parents will be available. Check that the appointment is still required, whether there are any particular difficulties with transport, and ask if they would like any extra information about the service. Practical information about the clinic attendance can be given – likely length of interview, where the clinic is situated, and an agreed procedure for cancellation agreed. Preferably, the appointment should be fairly soon after the call provided this is convenient. The prospect of an appointment can generate intense anxiety and long delays will probably result in a higher level of non-attendance.

USE OF QUESTIONNAIRES TO CLARIFY PROBLEMS AND PRIORITIES

Particularly where there are waiting lists for services the use of a purpose-designed postal questionnaire with those cases that are not obviously very urgent can help to clarify the problem and the actual urgency of referrals in order to manage the waiting list. These can also be used to obtain more detail about problems from carers and from schools where this is appropriate.

INITIAL INTRODUCTIONS

It is good practice to have a clear procedure for introductions which is welcoming but also clear about names and roles. It is also helpful to check basic data with the family at first contact, including names, date of birth of children, address, telephone, composition of family (including whether children are natural or otherwise) schools, and any other agencies involved or important carers who are not present. This establishes the basic facts in a professional way as part of an introduction which allows the family to settle.

THE USE OF PRELIMINARY INTERVIEWS TO ASSESS PATIENT AND FAMILY VIEWS

Many practitioners prefer to start with a relatively informal interview which allows the patient and family to speak fairly freely before using any more formal assessment procedures. Although less structured, it is still useful to follow some guidelines about the topics normally covered in the interview, such as:

- the experience and process of the referral (how, why now, whose idea, what did people think at first)
- views about the problem, from everyone (using the concepts of patient position)
- solutions already tried
- any previous experiences with other agencies
- expectations and ideas about what is needed to help
- who is willing to come regularly
- preferences about whether seen together or not
- how people might react to more formal assessments (e.g. forms).

This can outline specific areas where more detailed assessment would be helpful and also begin a flexible 'engagement phase' prior to using more formal assessment procedures which will be described in the next three chapters. The preliminary interview could be given as a home visit if appropriate. With older children and adolescents then some choice should be offered about whether people prefer to be seen together or separately.

THE USE OF VIDEO-RECORDING

Some clinics use video routinely. I am unconvinced that this can be justified in a public health context since it may prevent families attending for help if they are not able to exercise choice about this. The issues here are quite complex and legal problems can occur if policies do not distinguish between video recordings and other medical or professional records. In general it is important that:

- families genuinely exercise choice and informed consent
- preferably, the recordings are not treated as medical records
- ethically one way to do this is to identify the recording as the property of the family, so that they retain control of any use of the video.

Although the use of video is very valuable, people can react negatively to its use. Video can also affect behaviour in quite subtle ways, for instance to make some people who are in acute distress put on a more 'coping' front to the interviewers because of the camera's presence (which symbolizes 'the rest of the world'). Many patients have seen programmes on television and have very natural reservations about having a recording made of private discussions on such a medium. (Children may assume that this is what is happening.) Many families would refuse to attend if their treatment was routinely recorded. Hence careful consideration should be made of the reaction to the suggestion of video-recording before using it as part of an assessment procedure.

Summary

Chapter 6 has examined the topic of preparation for family assessment. This is complex because family members often have different views and the first part of the chapter examined ways to understand and work with patient views and motivations. Ethical dilemmas include dealing with privacy boundaries and conflicts of interest, welfare versus confidentiality, and dealing with unrealistic expectations. The wider system also has to be considered, and principles for convening family members were summarized. It has been argued that an initial interview understanding patient and family views which prepares for a contractual assessment (utilizing formal assessment methods as the practitioner thinks appropriate) has a number of practical and ethical advantages. Effectively, this preliminary client-centred interview is used to select more specific assessments if required. Finally, practical policies and procedures for preparation of families were specified.

7

USING A STRUCTURED INTERVIEW TO OBTAIN A BROADER ASSESSMENT

One of the fundamental choices during any assessment process concerns the choice between a broad or comprehensive view or a narrow focus. Chapter 6 described how the patient and family views can be used as a narrow focus, and this chapter will show how a broader assessment can be made which is still efficient and effective. A structured interview can be used to obtain a broader view of the child and family. This broader view is important because the level of public awareness about children's mental health problems is low, leading to a high rate of unrecognized problems, plus in health contexts there is an implicit professional duty to screen for health problems.

The interview is often regarded as a form of scientific or semi-scientific procedure. However, it is also a meeting of interviewer and interviewees – so that an interview with a child and family also becomes an important stage in the formation of new relationships between family and interviewer (as well as the opportunity to observe existing relationships in action). Hence there is a fundamental tension between the demands of the scientific method and those of relationship processes. This is the problem which is fundamental to all assessment interviews – how to reconcile a rigorous assessment with the flexibility demanded in a clinical situation.

This chapter will consider this basic dilemma from the point of view that either alone is inadequate, and that a balanced approach is desirable which combines the strengths of a scientific approach with flexibility and clinical skills.

Interviewing with families

The fact that an interviewer cannot be 'objective' or 'scientific' because of his involvement in the context of the interview is the fundamental problem facing those who wish to introduce a scientific approach to their practice. There are also the additional difficulties of the complexity of a family interview, and the problems of privacy boundaries and how they affect the interview.

However, there are ways to overcome these difficulties. First, the use of a standardized procedure in terms of the initial verbalizations of the interviewer will bring some uniformity to the situation. The structured family interview that was developed in Darlington provides a framework of similarity which appears to be clinically relevant to a wide variety of situations. None the less, this is only one aspect of interviewer behaviour. As important at least is the manner in which the interviewer relates to the family in his or her non-verbal behaviour or 'meta-communications', particularly his emotional style and expressions. This will tend to define to the family the types of relationships and behaviour that is expected of them by the interviewer, and is likely to influence the way that the interview progresses in a very powerful way.

General guidelines for the interviewer's behaviour

The following guidelines should normally be helpful in both facilitating clinical skills and assisting in bringing some standardization to the interviewer's non-verbal behaviours:

- the predominant attitude should be one of openness, friendliness, interest in and acceptance of the family as they are
- the interview should be conducted in a conversational manner rather than as an interrogation, using general interviewing skills
- in particular the interviewer should neither be so formal as to be aloof nor so informal as to destroy the family members' respect for him as a professional. He or she should be responsive to the family's preferred level of formality and intimacy, since this will assist the family themselves to relax. (If he or she behaves in the way that they hope for, they will have more confidence to be themselves.)
- the interviewer should also respond clearly but calmly when strong emotional behaviour is displayed within the interview situation, normally by explicitly labelling the behaviour, e.g. 'It sounds as if you are very cross about this'. In this way openness is accepted and modelled, rather than inhibition
- nevertheless, it is important to maintain some 'distance' from the family so that the interviewer does not become 'sucked into the family process' and side with particular individuals. It is equally important not to lose sympathy and openly criticize family members. If this seems a danger, remind oneself that no matter how bizarre the situation, there should be an explanation why the family is behaving in this way – and that one shouldn't make moral judgements until this explanation has been found
- the interviewer should pay close attention to what is said, particularly to statements about feelings and other self-revelations, which should be acknowledged as understood. It is also important to maintain eye

contact and not to interrupt unless this is clearly necessary (e.g. because of long, over-elaborated answers)

- every so often the interviewer should check his or her understanding by paraphrasing and summarizing what has been said, and inviting corrections by phrases such as 'Have I got that right?' With sensitive topics it is helpful to use the same terms as the family members use (e.g. 'getting heated') but to be clear and specific about what actually happens. The best way to do this is to encourage family members to talk about examples of what has actually occurred, for each topic
- the interviewer should be careful to take the family at their tempo, and particularly not to hurry through the initial joining or social phase of the interview until there is some evidence of the family settling down or relaxing. The use of very direct probes such as 'How did you feel?' is permitted but they should be used judiciously where there is a marked degree of defensiveness or inhibition
- the interviewer will need to be flexible and if topics are mentioned spontaneously it is sensible to listen to what is said at that point in the interview and omit any subsequent questions about that topic. Some other aspects of flexibility will be discussed later in the chapter.

The use of a supervisor

In order to obtain a more objective assessment of the whole situation, and assist those new to family interviewing, it is helpful to have an observer or 'supervisor' present in the interview situation. The supervisor's task is to observe, note and (if necessary to assist the interviewer) comment upon the processes and meta-communications. This also helps to deal with the inherent complexity of a family interview where there is much more to observe than in an individual interview. The use of one-way screens, video, and additional observers (if the facilities can accept them) can assist with this task. It has to be accepted that the interviewer's meta-communications or emotional behaviour cannot be standardized. However, the use of a supervisor can at least ensure that these processes can be considered in the assessment procedure.

From the clinical point of view (as opposed to the scientific one) the use of a supervisor is also helpful as it clearly gives a safeguard against problems arising in the relationship processes between the therapist and family members.

General format of the interview

The Darlington Family Interview Schedule (DFIS) consists of a 'script' to assist the clinician who is interviewing a family. The script shows the clinician's dialogue in block capitals in the main text. The interview is divided into twenty-five sections, consisting of the eighteen problem dimensions (see Chapter 5) and seven additional important aspects of clinical interviewing with families. The name of each section is shown in the margin to assist the interviewer.

There are certain characteristics to the format of the script. For each problem area, the script includes a carefully worded introductory statement to the topic which is followed usually by two probe questions designed to elicit information about that particular problem. The introductory statements are carefully phrased sentences which serve two purposes. First, they set the agenda for the probe question which follows; for the more complex topics they may also infer links between problems – in the second example given below there is an inference that parental disagreement about parenting models can cause problems with children. Second, the introductory statement is phrased in such a way that the problem is 'normalized', often by suggesting that the problem is very common, for example:

'Sometimes it is difficult for people to keep up a social life after they have children. Do you get a chance to go out together?'
'I don't believe there is a right or wrong way to bring up children. Lots of ways can work, but people often have different ideas about it. Do the two of you ever disagree about how to handle the children?'

This encourages more open disclosure, helps to remove inhibitions resulting from shame and guilt, and thus gives the family members implicit permission to discuss the topics more openly. How questions are asked is a crucial skill in interviewing; and in the author's view this use of normalizing statements is a crucial skill in clinical interviewing and a major feature of the interview.

The second major characteristic of the interview is an emphasis on seeking permission to make enquiries as part of the process of the interview. This also helps to minimize 'resistance' and reduce the risk of family members reacting to the therapist in a negative way.

The interview is also carefully structured in its sequence so that it moves in an easy and natural progression from simple aspects of problems to more complicated ones and from less threatening to more threatening topic areas. (In technical terms, the former progression reflects a move up through the 'systemic levels', i.e. from child focus through parental focus and parent–child focus to whole family focus.) This structure helps the clinician and family to discuss potentially sensitive topics in the first interview more easily. If the family begin to become highly stressed at some point, the clinician has some margin of error because of the gradual progression into areas of greater difficulty. She is thus more likely to be able to 'ease off' if she suspects that the family might become stressed to the point of 'no return', i.e. there is a risk of them not attending in future. From the family's point of view, this sequential progression can also help to begin the process of 'reframing' the problem by helping to understand the linkages between individuals, relationships, and whole family phenomena. Assessment and therapy cannot really be distinguished, and this assessment interview is designed to be potentially therapeutic. The perceived focus of the interview is, therefore, to relate individual problems to the functioning of the family as a whole in a way which the family themselves can understand.

The aim of the interview

The major purpose of the interview in terms of outcome is the formulation of a working therapeutic contract with the family members. In other words, the interview is designed to enable the clinician to make a thorough overview of the various factors which are assumed to be of critical importance in formulating an effective contract with a particular family. These factors can be summarized as:

- The clinician's view of the problems. Without a clear and comprehensive understanding of the problem, the clinician is clearly in danger of making an inappropriate, over-ambitious, ill-timed or otherwise inadequate intervention. This interview aims to cover eighteen problem dimensions in family assessment (see Chapter 5) which comprise a brief but efficient problem analysis. Provided that examples of problems are described the interview will elicit objective information about family life. The overall topic content is based upon seeing the family as a system but also looks at individuals and parts of the family in a way which is suitable for child-focused family problems.
- Family view(s) of the problems. The interview will also elicit information about members' attitudes and feelings about family life. However efficiently the clinician understands the nature of the problems, this is to no avail if she cannot 'sell' her ideas to the family. In order to do this, and thus to make an explicit 'contract' with the family about the work that needs to be done, she must understand their ideas about what the problems are.
- Certain other family characteristics which are critical in deciding the best therapeutic contract for a family. These are the family's strengths, motivations, and self-image.

These factors and how the assessment information is used will be discussed further in Chapter 9 in relation to therapeutic strategies (which may be part of the contract).

Finally, it does need to be emphasized that the major goal of the interview is 'assessment' and not 'therapy'. The clinician is encouraged not to be too rigid and in certain circumstances it may be necessary to alter the phrasing of questions or to omit or introduce additional questions in the process of exploring a topic. However, the major aim is simply to establish whether or not this area is a problem for the family and not to explore the ramifications of the problem in great detail. This is for two reasons. First, there are time constraints and elaborated responses to every problem area will result in a very long interview. Second, the practitioner is strongly cautioned against explicitly adopting a therapist role before a clear therapy contract has been negotiated with the family. Doing so is sometimes dangerous as it may be experienced as presumptuous and thus may damage the prospects of successfully establishing a treatment contract with the family later on. (To use an analogy, it is equivalent to asking a tradesman to visit to give an estimate for some work – and finding that he immediately sets to work knocking a hole in the wall without discussing the job or the price with you.) Many families who are referred with problems are wary of the possible 'costs' of therapy (real or imagined) and are naturally unsure of the benefits. Motivation may often be poor, particularly in public service contexts. Hence although one's initial interventions may be implicitly therapeutic, they are usually best made under the 'cover' of an assessment procedure.

The obvious exception to this position occurs where a family presents in an intense crisis, and in this situation a clinician may be required to work more rapidly and abandon the 'assessment' position, as discussed in Chapter 6. (Hence this interview is probably not suitable in these circumstances.) In addition, sometimes during the process of an assessment interview an issue may arise that seems so 'dangerous' that it must be tackled immediately. If so, the clinician should clarify the situation and explicitly seek permission to make a brief intervention by saying, for example 'This seems to be a very important issue and I'm not sure that I should proceed without making some effort to sort this out. Do you want me to try to sort this out now or would you rather I carried on with my assessment?' Usually, however, the clinician will attempt to 'store' key issues for future reference rather than dealing with them immediately.

Aspects of flexibility in using the interview

As mentioned at the outset of this chapter, it is important to apply the interview in a flexible and adaptive way. There are several issues that are particularly important.

The phrasing or target of probe questions   The clinician should also be flexible when deciding to whom the questions should be asked. The DFIS script is written 'as if' all questions are to be directed to the parents. Hence, the script as shown is suitable only for parents with very young children who would not normally speak for themselves. The interviewer will need to rephrase questions where it is more appropriate to ask the child directly, particularly with adolescents:

'How do you get on with other people of your own age?'

rather than

'How do you think the children get on with people of their own age?'

In general, the clinician should follow a 'structural' model of contacting children (i.e. first comments to the children made via the parents or with the parents' permission) but within the interview framework the interviewer should work hard to give permission to, and encourage, the children to participate actively in the interview. What is most critical here is that a certain amount of 'checking back' should occur, particularly where the parent makes a statement about the child or vice versa, for example:

'Your mum obviously thinks that you are very good at your schoolwork. What do you think is easy and what do you think is hard?'

This checking back also helps to clarify the nature of the parent–child boundaries and relationships.

Single-parent and step-families   Since many families, particularly in a clinic population, are single-parent or step-families the interview script needs specific modification in these situations. It is recommended that the questions during the 'joining' phase which enquire about the family composition are used to check the facts about the family history in a straightforward way using a sequence of questions phrased in an appropriate way, for example:

'Mrs Brown, I understand that you are the mother of all the children. Is that correct? Are you their step-father, Mr Smith?'
'Do the children see their natural father?'

Although this is often a very sensitive topic which in some ways is difficult to address so early in an interview, the issue is such a critical part of family identity that it is more naturally tackled as part of the process in which the family members identify themselves to the interviewer. From experience it seems clear that this usually seems to lead to a much more productive interchange with the family than an interview in which the topic is not addressed early on. Probably this occurs for several reasons. By ignoring the topic the interviewer unwittingly fails to recognize what the family members feel is different about themselves, and this leads the family members to feel a growing sense of frustration that he or she is not understanding them. In ignoring the topic the interviewer may also be unwittingly perpetuating family taboos about the topic which are a major source of tension. Or to put it more simply, the family may simply feel that the interviewer is making a lot of incorrect assumptions, but feel too embarrassed to correct him.

Redundancy of probe questions   With articulate and expressive families, the practitioner will find that towards the end of the interview he has already gathered enough information about several of the later topics. Certain probe questions may now be redundant since the family have already given an answer in the process of answering previous questions. Therefore redundant questions and sections should be omitted.

Use of preferred language and follow-up probes   It is recognized that local language and dialect differ widely and that certain modifications may be necessary to the phrasing of the questions to suit either the local population or the interviewer, who may feel more comfortable with certain phrases than others. Interviewers should also feel free to use their own accustomed follow-up probes where questions have not resulted in a clear answer.

Some generally useful follow-up probes are:

'How does that affect everyone else (or name of particular person)?'
'How much does that bother you?'
'How exactly does that happen?'
'Can you give me an example?'
'What's the worst thing about this situation for you?'
'I'm sorry I don't understand. Can you explain that again?'

Idiosyncratic qualities of families   Although the interviewer should attempt to adhere closely to the script, it has to be recognized that circumstances will arise which require several modifications of the script, or even make it down-right impossible to follow it. The commonest of these circumstances is when the interviewer may have to make modifications because of the idiosyncratic qualities of certain families. Sometimes a child is cared for by an extended family network. Imaginative rephrasing is required. Other families will have such pressure of speech about their experiences that it is probably more practical to let them talk with minimal interruption and abandon a more structured interview format. Generally, the interviewer should remain flexible and sensitive to the family's own rules and habits and willing to communicate about the ongoing process. When problems occur, discuss the process: for example if parents tend to interrupt and answer on behalf of the children it might be useful to highlight the issue by asking:

'I have some more questions concerning the children. I would like to see if they can answer for themselves first and then get your opinion. It may be difficult, but can we try that?'

Termination and contract formulation

At the end of the interview there is a choice about what to do next. Experienced practitioners may well have a clear idea about the next stage and be able to offer options and discuss these with the family immediately. Sometimes a short break can be taken in order to consider and analyse the information obtained and derive a formulation; this method is particularly useful when working in pairs or with trainees. Sometimes the information is so complex that more time is required to consider the implications, or there may be a need for more specific assessments (for example if a medical condition is one possible cause which needs to be checked) so that a contract for more specific assessment is the sensible option to offer to the family. The use of the Darlington Family Rating Scale (DFRS), which matches the interview content, can help to structure the formulation.

The first step is to assess the professional or 'objective' view of the problems in the family, using the ratings of the eighteen problem dimensions as a guide. In doing so the practitioner should be careful not to ignore the wider context, (e.g. the roles of extended family and other professional systems). The second step is to assess the family's 'position' on the problems. This includes the family's motivations and strengths but also other aspects of their 'view' of the problem.

If possible the practitioner should offer a contract for further assessment (in child work this commonly concerns an agreement to work with the child to understand their ideas, feelings and needs in more detail) or therapy which fits both with her own view of the problem and also fits with the family's position. The family position, in fact, is complex since it is often made up of several different positions held by various family members. However, the therapist will seek to offer a contract which will fit with the key members' positions (usually the parents though not always). Sometimes contracts may need to be negotiated separately ('splitting' the family) particularly with older children where conflict exists with their carers. When adolescents and their parents never agree about anything, it is unwise to expect them to agree to the same contract with a therapist.

If it is unclear what form the contract should take, the 'puzzle contract' may be offered (i.e. 'We're not sure whether we can help. Are you prepared to come back and talk with us again to help us decide whether we can help?')

Often no contract can be offered where views are rigid. It is best to be honest about this rather than to raise false hopes and waste time on both sides. The commonest 'no contract' situation is where the family do not consider themselves to have a problem at all, although the referrer does. The practitioner will need to be clear about his or her own views here before deciding what tactics to adopt. If there do seem to be serious problems which the parents seem to be denying, one tactic is usually to explicitly state and repeat the referrer's concerns for the future if the problems are not tackled. For example, 'You know, Dr X and I have seen a number of situations like this, and what worries us is that sometimes people either run away from home or try to kill themselves. Have you never worried about that?' Sometimes it may be important to work with the wider system (see

Chapter 6). As a matter of professional ethics it can be argued that the warning has to be clear and unambiguous and followed up in writing if serious risks are involved.

In summary, this interview should be viewed as another means of arriving at a helpful therapy contract for a particular family. It takes a broad overview of the problems. It can be used in conjunction with the Darlington Family Rating Scale – which can be considered as a record form particularly designed to assist with the decision-making processes involved in the formulation of the therapy contract.

In the process of doing this the interview should also delineate which particular problem areas will require detailed exploration or will be a focus for the goals of therapy in subsequent interviews. Sometimes it is possible to delineate a clear 'focal hypothesis' after this interview, but not always: in most cases it is safer to seek further clarification rather than risk making a premature hypothesis which may be rejected by the family.

The process of using the DFIS and DFRS will begin to delineate which particular problems and areas require more detailed exploration and, eventually, which may serve as the most useful focus for therapy. Sometimes it is even possible to delineate a clear formulation or 'focal hypothesis' after this interview. In most cases, however, the outcome is an agreement either to focus the work in some way or to continue in an exploratory manner if there is a marked degree of indecision and anxiety about collaborating in active work. In most cases it is safer to seek further clarification rather than risk making a premature hypothesis or other intervention which may be rejected by the family if made too early. Hence the DFIS is often the first step in a series of therapeutic efforts which may form a lengthy path. It should be regarded as a means of keeping to the most appropriate path and not as a short cut to the end. Initial agreements and contracts often change as therapy progresses, privacy boundaries loosen, and trust develops; this is a natural part of developing relationship processes. The important point is that although the DFIS is designed to formulate a working contract and strategy they should not be regarded as a fixed and final solution.

Advice to learners and common problems

For those contemplating using this method, there are some useful comments that can be made in the light of experience. There are two aspects to the approach which may be new to some people and it is worth distinguishing between them. First, following a 'script'; and second, the practice of interviewing the family together, some of whom may be there rather reluctantly.

In practice the 'learner' interviewer has a dual task of 'joining' with the family members to establish rapport despite any reluctance, while still following a structured format. This demands a great deal of the interviewer and it has been noticeable how much better structured interviews have been when an experienced colleague has been available to give live supervision. While the interviewer focused on following the format, the supervisor is then able to concentrate on the family members' reactions and help the interviewer direct attention to particular family members appropriately. Hence the first point about learning to use the interview is that it is useful to undertake this task in pairs using a live supervision model.

Second, and particularly for those less used to family interviews, it is also worth separating the learning process into stages, by focusing first on using the script with a parent on their own, then with two parents, and finally with family groups. Indeed the script can be used very flexibly, and readily adapts to interviewing parents separately or together, with or without the children. Some practitioners may feel more comfortable using the interview format with parents alone – good practice is partly dependent upon personal style, and preference. Although direct information about observed group processes is lost, it is probable that disclosures of personal experiences and feelings are more likely in individual or couple interviews. The sensible approach is thus to experiment with individual, couple, and group interviews in the normal course of practice with situations encountered. Certainly for learners it is sensible to take things in stages. It could be argued that a totally comprehensive assessment system would utilize individual and family interviews, if the time involved could be justified. However, in the next chapter we shall see how questionnaires can be used both as a preliminary screening and to collect more specific information efficiently.

Third, the most common problem that trainees encounter when using the interview is that they find it difficult to keep within the normal time limits because they attempt to do therapy rather than simply making an assessment. The interview often generates a rich amount of material and it is tempting to try to deal with it there and then. However, the purpose is to make an assessment – this entails simply discovering whether or not there is a significant problem for each dimension, not attempting to solve the problem. The task is therefore more akin to making an inspection, noting the necessity for further work, and moving on to the next area. Once this principle is grasped it becomes much easier to keep the interview to approximately one hour. However some verbose families will need two sessions.

Whenever new methods and techniques are used it is to be expected that other skills and abilities will suffer while the main strain of conscious effort is taken up with learning the new method. In other words, everyone will get worse before they gain the benefit of a new method. Indeed, it could be argued that the more complicated the method, the worse one will get. This is probably the biggest barrier that has to be overcome. The changes that are required in using this approach are quite substantial, and it is easy to abandon the approach in the face of these initial difficulties. This would be premature as there are benefits to the approach which become apparent as one persists with it.

As well as these general points, a specific problem arises when using the structured interview with clinical families who can be characterized as displaying an idealized view of themselves resulting in 'blanket denial'. Despite presenting for help, they give a pattern of 'ideal responses' within the interview and to the questionnaires – in a way which is simply not congruent with observations of them. Members of these families report subsequently that they feel uncomfortable in the structured interview. It is concluded simply that difficulties will be encountered in using these more formalized family assessment methods with families who have an 'idealized' view of themselves.

Advantages of the system

The assessment system has some specific advantages to balance the above problems:

- it allows a broader problem assessment at the outset – which particularly helps to ensure that problems are not missed, clarify whether the problems are specific or global, whether they are of severe or mild intensity, and understand links between key problem areas
- it immediately gives a clear sense of how supportive (or not) the family system will be in solving problems
- using the interview as a training tool helps to internalize the conceptual scheme which is at the heart of the system. Once this is internalized, it is much easier to cope with the confusing complexity of child problems
- using the structured interview regularly allows the interviewer to develop a standard of comparison between families – something which certainly is perceived to be useful by those who have used it.

Apart from the exceptions discussed earlier, the interview was also generally well received by patients and often elicited positive comments from them after the interview concerning:

- relief at being able to discuss difficult issues openly
- gaining a normalized perspective on their problems
- seeing connections between problems.

Taking a broad view of the whole department's work in which these methods were developed, the use of these methods seemed to help a much clearer focus for work to develop in most cases. It also encouraged a theoretical shift towards a 'developmental–social' model. The emphasis shifted towards focused problem-solving, rather than simple medical diagnosis and non-specific counselling. Problems were also more likely to be conceptualized in terms of psychological growth, development and interactions (rather than 'symptom-oriented' descriptions). The system also led to a more 'contractual' style of working in which terminations were more likely to be explicitly discussed rather than occurring by drop-out.

The Darlington Family Interview Schedule (DFIS) is reproduced in full at the end of this chapter. If the interview is to be used in a different type of working context then obviously some modifications may be necessary to the script. Different specialisms or contexts require a different emphasis or a modified set of problem dimensions.

The rating scale

The rating scale provides a purpose-designed record form to accompany the use of the structured interview. It does not replace normal record keeping as it is always useful to note down key phrases used by family members verbatim. Its main function is to provide a means for summing up the main features of a case and thus to guide decision making. It can be used independently of the interview although it is recommended that initially it is used in conjunction with it.

The Darlington Family Rating Scale (DFRS) is also reprinted after the interview schedule.

Summary

This chapter has discussed the application of a broader family interview schedule and an accompanying rating scale from the point of view that both scientific rigour and flexibility are needed by practitioners. A structured interview can be used to obtain a broader view of the child and family. This broader view is important because the level of public awareness about children's mental health problems is low, leading to a high rate of unrecognized problems, plus in health contexts there is an implicit professional duty to screen for health problems. The interview has three key principles: the use of normalizing statements, which facilitate disclosure, prior to the probe questions; an emphasis on seeking permission to make enquiries; and a sequential progression into more sensitive areas.

Certain general guidelines have been described for the interviewer, as well as the need to be flexible in relation to the target of the probe questions, the use of the interview with single parents or step-families, and the omission of redundant questions. In practice it is also helpful to learn to apply the interview in stages and with some form of supervision. Common problems and advantages are discussed.

The major goal of the interview is to help with the formulation of a therapeutic contract with the family. This will be discussed again in more detail in Chapter 9, which considers how assessment is used to determine therapy strategy. The next chapter will consider the use of more specific procedures as adjuncts to child and family assessment.

APPENDIX 1

DARLINGTON FAMILY INTERVIEW SCHEDULE

Induction phase

Hello . . . (*Introduce names, roles; ask family for similar.*)
As you know ——— (*referrer*) has contacted me/us to say you have a problem and that you are willing to discuss it with me/us. What I/we would like to do in the next hour is get a clear picture of the problem and its background, in your own words. I would like to be able to understand what it's like to be in your shoes. Is that all right with you? Does anyone want to ask a question?
(*Reply as necessary.*)

[Next, I'd better explain about this room and how we work . . .
(*At this point the interviewer can explain any special features of the interview, e.g. observers, video, etc., and check back with the family that they consent to these features. If relevant, the availability of play or drawing materials can be specified. Allowing the children (and adults) to explore the room or view special facilities such as one-way screens can help the family to settle.*)]

Joining phase (also gains social information)

Now before we start properly I would find it helpful to know a little bit of background about each of you as people. Mr and/or Mrs ———, are you (both) from this part of the world? Do you work? What as? Can you introduce each of the children and tell me a little about each of them – what they like to do, what they are good at, etc.

176

(Allow 5–10 minutes for a discussion which should aim to introduce each member of the family to the interviewer – who should aim to accept and confirm each member of the family in a positive way.)

OK, now we'll start. I usually go through a list of questions that I have found through experience to be important. I hope this doesn't put you off but I have a terrible memory. If you don't want to answer any of the questions, just say so.

Motivation: route to clinic (omit if covered previously)

Tell me, how did you come to be referred to us? *(Whose idea, how the referral was made; especially in relation to any discussions in the family.)*

Expectations (omit if covered previously)

What did you think about coming today? *(Have any of you seen anyone like me before? What sort of thing were you expecting?)* *(Establish any fears or expectations concerning the interview.)*

Family view(s) of problem

Now I would like to hear in your own words a description of the problems that you would like help with as *you* see them. I would like to take about ten minutes over this. Who would like to start? *(Allow parents to give their description and accept their description as far as possible. Try to make sympathetic or empathic comments. Establish and note the following:*

a) *Who is defined as the patient and how are they defined – as 'bad' or 'mad', i.e. are others sympathetic or not?*

b) *Is the identified patient concerned about the problem/liable to co-operate?*

c) *Who are the 'customers' in the family and who is not? Is another professional agency the real customer?*

d) *Particularly, how do the children view the referral and what, if anything, have they been told about it?*

e) *What solutions have been tried?)*

177

Child health	Now I'm going to talk about some general areas that can often be problems for parents. When children have health problems that can be very worrying. Have any of your children had any serious health problems? (What about when they were small?) (*If yes, check back with child,* e.g. can you tell what that's like for you . . . *prompt as necessary.*)
Child development	Children have to learn an incredible amount as they develop and grow up. Do you have any worries about their development? (*If yes, check back with child* and *acknowledge embarrassment and frustration.*)
Child emotional behaviour	The most common day-to-day difficulty for parents is when their children get upset – either angry, sad, or frightened. Can you tell when your children are upset? How do they show their feelings? (How do you cope with that?)
Child relationships	Making friends is very important but sometimes quite difficult. How do you think the children get on with other children of their own age? (Who do you think each of the children get on best with? how do they get on with each other?) (*Older children: rephrase as direct questions, e.g.* Has any of you got any important health problems? How do you get on at school? Do you find it easy or hard to make new friends? *Check back with parent(s) for their opinion.*)
Child conduct	Sometimes children do things which make problems for other people. Do your children have any habits that really bother you? (*If yes, specify the nature of the problem, who is affected most, etc.*)
Negative life events	Young people can get very upset by an emotional shock, like a bereavement or separation or seeing something nasty. Has anything like that happened to anyone?

Parents' health	Just as parents worry about children, so children worry about parents. Do (either of) you have any health problems? (How about the past? Any problems before or after childbirth?)
Parents' psychological health	Grown-ups can have problems too. How have you (both) been in your feelings lately? (*Specify reference to emotions if necessary.*) If (either of) you have got any problems that are bothering you, you can tell me privately if you wish. (*This allows privacy boundaries to be respected, although some parents may wish to speak at this point.*)
Parents' social support	Sometimes it is difficult for people to keep up a social life after they have children. Do you have any kind of a social life? Do you feel like you fit in where you live?
Parenting history and skills	I think being a parent is a *very* difficult task. The funny thing is that usually no one tells us anything about it, and we have to rely on what we remember about our own parents. Could each of you tell me a little about your own childhood and what your parents were like? (*Prompt each parent as necessary, e.g.* How would you describe your mum and dad to someone who didn't know them? Who were you closest to? How did your parents show their feelings to you?) How do you think this has affected you as a parent?
P–C control	First, some of the most common difficulties arise when children won't do what their parents wish. Is this a problem for you?
Over protection	The world can be a dangerous place. Do you worry a great deal if any of the children do anything a bit risky?
Over involvement	Do they tend to rely on you rather too much? (Do you ever think that you need them too much to let them go?)

179

Closeness and distance	You've already told us some things about how you all get on together. Who spends most time with whom in the family? Who does each of you go to when you're worried or upset? (Would anyone like to be closer to anyone else?)
Marital partnership	One last thing about being a parent – I don't believe there is a right or wrong way to bring up children. People often have different ideas about it. Do the two of you disagree about how to handle the children? (*If yes* – How do you resolve that?)
Marital partnership	(*If comfortable atmosphere*) Would you mind if I asked you a little about your relationship with each other? (*If consent given*) How would you describe your relationship?
Contextual stresses	Pressures from outside the family can often cause problems within it. Are there any particular pressures on your family? (*Acknowledge any obvious differences as appropriate.*)
Power hierarchies	Every family has difficult times. If there's an argument, who sides with whom? Who wins?
Emotional atmosphere	Feelings are very important but they can be very difficult to communicate. Does anyone find it difficult to show their feelings?
Family development	Every family goes through different stages – getting to know each other as a couple, marriage, the stage of little babies, childhood, adolescence, and leaving home. Which of these stages have you enjoyed most and which has been most difficult? (It's often said that when two people marry it's also the marriage of two families. How does each of you get on with your in-laws?)
Strengths	Tell me, what do you think are the *strengths* in your family?
Problem perspective review	We've just about finished now. Is there anything else you would like to say at this stage about your problems? Have we missed anything important?

Interview feedback Was this the kind of thing you expected today? Has anything bothered anyone about today? (*Closing statement as appropriate for context.*)

[Break for planning and contract formulation] [I would now like to take a short break to think about what you have said and discuss it with my colleagues. I'll come back in about ten minutes and let you know what we think about your problem(s) and what we might have to offer. (*Therapy teams can consult with each other at this point and decide on what, if any, therapy contract or message should be given to the family.*)]

APPENDIX 2

DARLINGTON FAMILY RATING SCALE – FORMULATION AND STRATEGY

SPACE FOR FAMILY SOCIOGRAM:

1 HISTORY AND DEVELOPMENT OF PROBLEMS
   a) Distant history (+2 years) – key events

   b) Recent history – onset; duration; maintaining factors etc.

2 KEY PROBLEM AREAS FOR INDIVIDUALS AND THE FAMILY SYSTEM
   a) Family perceptions: problem(s) as seen by family member(s)

   b) Observer perceptions: key problems (see ratings)

   c) Attitudes to therapist/other agencies

3 MOTIVATIONS AND STRENGTHS IN FAMILY

4 KEY PROBLEM AREAS (see ratings)

5 THERAPEUTIC STRATEGY
   a) Therapist's understanding of problem

   b) Plan for next session

   c) Explanation(s) to family

CHILD-CENTRED PROBLEMS

CHILD HEALTH (PHYSICAL)

A Good or average health
B Persistent but minor health problems
—— C Acute illness requiring specialist help
D Chronic illness or disability
E Life-threatening illness or serious disability

CHILD DEVELOPMENT
Consider the following areas:
Physical growth/motor skills/
self-care skills, especially
toileting/intellect and
education/speech and language/
general independent
functioning

A Age appropriate development or better
B Specific developmental delay (one area)
—— C Delay in two areas
D Delay in three areas
E More than three areas delayed

EMOTIONAL DISTURBANCE
Consider the following areas:
Mood disturbances/activity
levels/concentration/tics/
psychosomatic pains/sleep
pattern/eating behaviour/self-
injury/phobic behaviour/
obsessions and compulsions

A Age appropriate emotional behaviour
B Specific problem (one area)
—— C Problems in two areas
D Problems in three areas
E Problems in more than three areas

CHILD RELATIONSHIPS
Consider relationships with:
 father/mother/siblings/ peers/
schoolteachers

A Relates satisfactorily for age
B Problem in one area
—— C Problems in two areas
D Problems in three areas
E Problems in four or more areas

CONDUCT

A Average conduct for age
B Misconduct specific to certain situations,
  e.g. theft from parents
—— C Generalized misconduct, e.g. theft in various situations
D Evidence of dangerous misconduct, e.g.
  solvent abuse
E Potentially lethal misconduct, e.g. fire-
  raising

NEGATIVE LIFE EVENTS
Consider: Bereavement (family
or friend)/separation from parental carer/sibling separation/
peer separation/physical abuse/
sexual abuse/neglect or emotional abuse

A None
B One event
—— C Two events
D Three events
E Four or more events

PARENT-CENTRED PROBLEMS

PARENTAL HEALTH (PHYSICAL)	A Good or average health
	B Minor persistent health problems
———	C Illness requiring specialist help
	D Chronic illness or disability
	E Life-threatening illness or serious disability

PARENTAL HEALTH (PSYCHOLOGICAL)

A Good/average psychological health
B Anxiety/depression in one parent
——— C Anxiety/depression in single or both parents
D Serious impairment of parenting ability in one parent
E Serious impairment of parenting ability in single or both parents

MARITAL PARTNERSHIP

A Average or good relationship
B Problems apparent but neither admit dissatisfaction
——— C One partner dissatisfied
D Both partners dissatisfied
E Breakup threatened or probable

PARENTING HISTORY

A Good or adequate parenting history
B One parent reports difficulties in childhood
——— C Both (or single parent) report difficulties in childhood
D One parent abused or other severe disruption in childhood
E Both (or single parent) abused or other severe disruption in childhood

PARENTS' SOCIAL SUPPORT

A Average or good social support
B Poor social support – one parent
——— C Poor social support – single or both parents
D Isolated from community – one parent
E Isolated from community – single or both parents

PARENT-CHILD INTERACTION

If the description applies to only one parent/carer (of two) use the left hand column; if the description applies to a lone carer or both parents use the right-hand column.

CARE (quality of attachment)	A	A	Good or average care
	B	C	Mild attachment problem = rigidity/ excessive demands for conformity
	—— D	E	Severe attachment problem (non-accidental injury, threat of abandonment or overt attachment disorder)
	B	C	Mild over-involvement = clear tendency to act for child
	D	E	Severe over-involvement = separation problem + intrusiveness
CONTROL	A	A	Good or average control
	B	C	Mild lack of control (not to dangerous level)
	—— D	E	Severe lack of control (to dangerous level)
	B	C	Mild over-control/protection, i.e. restricts activities inappropriately for age
	D	E	Severe over-control/protection preventing individuation

WHOLE FAMILY FUNCTIONING

CLOSENESS AND DISTANCE		
		A None of these
Consider: Enmeshed relationship(s)		B One of these
Disengaged relationship(s) Severe jealousy		—— C Two of these
Family split threatened Absent family members		D Three of these
Lack of affection		E Four or more

POWER HIERARCHIES		
		A None of these
Consider: Dominant family 'controller'		B One of these
Scapegoat Fundamental role conflicts		—— C Two of these
Lack of compromise Parental child		D Three of these
Abdication of responsibility Ambivalent power		E Four or more

EMOTIONAL ATMOSPHERE		
		A None of these
Consider: Tense atmosphere		B One of these
Hostile atmosphere Depressed atmosphere		—— C Two of these
Repetitive conflicts Pseudomutuality		D Three of these
Lack of affection Lack of humour		E Four or more

CONTEXTUAL STRESSES		
		A None of these
Consider: Living conditions		B One of these
Poverty Employment/school stress		—— C Two of these
Cultural difference Disaster/trauma		D Three of these
Stigmatised or persecuted		E Four or more

SUMMARY OF FAMILY DEVELOPMENT

    A One or two specific problems, typical of present family developmental stage

—— C Evidence of several problem areas in family life and unresolved tasks from previous stages

    E Global problems with few healthy areas and/or evidence of strong transgenerational problems (e.g. child abuse on parents)

8

USING ADDITIONAL ASSESSMENT PROCEDURES FOR MORE SPECIFIC INVESTIGATIONS

The first three chapters of this part about practice have described the development of a conceptual framework for assessment, preparation for assessment, and a procedure for a family interview with an accompanying rating scale which gives a broad overview of the problems. This chapter deals with the use of more specific assessment methods which can help to:

- investigate particular problems
- clarify particular viewpoints, especially that of the child
- allow comparisons to normal scores and the evaluation of change.

The first part of this chapter describes the development and use of the original Darlington Family Assessment System package. This was a project which had a clinical aim of clarifying what was good practice and a research aim to investigate the applicability of multisystem multimethod assessment in a clinical context. Using what was learned from this work (and subsequently) the second part of the chapter moves on to consider the issue of communication with children before examining how the addition of other more specific procedures can form the basis for a skilled and professional approach to assessment with children and families.

The original package of measures

In order to evaluate formally the interview and rating scale it was necessary to use them with other established measures to establish that they would give comparable results to instruments that had already been proved to be useful (concurrent validity). Since the other measures had to be carefully selected to relate clearly to the dimensional system, this created a co-ordinated 'package' of assessment methods. At the very time that the other measures were being selected Cromwell and Peterson (1983) wrote about 'multisystem–multimethod' (MSMM) assessment, the principles of which can be summarized as:

187

- the use of strategies to understand wholeness, hierarchy and parts of the system
- the use of formal assessment methods as clinical aids
- the correct matching of assessment methods to the information required
- the need to develop links between research, theory and practice.

The original package of assessment methods therefore fell into place as an example of MSMM assessment and their use in clinical practice became an evaluation of this approach in clinical practice. The package took the format shown in Table 12 below:

The questionnaires used in the original 'package'

The particular questionnaires used were chosen on the criteria that they were brief, easy to complete and score, and clearly relevant to the dimensional scheme used. After testing a number of different instruments the following questionnaires were selected, which a literate person could complete in about twenty minutes.

Eyberg Child Behaviour Inventory (the ECBI, short version: Eyberg and Ross, 1978; Robinson, Eyberg and Ross 1980) This questionnaire comprises a checklist of thirty-two problem types of behaviour often displayed by children, including items which refer to emotional problems, relationships with others and conduct difficulties. Examples are 'has temper tantrums', 'teases or provokes other children' and 'is cheeky to adults'. In the short version of the questionnaire, the response requested is simply 'yes' or 'no' (whereas in the full version, a seven-point scale can be used if information about the frequency of occurrence is required). Norms were available (from American populations) both for smaller children and for adolescents.

Goldberg's General Health Questionnaire (the GHQ, 28-item version; Goldberg, 1978) This questionnaire comprises four sub-scales with seven questions each about common symptoms which are associated with neurotic or psychological problems, and high scores can result from either general

Table 12 Summary of Darlington family assessment procedures – components of original 'package'

	Family perspective	Observer perspective
Cognitive understanding	Questionnaires (five in all)	Family rating scale (DFRS)
Behaviour processes	Structured interview (DFIS)	Task + coding system (Eyberg)

mood disturbance or physical health problems. The sub-scales are somatic symptoms, anxiety and insomnia, social dysfunction, and severe depression. Items are in the form, for example 'Have you recently been getting any pains in the head?' with a four-point response scale for each item to specify the frequency of the symptom. A manual is available with details of scoring methods, validation and standardization.

Marital Satisfaction Index (the MSI; derived from Azrin, Naster and Jones, 1973 and modified by this author) This questionnaire delineates and describes ten different 'areas' within the marital relationship (household responsibilities, child-rearing, social activities, money, communication, sex, study or work, my independence, spouse independence and overall happiness) and then requests a rating for each area on a five-point scale. No extensive normative or standardization data is available but the clarity and simplicity of the scale made it seem more practical than the other marital instruments considered. The scale is reproduced in full at the end of this chapter.

A brief index of social support (denoted as the SSI; derived by this author from the work of Brown and Harris, 1978) This questionnaire gives a brief summary of the amount of contact with relatives, friends, and other important information noted by Brown and Harris to be important in relation to the degree of social support available to a person. As a new instrument no normative data was available but no brief measures were located at the time. This measure is also reproduced in full at the end of this chapter.

The McMaster Family Assessment Device (known as the MFAD; Epstein, Baldwin and Bishop, 1983) The MFAD is a 72-item questionnaire comprising statements about family life such as:

> 'We are reluctant to show our affections for each other.'
> 'We discuss who is to do household jobs.'

Each statement has a four-point response scale, 'strongly agree', 'agree', 'disagree' and 'strongly disagree'. The items can also be grouped to form seven sub-scales with varying numbers of items in each. The sub-scales are problem-solving, communication, roles, affective responsiveness, affective involvement, behaviour control and general functioning. In theory, therefore, the MFAD will give not only give an overall index of family functioning but can also specify particular problem areas.

The task and coding system used in the original 'package'

Since no satisfactory family coding procedure was available at that time it was decided to use behaviour coding to examine the parent–child problem dimensions using the Eyberg behaviour coding procedure (Eyberg and

Robinson, 1981). This procedure examines parent–child relationships by assessing the type and quality of communications during fifteen minutes of play under three different conditions (child leads, parent leads, and child tidies up). It can be viewed as a standardized task (enactment) with a built-in method of analysis. For adolescents a modified approach was used in which discussion tasks were used rather than play, under three equivalent conditions. In the first condition the adolescent leads a discussion in which imaginary choices need to be made by the adolescent, in the second the parent leads and chooses, and in the final section the parent has to discuss the topic of adolescence with their offspring. The interaction is video-recorded and analysed using a behaviour coding system which uses event codes such as 'labelled praise', 'reflective statement', 'indirect command' (parental actions), 'non-compliance' and 'smart talk' (child behaviours). The codes clarify the style and manner of interaction between parent and child. Some codes such as 'physical positive' (affectionate touch) or 'labelled praise' are clearly relevant to aspects of caring. Other codes such as 'direct command' and 'compliance' are clearly relevant to control.

Using the complete 'package' in practice

The entire package of interview, rating scale, questionnaires and coding system was used with thirty families, fifteen from a normative sample and fifteen families referred to a child and family mental health clinic. Usually this involved two clinic visits by the family – the first involved the whole family in the structured interview, from which the rating scale was completed. The second visit involved the parents and the identified (referred) child only to complete the questionnaires and tasks (from which the behavioural coding was scored).

Our impressions about the package from a scientific point of view have been reported elsewhere (Wilkinson and Stratton, 1991). From a practitioner's point of view there were a number of advantages and disadvantages which will be summarized by considering three case examples and some other data relevant to practice.

CASE EXAMPLE 1: THE JONES FAMILY

This comprised a family whose youngest daughter Anne, aged 15, was refusing school. There was one older son of 19 at home and several other grown-up children. In the interview Anne was very passive and non-committal about her problem, while her parents complained about her not growing up: her mother particularly complained that

Anne had 'bad nerves' and there was 'something wrong with her'. A number of other problems were observed, including a general passivity and depressed atmosphere. There also appeared to be a marked denial of problems; conflict avoidance among family members; and a family pattern of enmeshment. Mrs Jones particularly appeared to deskill her daughter and emphasize her inability to cope with normal demands.

On the questionnaires, both parents had zero scores on the GHQ despite Mrs Jones appearing quite depressed. Both parents also reported high levels of marital satisfaction (at maximum scores, this could be construed as quite unrealistic!). However, Mrs Jones did report a low degree of social support, and also reported a very high level of behaviour disturbance for Anne. By contrast, Mr Jones had moderate social support and reported little behaviour disturbance for Anne. On the family questionnaire, both tended to report an idealized situation although Mr Jones admitted to some problems to do with emotional expression.

During the interaction task, Mr Jones had a warm interaction with his daughter (who displayed a good sense of humour when alone with him). However, when Anne gave clear cues about issues that really concerned her he appeared to miss them completely. By contrast, Mrs Jones displayed a marked lack of enthusiasm for the task and approached her daughter in a dictatorial fashion throughout, carefully explaining to her daughter exactly why she was not allowed to do a number of activities that would normally be considered appropriate for a girl of her age.

There were two difficult contractual issues that emerged from this assessment. First, it appeared that the family had come mainly to enlist support for continued school avoidance in general, and to obtain a home tutor in particular. Second, although there were some problems for Anne in terms of individuating from an enmeshed family system, the general attitude of denial of problems and lack of customerhood made it unlikely that any form of therapy was going to be productive in the long term. The parents' difference of opinion about Anne's behaviour and Mrs Jones' lack of social support gave a focus for a brief intervention in the short term, which led to some positive changes. As predicted, once Anne reached school-leaving age the family ceased attending on the grounds that her problems had resolved.

CASE EXAMPLE 2: THE SMITH FAMILY

This comprised a family with three children, Claire aged 13, Jimmy aged 11 and Ruth aged 9 (who had been referred for bedwetting). The interview began with complaints about the children but as the interview progressed to look at other areas of family function the marriage became the main focus of discussion well before the end of the interview. Mr Smith complained his wife was both clinging and domineering towards him. She justified her behaviour by saying she was worried about her own health problems (she was due for a hysterectomy but was afraid of surgery). She felt guilty that the children might be missing out because of her problems and felt compelled to pester her husband about them. She admitted she needed more affection herself.

On the questionnaires Mr Smith reported a mild degree of mood disturbance – whereas his wife showed very high levels of symptoms, some of which were to do with her physical health. She also reported higher levels of disturbance in Ruth's behaviour than her husband, due to her low mood and lack of firmness. Both parents agreed in reporting low levels of social support, high levels of family disturbance, and very low levels of marital satisfaction.

On the interaction task both parents demonstrated a warm and caring interaction with their daughter.

The major contractual issue in this case was remarkably simple, since both parents stated at the end of the interview that they felt we should focus upon their problem and not upon the children. This was agreed, and therapy went on for some time and went through several stages of marital, individual and family work.

CASE EXAMPLE 3: THE BELL FAMILY

This was a young couple with two small children, John aged 3 and Claire aged 2. John had been referred because of overactivity, aggressive behaviour to his sister, and general management problems. In the interview, it was clear that there were multiple problems including a marital crisis but that John was clearly labelled as the cause. His behaviour was referred to as 'turns' and he had in fact had some febrile convulsions as an infant. The couple had long-standing sexual difficulties arising from gynaecological problems and it seemed that they had difficulty in resolving disagreements. The two children behaved well in the clinic situation.

Both parents indicated high levels of their own mood disturbance using the GHQ, disturbed behaviour by John (ECBI), marital dissatisfaction (MSI) and family disturbance (MFAD). Mr Bell described himself as a loner and had low social support, whereas Mrs Bell had good social support. In the task situation, both parents appeared concerned and willing to play with John but both seemed rather afraid of him and they allowed him to insult them and display other behaviours which appeared to be a way of showing off to anyone watching.

The main contractual problem was that John was so clearly labelled as the problem whereas it was clear there were other contributing issues. In addition, Mrs Bell seemed preoccupied with the idea that there was something physically wrong with John which explained his behaviour and which would be impossible to change. An agreement was made that John was seen regularly to thoroughly assess his problem (including an EEG) while his parents were also seen separately. Initial discussions about managing his behaviour led into discussion of their differences of opinion and ultimately into more formal marital work. This case illustrates how a contract for more specific child-focused assessment helped to clarify that he was not physically ill and also gave the parents a sense of being taken seriously, so that the contract and focus of therapy shifted. John was probably also an early presentation of ADHD (Attention deficit hyperactivity disorder) and acknowledging that he was not an easy child to manage also helped in giving a focus for the child management problems.

Comparing the clinical and healthy families

The package did show clear differences in the average level of reported problems between the two groups of families (see Wilkinson and Stratton, 1991 for details). However, there was a wide variation in the patterns and levels of problem reported within the clinical group. This means that some of the clinical group had healthy family functioning, as would be expected – sometimes health problems are not caused by (or maintained by) family factors, but by other causes either focused upon the individual or external to the family. Clinical families are a mixed bunch. Using the package made these differences clear.

Evaluating the outcome of therapy

The other procedures were also used to evaluate the outcome of work with families by repeating their use at baseline, discharge and follow-up after therapy. In the research study each of the fifteen clinical families were subject to this procedure for all of the questionnaires used in the original package.

The number of parents showing measurable changes at follow up, detected by a change of one standard deviation or more on one of the questionnaires, is summarized in Table 13. Each measure is shown separately, as is each sex of parent: deterioration effects are also shown.

In general, therefore, using the package demonstrated that the interventions used generally had positive and measurable effects, showing how this approach can be used for service evaluation (there was an overall positive and measurable change at follow-up in 11 out of 15 cases). The type of change reported varied from case to case and the package approach helped to capture some of this diversity while still allowing comparison between cases. The mothers in the clinical group reported more problems and also more changes than the fathers; an interesting result which probably reflects traditional roles – the females being more likely to feel initially disempowered, more involved with relationships, and more empowered after therapy.

The advantages and disadvantages of the package are summarized below.

ADVANTAGES

- different families have different problems and different needs – what one part of the assessment missed, another part of the package detected
- the overall pattern of results from the package helped to clarify differences between functional and dysfunctional families – with all high scores indicating a crisis
- the package was also useful to clarify and compare explicitly important differences of opinion between family members (usually parents) and with the views of the clinical worker. This clarification and comparison was helpful in relation to the practical issue of formulating the 'therapeutic contract'
- using the package allowed other problems to be identified which could then be used to shift the focus of concern where it was therapeutic to do so

Table 13 Summary of measurable changes at follow-up among clinical parents using questionnaire scores

Measure	Number of mothers showing change (out of 15)	Number of fathers showing change (out of 12)
GHQ	8 (–2)	4
ECBI	7 (–1)	3
SSI	5	3 (–1)
MSI	3	1
MFAD	3	3

Note: minus figures indicate deterioration effects

194

- using the package often clarified the intensity or severity of problems
- the package helped with evaluating outcome.

DISADVANTAGES

- the package was rather formal and complex to administer when used in full
- the wide variety of problems meant that often parts of the assessment package were irrelevant to some families
- this perceived irrelevance was clearly irritating for some people
- some families reacted with defensiveness (usually denial) to a formal assessment interview
- the package approach is difficult for parents with literacy problems
- the comprehensive (full) package demands a lot of time to score and analyse the results.

Implications for the use of additional assessment procedures

The contents of the original assessment package are not sacred. It is obviously possible to utilize the principles of the package but modify the particular format to suit a particular case or working context. In relation to services, the package will need to be modified to suit particular specialisms or contexts. Furthermore in the interests of efficiency it is sensible in clinical practice (as opposed to research) to avoid using assessments which are irrelevant for a particular child and family. On a case-by-case basis, a more constructive approach is to select and use only those assessments which are most likely to be relevant for that case.

Most beginning practitioners find the full interview structure useful (as would be expected since it was intended to be a training device). More experienced practitioners may find the principles of the interview and the broad problem structure useful, although they may not wish to use the full text of the interview. The rating scale similarly may appeal to some practitioners (but not others) as a device to summarize a case and plan a strategy. The questionnaires are not universally applicable and their utility varies from case to case. Each one may be relevant and important with some cases but not relevant, or important, with others. As a general strategy questionnaires should therefore be used either as screening devices to check for the possibility of severe or complex problems or for more specific information-gathering devices about an identified problem. Provided a set of brief instruments is used, in general, the time employed in using them is likely to be labour-saving. Furthermore, they can be used again after discharge as a brief evaluation of outcome. If this is the case, it is sensible in routine practice only to repeat those questionnaires that are relevant to the work done or the improvement reported. It is also very important to check whether people are literate before giving question-naires. With children or parents who are very defensive and present ideal-ized views of themselves, it is probably better either not to use structured methods initially but to wait until they are more relaxed and engaged with the practitioner.

Communicating with children – a brief summary

Some young adults in professional roles have had relatively little contact with small children and worry that they will not know how to make a relationship with them. The next section gives some brief guidelines for communicating with children since these are essential skills within the assessment process. For more details see McMahon (1992).

These guidelines should help to make the experience a more satisfying one for both the practitioner and the child. Communicating with children can be an enjoyable and interesting experience. It can also be funny, moving, hum-bling and frustrating. It is not difficult to communicate with children once the right approach is used.

Preparation

Ensure that the environment where you are to meet the children, is as child-friendly and age-appropriate as possible:

- with the minimum of hazards for them
- where the minimum restrictions need be placed on their activities
- where there is suitable play equipment available
- use puppets, dolls, telephones and any other suitable play equipment as a means of communicating with children.

This may make communication less threatening for them and also more fun or interesting, thereby keeping their attention.

Introductions and welcome

- Explain to the children what is going to happen – explain anything which may be unfamiliar. Encourage them to express any worries which they may have about the situation in which they find themselves.
- Give the child a consistent message that they are welcome and you are interested in what they have to say (and what they do).
- LISTEN to the children.
- Reflect back what the children say – as a means of checking that you have understood correctly; as a way of encouraging them to expand on what they have said and to let them know you are listening.

- Use your non-verbal communications (facial expression, posture, affective tone) to match and reinforce what you say.
- Present yourself in as non-threatening a manner as possible – i.e. get down to the children's height; play on the floor; mimic their posture.

Awareness of the child

- Note, and if it feels comfortable, comment on the child's non-verbal communications (facial expression, posture, affective tone).
- Be aware of the impact of the power differential between adult and child. Try to understand what expectations the child has of adult behaviour, especially whether there is significant anxiety or not.
- Without being patronizing convey a message you know you are different but you still regard them as equal.
- Consider the child's emotional behaviour and development very carefully. Is affect openly shown and experienced, hidden and denied, or acted out? Can it be accepted and described as a normal experience or are defences too strong to admit feelings? If so, which emotions are acknowledged and which are not? Are feelings accepted as a normal experience or as something pathological or undesirable? What language is used by the child to describe feelings?
- In relation to cognitive development, assess the child's understanding of and general use of language, and ability to use concrete or abstract ideas.
- Consider also moral development, particularly in relation to the level of egocentricity and ability to use empathy.
- Be sensitive to the level of touch appropriate for each child. Some children do not like being touched. Be alert to cues from them as to what is acceptable to them. Be especially alert to 'startle' responses or, conversely, 'over-friendly' behaviour.

General principles for actions

- Let the children set the pace – do not force communication upon them.
- Unless there are specific reasons to the contrary, be non-directive and follow their lead in play.
- Keep your sentence structure simple for younger children. Pitch the vocabulary and the concepts you use at an age-appropriate level.
- Avoid criticizing mistakes or odd behaviour.
- Try to frame comments about the child positively. Use praise specifically for things they do well.

Analysing the interaction with the child

The following ideas give a framework for understanding and analysing interaction with a child, from the work of Eric Shepherd (1987, 1993). First, it is useful to consider the willingness to communicate as well as their ability with language as shown in Figure 5.

Certain other barriers to conversation can be identified. A general principle is that conversation is satisfying when there is a reciprocal commitment to communicate effectively through a balanced interplay of mutual control and reward. In other words, the child should be encouraged to have some active control of the conversation rather than simply answering questions, and the practitioner should be responsive and encouraging to the child's contributions. Key attitudes are:

- openness
- supportiveness
- flexibility
- positive regard
- empathy
- equality without ignoring differences
- a balance of control
- neither unresponsive nor invasive.

It is important to avoid interrupting, over-talking the child, changing topics abruptly or giving abrupt or minimal responses to the child's contributions. The aim is to achieve some symmetry in the conversation.

Key processes in conversation are attending and listening, clarifying and summarizing, taking turns, and what is known as back-channel activity. The latter consists of feedback given by the listener to encourage the talker, mainly by eye contact, nods and other non-verbal activity. Back-channel

	Willing to communicate	
Co-operative and responsive in play only		Co-operative and responsive in play & conversation
Unable to talk		**Able to talk**
Resistant and unresponsive in play & conversation		Understands but unresponsive in conversation, and may play benign games, but avoids active communicating through play
	Unwilling to communicate	

Figure 5 Dimensions of child's conversational ability
Source: Shepherd (1993)

behaviour does not normally develop in children until late in childhood (early teenage years). Therefore it can appear that younger children are not interested or not listening. Always assume they are, although they may not seem to be. Be patient, and wait for a sign that they have listened in the content of what they say when they feel it is their turn to speak. Another major difference is that adult conversations are characterized by short pauses and few gaps in the conversation. Child conversations are characterized by long pauses and noticeable gaps are accepted without discomfort. If adults are not aware of this they can wrongly assume the child is uncomfortable or hostile, which can lead to the practitioner in turn becoming anxious or frustrated. This in turn can communicate to the child, causing a blockage in communication. Therefore if the process appears slow initially, with pauses and gaps in conversation and apparent disinterest from the child, do not worry unduly.

Generally, the interaction should follow a sequence of greeting, explanation and orientation, mutual activity, and closure.

Using other assessments

The rest of this chapter will be used to give an overview of other recommended methods for assessment with children and their families.

Questionnaires

Interviewing family members together has the advantage of allowing direct observation of family processes but it can lead to difficulties in the disclosure of information. One of the most important qualities of questionnaires, often overlooked, is that they provide a safer medium for disclosing information which might not be readily disclosed in an interview. (Indeed there is evidence to suggest that under certain conditions people disclose information more readily to a pencil and paper form than to a person.) This is particularly true when family members are given the questionnaires separately, under conditions where they can complete them independently, and told that information is confidential. Under these conditions the questionnaires provide a brief and more efficient alternative to that of having a number of separate interviews with each family member. Questionnaires can also provide a screening device to identify family members who may need a separate interview as part of the assessment – where the questionnaire results either indicate severe disturbance or are markedly discongruent to the impression gained in the interview. This separate interview then explores the reasons for the disturbance or discrepancy, and whatever ramifications this may have for therapy.

The second use of questionnaires is their value in giving clear information about the perceived intensity of the problems. This is extremely valuable for two reasons. First, the particular concerns of the individual are specified in detail, for example by clarifying which behaviours are perceived as a problem for parents and which are not. Second, the overall score pattern enables a further standard of comparison to be used, in relation to the normative scores for a particular questionnaire. For example, when a parent appears depressed it is useful to know at what level the depression is, so that potential risks can be assessed.

As a result of this clearer specification of the problem, two more issues arise in relation to therapy. The questionnaire scores may help to plan the particular nature of an intervention by specifying target problems more clearly. In addition, the questionnaire scores provide a very efficient means of evaluating the outcome of therapy. By repeating their completion during and after therapy it is possible to evaluate what progress has been made in the view of the client.

Irrespective of the other qualities they may be felt to have, there is no doubt that questionnaires are often a cost-effective way of collecting information. In a busy clinical setting they do provide a very effective means of gathering basic data about the problem. With carefully selected questionnaires (or other suitable methods) for each case, it is possible to save a lot of time.

Child-centred assessments

As discussed, younger children can be encouraged to make use of play and drawings as a medium for communication, as exemplified in the 'bag of feelings' drawing task developed by Binney and Wright (1997).

There are also some very useful structured methods for gaining broader perspectives about the child's view of the world. In relation to the child's view of their family, the Bene–Anthony Family Relations Test (Bene, 1978, available from NFER-Nelson) remains a classic method. This is a semi-structured interview task (adapted to the child's developmental level) which, when used in a conversational way, becomes an elegant clinical and therapeutic tool. The manual is dated and technically weak, so that interpretation of results needs some experience of using it over time. However, as a clinical tool for exploring the child's view of the world it is excellent.

Although it also takes time to administer, the Children's Depression Scale (Lang and Tisher, 1978) provides a more detailed means of understanding the child's view of the situation which is much broader than the word depression implies. Sixty-six items are grouped into eight sub-scales denoted as affective response, social problems, self-esteem, preoccupation with sickness or death (sleep problems and anergia), guilt, miscellaneous depressive items, pleasure and enjoyment, and miscellaneous pleasure items. Norms are available for normal and depressed children. Given in a conversational manner with an emphasis upon developing empathy, this assessment technique is often a very therapeutic procedure.

From the child's own perspective of themselves, it can also be useful to get the child to complete a short scale such as the Culture-Free Self-Esteem Inventory (Battle, 1981) if the child is old enough to do so. This scale examines 'the perception the individual has of his own worth' and contains a lie scale plus four sub-scales of general self-esteem, social/peer-related self-esteem, parent/home-related self-esteem and academic/school-related self-esteem. Two forms are available of either 30 or 60 items.

For adolescents with complex problems, personality scales can be very useful to define problems and produce detailed formulations. Since the development of a separate and coherent sense of self is the main developmental task in adolescence, using personality scales in a way which gives constructive information back to the young person can have profound benefits to troubled youngsters. Two useful scales are the Millon Adolescent Personality Inventory (Millon, 1993) and the Adolescent version of the MMPI (see Archer, 1992). Both scales are available from NCS assessments.

Another useful scale with adolescents is the Adolescent Coping Scale (Frydenberg and Lewis, 1993) which measures the kinds of coping strategies used by adolescents in a way which encourages them to use new or alternative coping strategies.

The single most useful package of assessment instruments for children and young people has recently been developed by NFER-Nelson in collaboration with the UK national special interest group for clinical psychologists who work with children and young people. Known as the Child Psychology Portfolio (CPP) it consists of a selection of recommended measures for child assessment covering six main topics. Each topic has a general overview and each assessment method is presented with a review of information on the main uses of the scale, normal scores, and comparison with other measures. It is intended to provide a convenient, comprehensive and accessible resource for those concerned with the mental health of young people. It contains a wide range of measures in child psychology, covering health, social behaviour, family support and relationships.

The CPP consists of an introductory booklet (a general introduction to child psychology and an overview of the portfolio) authored by Irene Sclare, the editor, and six themed units, each containing a number of measures and scoring keys, background information, normative data and details on administration. All measures are presented as a photocopiable master with supporting information on how to administer, score and interpret the scale. Many are accompanied by acetate scoring keys to aid quick scoring. Each booklet has a table which provides an 'overview' of what scales are in the booklet, what they can be used for, by whom and for whom.

The themed units and their authors and contents are as follows:

Child Health – Jim Stevenson:

- Children's Headache Assessment Scale
- Functional Disability Inventory
- Child Health Related Quality of Life
- Behavioural Upset in Medical Patients – Revised
- Paediatric Pain Questionnaire
- Children's Health Locus of Control

Behaviour Problems in Children – Caroline Hogg, Naomi Richman and Michael Rutter:

- Revised Rutter Scales versions A and B, Preschool and School age
- Behavioural Screening Questionnaire
- The Child Behaviour Checklist
- Werry–Weis–Peters Activity Scale

Parenting Coping and Support Measures – Helen McConachie and Martina Waring:

- Family Crisis Oriented Personal Evaluation Scale
- Coping Health Inventory for Parents
- Family Support Scale
- Social Support Resources
- Questionnaire on Resources and Stress – Friedrich Short Form

Children's Social Behaviour and Competence – Kathy Sylva and Jim Stevenson:

- Taxonomy of Problem Situations
- Prosocial Behaviour Questionnaire
- Kidcope
- Locus of Control Scale for Children
- Life in School Checklist
- Target Children Observation Schedule

Families and Relationships – Ian Wilkinson:

- Darlington Family Assessment System
- The Family Grid
- The Family Health Scales
- The Beavers Interactional Scales and Family Competence Scale

Anxiety, Depression, Fears and Traumatic Stress in Children – Bill Yule:

- The Spence Children's Anxiety Scale
- The Fear Survey Schedule for Children
- The Children's Impact of Events Scale
- The Birleson Depression Scale
- The Brief Grief Index

This portfolio can be regarded as an essential toolkit for practitioners working with children since it provides a good collection of more specific measures for more detailed assessments once a general problem area is identified. It is in many ways complementary to this book as a technical resource for assessment tools.

Most recently, Calam (1997) has also reported on the development of a computer-assisted interview for children which is targeted at children who would otherwise be very difficult to communicate with or engage in assessment, such as those with learning difficulties, psychosomatic problems, or involved in child protection. The package has been well researched and piloted by practitioners in various settings with good results and should also be available soon.

Parental reports of behaviour

In child-centred work, the ECBI clearly is a brief and useful tool. It helps to clarify the degree to which each parent views the child's behaviour as a problem, and any major discrepancy between parents can often provide a useful initial focus for discussion. Other alternatives are available in the NFER-Nelson portfolio. Specific methods for the assessment of Attention deficit with hyperactivity and related disorders are contained in Barkley (1991).

Parental mood

A measure of adult mood such as the GHQ is also useful. Whether the child or the adult is identified as the problem, it is important to know exactly how stressed the parent feels, and the results can often be surprisingly different from the impression conveyed in an interview. A more detailed alternative to the GHQ would be the SCL 90 (Derogatis, Rickels and Rock, 1976). The full version of this scale is particularly useful for screening symptoms that may be psychiatric, since the scale comprises a number of sub-scales that are relevant to diagnostic classifications (somatization, obsessive–compulsive, interpersonal sensitivity, depression, anxiety, anger, phobic anxiety, paranoid ideation, psychoticism, plus 'additional' items). It would be feasible to select out relevant sub-scales that are specific to a particular case to give repeat measures for outcome assessment.

Social support

The discriminatory power of the social support measure (SSI) between clinical and normal families (despite its brevity) suggests that this can be an important topic to assess. It has proved very useful to identify to parents that they found the stresses of parenting more difficult to cope with because they had so little social support. The parents are then encouraged to attempt to improve their social life. A rather more detailed measure of social support for adults has been produced by Power, Champion and Aris (1988). However, the full version of this scale is very detailed as it distinguishes between five types of emotional support and five types of practical support, applies these to eleven types of relationship, and distinguishes between actual and ideal support: but the scale could be adapted and shortened for routine practice to provide a more powerful measure than the SSI.

Marital assessment

The marital satisfaction measure (MSI) also proved useful in a number of cases – not only to clarify marital satisfaction level (often providing a means of disclosure) but also to specify particular problem areas. Often dissatisfied partners have used the framework of the scale to specify the kinds of changes that they felt were necessary for their spouses to make in order to continue the marriage. Therefore, like the SSI, the MSI performs well as a clinical tool despite not being particularly well validated in a formal sense. Alternatives are myriad but the most useful are likely to be the GRIMS for assessing general marital satisfaction (Rust, Bennun, Crowe and Golombok, 1988) and the GRISS for specifically sexual problems (Rust and Golombok, 1986).

Family and relationship measures

The MFAD was the least satisfactory of the questionnaires used in the original package. Part of the problem was that it is too long and therefore tedious both to complete and score. Also, with most of our parents the scores on the MSI and MFAD were closely associated, so that if marital satisfaction was low then family disturbance was often perceived as high. The extreme scores at this end of the range on both questionnaires were attained by the same individuals, and the overall correlation between the scales was -0.72. (In single-parent families, elevated MFAD scores seemed to reflect a dissatisfaction with the identified child.) This high association seems to stem from the fact that this kind of questionnaire does not really measure family functioning – rather it measures an individual's view of family functioning, and this is likely to be highly influenced by problems within relationships between that person and their spouse or child. In the research cases the result of this was that MFAD scores did not reveal any problems that had not already been detected by either the MSI or the ECBI scores. These problems are likely to result from the problem of validity that self-reports of the family have. Self-report methods are likely to be most valid when used with adults or adolescents to collect information about their personal experiences.

For this reason it seems better in clinical practice to use relationship or family measures which explicitly focus upon the experience of the person completing it. The Family Grid (Davis and Rushton, 1991) which is included in the Child Psychology Portfolio is a brief, easy to complete, and effective self-report method for parents which focuses on the three key areas of self-esteem; satisfaction with partner relationship; and satisfaction with child relationship.

The Parenting Stress Index developed by Richard Abidin (1992, also available from NFER-Nelson) is another self-report questionnaire for parents based upon a clear model which also uses a dimensional analysis including child behaviours, temperament, relationship issues between child and parent, and parental supports. It is recommended as a more detailed self-report measure at the parental level which gives information relevant to many of the problem dimensions used by the DFAS. Both the Family Grid and the Parenting Stress Index combine assessment of the parent as an individual and their opinion of the parent–child and partner relationship.

Those interested in observing family functioning from a systemic point of view should consider the family tasks developed by Kinston and Loader (1988). Unfortunately these do not have the built-in method of analysis that the parenting tasks possess. A more recent alternative would be the Family System Test (FAST) developed by Gehring and Marti (1993). This is a simple representational task using figures on a board which can be used by children or adults to show their view of the patterns of closeness and distance (cohesion, or attachment patterns) and the (power) hierarchy in the family (shown by elevating the figures with blocks). Family members are asked to represent their current relationships, their ideal relationships, and a typical conflict scenario. Used in a conversational manner, this is likely to generate important material, and the task can also be used with the family group to generate observations of family process. Methods are suggested for scoring and categorizing families.

Assessment of parenting

Behavioural tasks and coding systems for parents and children give some clear, objective information about the style of parenting. They allow an objective assessment of parenting behaviour – the pattern of codes obtained is often highly relevant to the ongoing relationship quality, and type of attachment. If using video, it is often useful to replay the task to members of the family during therapy. The Parent/Child Game (Forehand and McMahon, popularized in the UK by Jenner, 1992) is an alternative to the Eyberg coding system (Eyberg and Robinson, 1982). They do demand time and resources to use effectively but the methods appear valid, reliable and clinically potent.

However, many people find task approaches very uncomfortable as they feel on trial and of all the procedures these should be used most carefully.

Expressed emotion

An alternative approach to assess the family process would be to use the expressed emotion (EE) coding system which is described in some detail below.

There are, in fact, five separate scales, two of which are frequency counts of events and three are global rating scales (warmth, hostility and emotional over-involvement) intended to reflect the degree to which emotion was observed during interview. The scales are designed to be applied to the relative of a patient during an interview.

The two frequency scales comprise counts of

a) critical comments

b) positive comments

In brief, a critical comment is a clear and unambiguous negative comment about the behaviour or personality of the patient – usually with an element of blame. It expresses an intense and emphatic dislike, disapproval, or resentment; or some clear element of rejection. Critical comments may be rated on content only (meaning of speech) but usually require vocal aspects (negative tone indicated by change of pitch), speed or inflection of voice.

A positive comment expresses praise, approval or appreciation of a person or behaviour; unlike critical comments, positive comments are rated primarily on speech content although positive voice tone is required when a positive comment refers to physical characteristics such as looks.

Two of the global rating scales (hostility and warmth) are likely to be associated respectively with critical and positive comments, although not in every case. Hostility refers either to a clear and generalized emotionally critical attitude to a person, to a statement of frank rejection, or both. Warmth refers to a clearly positive emotional attitude to a person, as reflected in tone of voice, sympathy, concern, empathy, interest in the person, and spontaneous expressions of warmth.

The final global scale of emotional over-involvement concerns behaviour by the relative which is unnaturally 'overclose', self-sacrificing or overprotective. Examples would be relatives who cannot separate from the patient, who give in to their every demand, or who assume them incapable of actions or decisions of which they are capable. With any real 'illness', a degree of over-involvement is normal during the acute phase, but the degree to which this initial response is subsequently generalized appears to be crucial to recovery and rehabilitation. Therefore emotional over-involvement is a key aspect of adjustment to chronic illness. Familiarity with these scales would have obvious benefits to practice. This would help to sharpen up observations of behaviour; helping relatives to give feedback without being critical or hostile, and to reduce over-involvement would be generally useful in therapy.

The major problem with the EE scales is that like most coding methods they can be very time-consuming. In order to obtain the levels of accuracy required for research purposes potential users attend a two-week course to learn how to make the EE ratings. Whether this degree of training is justifiable for more routine practice is debatable, but the judgements are complex. Some training and careful practice are certainly required, as well as the time to observe interviews or review tapes of them.

Practical issues in using other procedures

It will be obvious that the widespread use of more systematic assessment can entail the use of a large number of standardized forms. Therefore a department will find it essential to have adequate secretarial support, word-processing, copying and printing facilities, and a budget to buy in those assessment materials that have to be purchased through a supplier. Anyone wishing to keep records of the data for the evaluation of outcome would need a computer and secretarial assistance for routine input of data. These economic factors are undoubtedly very important in limiting a more widespread use of standardized assessments; some NHS departments in the UK could not meet these criteria. However these are not the only factors. The author's perception is that there is also a great deal of covert resistance to assessment which seems to arise from two sources. First, a general fear of the technical approach among all professions stems from worries about having one's own competence put under scrutiny. Second, among non-psychologists a lack of confidence in using these methods stems from a lack of experience in interpreting the results of formal assessments. Psychologists should be used in a consultative role to demonstrate and supervise their use.

How are the various results and the information they give to be integrated and interpreted? How is the assessment linked to choice of therapeutic strategy? These questions will be examined in the next chapter.

Summary

The first part of this chapter described the use of the original Darlington Family Assessment System package and the lessons that were learned for clinical practice from its use. The advantages and disadvantages of formal assessments are summarized. The second part of the chapter considered the issue of communication with children as a special topic and gave a summary of the main principles for effective communication with children. Finally the use of other more specific procedures is considered and some particularly useful methods for clinical practice described. A selective and informed use of these methods can form the basis for a skilled and professional approach to assessment with children and families.

APPENDIX 1

MARRIAGE SATISFACTION INDEX

This is a brief measure of your contentment with various areas of your marriage or partnership. For each of the ten areas, please put a score as follows:

0 = very dissatisfied
1 = room for improvement
2 = average
3 = better than average
4 = very happy

HOUSEHOLD RESPONSIBILITIES

(Which includes cleaning, shopping, cooking, washing up, laundry, car maintenance, etc.)

CHILD REARING

(Which includes watching over, feeding, bathing, disciplining, playing with, and helping the children)

SOCIAL ACTIVITIES

(Which includes going out together, e.g. going out to the pictures, to dinner, to friends together, for walks, doing sports together)

MONEY

(Which includes having your own money, buying and getting presents, budgeting and saving, buying clothes, and deciding how money is spent)

COMMUNICATION

(Which includes time to talk together, arguments, being tactful, getting the wrong end of the stick, talking things out)

SEX

(Which includes anything to do with sexual habits, but also to do with jealousy and showing affection in public)

STUDY OR WORK

(Which includes spending too much time on it [or too little], complaining about work, being away from home, putting work off all the time, etc.)

MY INDEPENDENCE

(Which includes going out alone, having the car or learning to drive, asking advice or having to ask permission, having to check everything is OK before making a decision)

SPOUSE INDEPENDENCE

(Which includes being relied on too much or too little, being left alone too often or too little, possessiveness, lack of discussion about decisions, partner has no life of their own or too much without you)

GENERAL OVERALL HAPPINESS

APPENDIX 2

SOCIAL SUPPORT INDEX

QUESTION	SCORE (if Yes)
1 Do you have a confiding relationship, i.e. someone you can discuss personal problems with?	2 points
2 How often do you have regular contact with friends?	
At least once a week	2 points
At least once a month	1 point
3 How often do you have regular contact with relatives?	
At least once a week	2 points
At least once a month	1 point
4 Do you have any interests/hobbies?	
2 named	2 points
1 named	1 point
5 Do you have a job?	2 points
6 Have you had a holiday in the last 12 months?	1 point
7 Do you enjoy your job?	1 point
8 Are you friendly with your work mates?	1 point
9 Are you satisfied with your house/flat?	1 point
10 Are you satisfied with your money situation?	1 point

9

INTEGRATING AND APPLYING ASSESSMENT INFORMATION

The crucial test of any assessment is whether it is useful and efficient as a means of deciding what action is appropriate to solve problems. In clinical work, the assessment should provide a means for choosing an appropriate treatment or therapeutic strategy. For a practitioner using a single theory or therapeutic method this is a relatively straightforward process. However, most practitioners in non-academic or non-specialist settings use a number of different approaches in an attempt to meet the needs of individuals in a flexible way (the 'eclectic' position). Working from an eclectic position makes the process of choosing a therapeutic strategy very complex, since any particular case can be viewed from a number of theoretical perspectives and thus approached using a variety of therapeutic methods.

Therefore the assessment process is a crucial one for practitioners. From a theoretical point of view, most of the literature on the efficacy of psychotherapy concurs that, while many methods have been shown to be generally effective, there is still much uncertainty about when a particular method will be effective and when it will not, particularly with respect to children and families. Hopefully this situation will improve in the long term as services move towards clinical guidelines based on evidence of clinical outcome. However, from the practitioner's point of view, the choice of therapeutic strategy stares him in the face every working day.

Most of the existing literature about choosing a therapy strategy focuses upon patient and family characteristics. This has neglected the issue of variation in practitioner characteristics; a strange omission, since it is patently absurd to assume that every practitioner has the same knowledge base or personal skills. This important issue will also be considered in this chapter. An interactional framework between practitioner and family is used to examine and explore the process of choosing a therapy strategy in a way which suits the needs of the patient and his or her family.

Two underlying purposes guided the development of this assessment system. One was to provide a method for training beginners which was comprehensible but also reflected the complexities of family work. The other purpose was the hope of providing a better way of choosing appropri-ate therapeutic strategies for patients, rather than by prejudice, evangelism or fashion.

Assumptions underlying this approach

The assumptions or paradigms underlying the approach described in this chapter can be summarized as shown in Figure 6.

In effect this represents the interaction of two polarities: the practitioner and the family, and subjective and objective perspectives. This can be restated as four sub-assumptions:

1   It is important for the practitioner to look at problems within the family from various perspectives, e.g. the individual; the dyad; the family network.
2   It is also important to understand problems both subjectively and objectively, i.e. by looking at the family members' views and beliefs about their problems as well as their behaviour (and the influence of any previous experiences of the therapy situation).
3   A practitioner's 'repertoire' of actions and responses will be determined by his or her skills, resources, training experiences and personal style.
4   Similarly, family members actions and responses will be limited by their resources, skills, and personal styles.

Underlying this is another assumption derived from the realist philosophy of science: that theories represent the real world – therefore no theory is an absolute truth. Furthermore no therapy is inherently 'better' but some work better in particular circumstances. As O'Hanlon (1989) pointed out in an eloquent address to the first World Family Therapy congress, schools of therapy are cultural belief systems, like churches. A strict adherence to a particular school can lead to 'delusions of certainty' and 'hardening of the

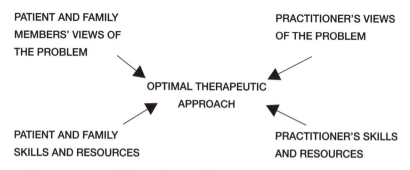

Figure 6 Assumptions underlying choice of therapy strategy

categories', leading to a rigid and inflexible approach which will be damaging for some patients.

Stages in choosing an appropriate therapeutic strategy

It is useful to consider the process of choosing an appropriate therapeutic strategy in six distinct stages.

1   Examining the practitioner's competencies and style.
2   Describing the family.
3   Fitting the practitioner and family together.
4   Understanding the family members' subjective views.
5   Comparing family versus practitioner views.
6   Formulating an appropriate therapeutic contract.

Stage 1: Examining the practitioner's competencies and style

This is something that every practitioner should do periodically, as Liddle (1982) suggested. The essential task for the practitioner is to:

- list each of his or her 'options' in terms of the therapy approaches that he or she commonly uses;
- clarify the amount of confidence the person has in their knowledge and competence in each of these approaches – particularly, on what training and experience is that competency based?
- clarify the practitioner's attitudes to each of these approaches, positive and negative, particularly in relation to the practitioner's own personal style, i.e. what aspects of each therapeutic approach fit comfortably with the practitioner's personal style and what aspects are more difficult?

It is useful to do this as a discussion exercise with a colleague.

Stage 2: Describing the child and family

In order to do this effectively, a proper framework for describing children and their families, such as that outlined in Chapter 5, is required. The dimensional scheme (Table 8 at the beginning of Chapter 5) and the associated assessment methods described earlier can be used as tools with which to obtain and organize such a description.

Once the overall description has been obtained, then it is necessary to sum up the important features of the case. In summarizing the information available, the following questions help to identify the most salient features of a case:

1   Is the presented problem a relatively isolated one or is it part of a broader pattern of problems? If the problem is discrete such as a grief reaction, it is more likely to respond to a direct and straightforward intervention such as individual counselling or advice to parents of young children. Conversely if there is a complex pattern of problems there is a greater need to understand the family functioning and system characteristics carefully before acting. For example, an older child with psychosomatic headaches in the context of a family with apparently warm, supportive relationships and few other problems might respond fairly easily, and on a lasting basis, to straightforward counselling which focused upon accepting and expressing emotions combined with relaxation exercises. The same problem occurring in the context of a multi-problem family characterized by repetitive conflicts would be unlikely to be resolved by this approach, except in a transient way. In this case it might be necessary to find a way of preventing the scapegoating, which would entail a greater emphasis upon understanding the family system. Hence the broader the pattern of problems, the more necessity there is to use the family level perspectives to understand the problems.

2   If there are multiple problems, first, what – if any – causative links are perceived by the family members and the practitioner between the various problems? Causation may be viewed as either linear or circular. Most people understand the concept of a vicious circle or can certainly grasp it enough to comment about whether one problem preceded another, or both started out small and grew together in a vicious circle. For example, if a parent is depressed and the child is seen as unmanageable, is one of these problems perceived as the cause of the other? Or do the family members admit they were not sure which came first? Second, it is important to distinguish between maintaining factors and original causes. The parent may agree that the problems have become a vicious circle but say that in fact the behaviour originally started in response to some life event such as separation from a best friend. Third, does the practitioner have any particular evidence for an alternative view of causation to that of the family members (evidence here might consist of facts reported about the timing and sequence of events or knowledge about life events, such as bereavements, whose effects are often underestimated)? For example the death of a grandparent may have happened around the same time as the friend moving away, and the significance of this partial cause has not been understood. The use of a general developmental framework within the assessment helps to clarify these important issues of sequence and causation. An overall view of this family's formation and development in relation to the problem is achieved.

3   Do the measures point to a need for further work or investigation with any particular individuals in the family? For example, is there a

possibility of medical illness or some form of abuse? Does the child or either parent exhibit specific problems such as peer difficulties, low levels of social support or high levels of mood disturbance? In the case of adults with low social support, long-term goals of the intervention should include encouraging and/or assisting that person to develop their social relationships. Children with global difficulties in peer relationships could also be given specific help with this aspect of their development. Significant mood disturbance in adults or children requires further investigation both to clarify the perceived cause and to ensure there is no formal medical or psychiatric condition.

Stage 3: Putting the practitioner and family together

At this stage the information about the child and family, having been organized, is now interpreted; hypotheses are formulated about the problem and the characteristics of the family system: what are its strengths and weaknesses, and how supportive will it be to various types of therapeutic input?

It is difficult to discuss the notion of hypothesizing in the abstract, so in order to take an example of the principles involved, consider a situation which is fairly typical for a practitioner with a child-focused problem. A young child has a severe conduct problem which appears to be caused and maintained by differences in parental management which in turn can be summarized as a circular causality. A very good example of this kind of problem was illustrated in one of the classic videotape demonstrations of structural family therapy entitled 'Taming Monsters' which features Salvador Minuchin. For those who do not know the case, a circularity diagram which sums up the essential features of the case is shown in

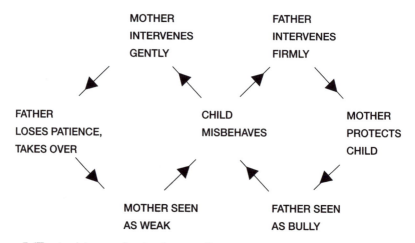

Figure 7 'Taming Monsters' – circular causality

Figure 7. This is also an interesting example of a more complex (in this case double) circular diagram.

The next step is to consider the role of the practitioner in limiting the therapeutic possibilities available. Every practitioner has a certain repertoire which is determined by the particular training and subsequent experience that practitioner has received. Most practitioners in practice have a specific range of therapy methods with which they feel comfortable and competent, and they will tend to use these as a set of options from which they select a method that seems appropriate to a particular case. Therefore if we assume that a typical practitioner is comfortable with five methods of interventions, he or she might have the following options:

- formal behavioural approach
- counselling the parental dyad to encourage consistency
- formal marital therapy
- structural family therapy
- play therapy.

These options are a random but somewhat typical set of options. They are not selected for any reason of presumed merit in themselves.

Depending upon the details of the case (and the particular skills and training of the practitioner) there are many potential interventions, each of which is likely to work best given a particular set of conditions. It is assumed that for each of the five therapeutic options available, certain general conditions in the family context facilitate the effectiveness of a given strategy, and other conditions inhibit it, as shown in Table 14.

Similar principles are beginning to be used to establish clinical guidelines for who should receive which type of psychological therapy (Cape, 1997) and this is now a main focus of professional activity in the UK, where the BPS has set up a special unit known as CORE (Clinical Outcomes, Research and Effectiveness). The aim of this centre is to encourage the application and utilization of outcome research into clinical practice. One example already produced gives guidelines for choosing between counselling services, cognitive behaviour therapy and psychodynamic psychotherapy (Cape et al., 1996). Underlying this approach are the principles that facilitating and inhibiting conditions exist, and that they should be definable for each therapy option. The principles can be applied to an individual practitioner as well as to choices between particular specialist services.

Advanced specialists and proponents of particular theories may dispute some of the inhibiting conditions shown; however, there are likely to be differences between practitioners who specialize in a particular method and those who do not. Practitioners who specialize in a particular method are likely to become more proficient so that they may be successful despite

Table 14 Facilitating and inhibiting conditions

Therapeutic strategy	Facilitating conditions	Inhibiting conditions
Behavioural therapy	Reasonable compliance. Realistic view of problems.	Severe conflicts. Power struggles. Rigid attitudes to child management.
Counselling parental dyad	Insight into different values within committed marriage. Child conduct problem.	Global marital problem. Poor parent–child relationships.
Formal marital therapy	Acknowledgement of global and primary marital problems. Compliance.	Child labelled as the problem. Difficulties secondary to life event.
Structural family therapy	Some compliance. Ability to convene core family members.	Transgenerational themes and unresolved bereavements.
Individual (play) therapy	Specific traumas/events. Child does not readily communicate – or has general social problems.	Chronic scapegoating. Symptom reflects family function.

inhibiting conditions. Conversely, practitioners who do not specialize are likely to be more sensitized to inhibiting and facilitating conditions.

The general assumption that facilitating and inhibiting conditions are likely to exist for each type of therapy is hard to dispute; the evidence on the efficacy of therapy would generally tend to support it. A therapeutic method is a kind of tool, and all tools work better under some conditions and suit certain tasks better than others. If this assumption is accepted, there are a number of implications. For researchers, it underscores the need expressed in Chapter 2 to focus upon processes within therapy (to clarify what actually does facilitate and inhibit a particular method) rather than simply looking at general efficacy. For practitioners, there are two major implications. First that all practitioners with children do need to consider the general context of the problem (the family system) as part of the process of selecting interventions. Second practitioners should carefully examine their own 'options' for therapy and specify what sorts of conditions are facilitative and inhibiting to their practice for each option.

To return to our example: what the practitioner must do at this stage is to use the information about a particular family to hypothesize which strategies are more likely to succeed out of the range available. Effectively this means that certain options can be discounted and others remain. In the 'Taming Monsters' video, Minuchin concluded that in that particular case the parents' relationship was basically sound but that they had certain dysfunctional beliefs about each other (the husband believed that the wife was

218

weak and the wife believed that the husband was violent). These beliefs perpetuated the problem, which appeared to be fairly specific. He therefore set about attacking these dysfunctional beliefs by first demonstrating within the session that the wife was capable of controlling the child without assistance, and that the husband was capable of gentle play. He was then able to forge a parental alliance after explicitly pointing out to the parents that they had certain myths about each other.

Some further illustrations can be considered using the case examples given in Chapter 8.

CASE 1: JONES FAMILY

Mr and Mrs Jones would not have complied with a behavioural approach because they had very rigid views about child management. There were certain unacknowledged differences of opinion (i.e. Mr Jones overtly supported his wife but indicated via the questionnaire that he did not really see Anne as a major problem). Therefore a parental alliance was unlikely to be achieved even if the practitioner had felt that Anne's conduct was a genuine problem, which it was not. Her conduct seemed to be part of a normal and healthy individuation process. The parent's idealization of their marital and family relationships made a marital or systemic approach difficult. A combination of some individual sessions for Anne to help her cope (with her mother's covert rejection) combined with some sessions to activate support from father (who was willing to come with Anne) to both daughter and wife appeared to be the best option.

CASE 2: SMITH FAMILY

In this case a behavioural approach appears difficult because of the complexity of the problems. Forging a parental alliance was impossible because of the bitter marital conflict, but at least this was openly discussed with the practitioner. It would have been inappropriate for whole family sessions to focus upon parental conflicts in detail, and Claire did not appear to need individual help except in so far as dealing with her anxiety about her parents' conflict. Marital therapy therefore clearly appeared to be the best option.

CASE 3: BELL FAMILY

A formal behavioural approach might be useful in this case as a starting point of discussion because of the mother's need to perceive that she was getting some practical assistance for John. Since John was so clearly labelled as the problem (probably owing to privacy boundaries since both parents disclosed other problems on the questionnaires) it was difficult to use a marital approach immediately. However, differences of parenting style were openly acknowledged so that the prospect of counselling the parental alliance was good and this in turn was likely to lead to more general marital issues being discussed later. Some individual sessions for John were also felt to be of value in clarifying his problems and feelings, as well as reassuring his parents he was not ill via medical investigations. Convening the whole family reliably appeared difficult, so that the structural approach was likely to be less useful in this case.

Stage 4: understanding the patient's (and family members') subjective views

One of the golden rules of successful therapy is a continuous negotiation with the client(s) about the aims and ongoing process of therapy. The principle applies to assessment as well as therapy. Therefore the third stage of choosing an appropriate therapeutic strategy focuses upon using the family members' views to select and discard therapeutic 'options' from those remaining. In order to obtain an agreement to continue work, the practitioner must explain his approach in such a way that the family members wish to continue. The style and method of therapy must achieve a reasonable fit with the family members views and preferences or they will cease attending. In particular, there needs to be some tacit or explicit agreement about who comes, what happens, and with what aim. There should be a very clear negotiation about who wishes or expects to be involved in any work and any other particular preferences that the family members feel strongly about. Clinical experience generally teaches that if patients or parents have a very strong preference for a particular style of therapy then that type has a good chance of success.

The concept of 'patient position' (Fisch et al., 1982) was presented in detail in Chapter 6 because it is an extremely useful means with which to understand family members' views and obtain an initial contract with them.

'Patient position' can be summarized as:

1   Whether a particular person is defined as part of 'the problem';
2   If so, whether they accept this role willingly or reject it;
3   If not, the degree of sympathy with which they view the person who is labelled as the problem – e.g. as sick (sympathetic) or bad (unsympathetic);

4   Whether they are a 'customer', i.e. whether any changes are desired, how strong this desire is, and the exact nature of the changes desired;
5   Whether the person is optimistic or pessimistic about the possibility of change;
6   Key self-concepts with which the person tends to identify themselves e.g. 'caring mother', 'working man' or 'honest and straightforward'.

Where views differ radically betwen family members, it is sensible to rephrase the way the contract is offered to different members of the family.

Using the six dimensions of patient position to negotiate a contract

By using all these six dimensions carefully, a message which reflects the person's view of the problem can be constructed which maximizes the chance of gaining their co-operation. In effect, the concept of patient position helps to construct the form of the therapy contract offer.

> Liam, and Mr and Mrs X, I can see that you have been very puzzled about the effect of the accident upon all of you and Liam in particular. All I can say is that in my experience it is not uncommon for very frightening events to affect people very badly for a long time. He also feels blamed at school and I would like to investigate the reasons for this to check there are no other problems there that we don't know about. I can see you are not very optimistic about coming here but I do not think he has anything to lose by having four sessions with me as a sort of trial period, after which we can meet again together and report back. I can see you and he need to decide this yourself, so perhaps you should think it over during the weekend and let me know.

Narrowing the choice of therapy strategy

These ideas also help with the choice of therapeutic strategy since certain strategies will be incompatible with family members views or beliefs about the problem. Therefore some therapeutic strategies can be discounted immediately, for example in the case of the Bell family, Mrs Bell was so concerned about the prospect of an organic condition that a formal family therapy approach would not have been accepted – it was tactically important to be seen to be 'investigating' John, even though it was felt unlikely he had an organic problem.

The use of patient position further narrows the potential choice of therapy strategy. The most important aspect of this is in relation to motivational issues, where the idea of customerhood helps to select those family members who will be most likely to engage in productive therapy. In addition, the concept helps to phrase the offer of a treatment contract in a way which matches family members' beliefs and therefore maximizes the likelihood of engaging them in therapy.

Organizing and summarizing the family members' views

Once the concept of patient position has been used to understand and summarize the views of family members, it should now be possible to work out which of the therapy 'options' used by the practitioner will be acceptable to the family. However there are three other issues that should be considered very carefully:

1   Is there agreement within the family about the nature of the problem(s)? For example, do the parents agree with each other about the nature and/ or severity of the problems? Does the child or adolescent accept the parents' views or not? Are there any other differences of viewpoint (e.g. siblings, grandparents)? If there is a high level of agreement, then once again a direct approach is more likely to succeed, whereas if there are a number of diverse views then the therapeutic strategy will need to take this into account and is therefore likely to be more complex. For example, if two parents agree about the nature of a child's problem it is obviously much easier to agree to a direct strategy, which could entail some play therapy with the child combined with a method of helping the parents to work together in some way to help deal with the problem. Conversely, if the parents disagree significantly about the nature or severity of the child's behaviour problem this suggests either a difference in standards of expected behaviour, parenting style, or a deeper problem in the marital relationship which is expressed in conflict about the child. A direct approach to the child's problem is unlikely to succeed (and certainly difficult to negotiate owing to parental differences of opinion). Other types of disagreements about the nature of the problem can be equally significant. If reports of marital satisfaction are very different, this would suggest an unresolved issue in the relationship (such as a power imbalance) which may be affecting the family in diverse ways. If the satisfied partner has little or no appreciation of their spouse's discontent the practitioner has to handle the case with some delicacy. In some ways the situation is more straightforward when both partners are dissatisfied, as it is easier to adopt a straightforward marital therapy approach if this is requested by the spouses. Therefore, the more agreement there is within the family about the nature of the problem the more likely a direct or straightforward approach to therapy is to succeed.

2   Are there any major discrepancies between the information obtained in different contexts of disclosure, i.e. differences between what is reported in a family interview and what is reported either in a questionnaire or in

a separate interview? For instance, a husband may appear to concur with his wife's complaints about a child in the interview but then privately indicates that he does not view the child as a problem at all. There are several possible explanations. It could be that the husband disagrees with his wife privately, but is reluctant to do this publicly; that he himself never sees the problems, although he accepts his wife's account; that in reality he would accept that there is a problem but he does not like to admit this publicly and explicitly; that he covertly disagrees with his wife but is avoiding conflict; or that he wishes to terminate the contact with the practitioner but is unwilling to say this openly. The first possibility illustrates the use of an alternative context as a deliberate means of disclosure, i.e. disclosure of a conflict of opinion between the spouses. The other possibilities are also common. Therefore if discrepancies are noted which are due to differences in the context of disclosure, it is useful to ask the following questions. How global is the discrepancy? Is it likely to be due to privacy boundaries; lack of insight or unconscious denial; loyalty to, or fear of, another family member; or deliberate deception?

3   What issues are seen as most important by family members – do they have any priorities for action? If so, it is sensible to take these into account provided they are not likely to interfere with the efficacy of the therapy offered.

Stage 5: Comparing family versus practitioner views

A second type of discrepancy resulting from the use of different views concerns differences between the subjective (family) and objective (practitioner) views of the problem. For example, what implications does it have for therapy if a parent views his relationship with his child as normal but we observe signs of distress in the child and of disengaged and punitive interaction in the family? What if a child's behaviour appears normal to us, but unacceptable to the parents? As illustrated in Table 8 in Chapter 4, the matching of subjective and objective views has implications for the type of change required in therapy.

Where there is agreement from both viewpoints, behavioural change is required. Where there is clearly an objective problem but the family members do not acknowledge it, cognitive change (understanding that there is a problem) is likely to be required as a precursor to behaviour change. Where family members complain about a problem which does not seem to be observable, then it is likely that cognitive change (understanding that the problem is one of attitude or belief) is the main requirement in therapy. As with the contextual discrepancy, however, the differences may arise for a number of different reasons and it is important to try to understand these. Family members may in fact agree with the practitioner privately but consider the problem is too personal to acknowledge publicly; they may have different expectations or standards of behaviour so that the problem to them is normal behaviour or vice versa; they may be unable to admit to this problem consciously as it is too threatening to them; they may be aware of it but under covert or overt pressure from others not to admit to the problem; or they may be indirectly expressing a wish (to terminate contact). Therefore when these differences arise it is useful to ask whether the discrepancy is likely to be due to privacy boundaries, lack of insight or unconscious denial, loyalty to or fear of another family member, or deliberate deception?

There are complex ethical issues involved here. When does a practitioner have the right to assume that his view is more correct than the family's views? As discussed earlier, it is felt that the main judgement required is whether there is a serious risk of harm occurring to a family member. If so, it can be asserted that the practitioner has a moral duty to act, even if this may be against the wishes of other family members.

This issue can be further examined using Tomm's categorization of ethical postures (Figure 1 in Chapter 3). Tomm suggested that therapies can be described according to the ethical posture of the practitioner as either empowerment (increasing options, conscious change), succourance (increasing options, unconscious change), confrontation (reducing options, conscious change), or manipulation (reducing options, unconscious change). Ideally Tomm suggests that practitioners should adopt an open and 'empowering' attitude to their patients and adopt therapy strategies which contain this attitude. However there certainly will be occasions where family members require emotional support rather than ideas (the solution to their difficulties may be obvious) and on these occasions the posture of succourance is clearly appropriate. The other two postures appear to be necessary where the family members have a markedly unrealistic view of the problem which is in some way harmful so that it is felt to be necessary to reduce the risk of harmful actions. If the family members are resistant to reality, but it is felt they will be able to accept and learn from a confrontation, then the posture of confrontation should be adopted. However there will be occasions where the family members have such an unrealistic view and/or a resistant attitude to the practitioner that they are not felt to be capable of learning from a direct confrontation. In these circumstances, the only option will be to use some form of paradoxical or other type of intervention which involves a manipulation of the family members' actions to reduce the risk of harmful outcomes.

Stage 6: Formulating an appropriate therapeutic contract

The practitioner should now be in a position to offer a contract for therapy which fits both with his own view of the problem and also fits with the family members' positions. The 'family' position, in fact, is complex since it is often made up of several different positions held by various family members. However, the practitioner will seek to offer a contract which will fit with the key members positions (usually the parents though not always). Sometimes contracts may need to be negotiated separately ('splitting' the family). Usually the contract will be an agreement about who will attend, how often, and what the goals or purposes of further attendance are.

If it is unclear what form the contract should take, a 'puzzle contract' may be offered (i.e. 'We're not sure whether we can help. Are you prepared to come back and talk with us again to help us decide whether we can help?') Contracts may be formal or informal and may be as simple as 'to discuss the problems again'.

Sometimes no contract can be offered. It is best to be honest about this rather than to raise false hopes and waste time on both sides. The commonest 'no contract' situation is where the family do not consider themselves to have a problem at all, although the referrer does (see Chapter 6). The practitioner will need to be clear about the strength of her own views here before deciding what tactics to adopt.

Sometimes it is possible to delineate a clear 'focus' for therapy after the first interview. In most cases, however, the outcome is an agreement either to focus the assessment in a particular way, begin therapy in a provisional way, or to continue in an exploratory manner if there is a marked degree of indecision and anxiety about collaborating in active work. In most cases it is safer to seek further clarification rather than risk making a premature hypothesis or other intervention which may be rejected by the family if made too early.

Hence the outcome of the first assessment is often the first step in a series of therapeutic efforts which may form a lengthy path. It should be regarded as a means of keeping to the most appropriate path and not as a short cut to the end. Initial agreements and contracts often change as therapy progresses, privacy boundaries loosen, and trust develops; this is a natural part of the relationship processes that make up good practice. The important point is that although the DFAS is designed to formulate an initial contract and strategy, these should not be regarded as fixed and final, but as a step along the way.

Using written reports for the patient or family

One core professional skill is the ability to utilize and integrate theories and methods derived from several perspectives in a way that meets the particular needs of the situation concerned. In relation to children and families, this can mean using a variety of assessment methods and therapeutic models (medical, behavioural, cognitive, psychodynamic and systemic) in creative ways which meet the particular needs of the child and family.

Other writers (e.g. Wynne, McDaniel and Weber, 1986) also refer to the concept of family consultation. This aims to give a clearer definition of the problem back to the family, which may be all that is required for the family members to deal with problems themselves. Other families do need more intensive help, but may need time to consider choices before committing themselves. Giving an assessment back to the family in a collaborative, contractual, and empowering way is therefore very important.

Another point is that because of anxiety many people often do not understand or remember the outcome of verbal discussions with practitioners. Philip Ley's (1988) work on communicating with patients shows how the use of written information increases both satisfaction, compliance, and the effectiveness of services. The use of a written report, using plain English and avoiding jargon, to follow up verbal discussions is highly recommended.

Therefore the use of appropriate assessment methods, combined with a written report to the family (as in Street, Downey and Brazier, 1991) can be an effective way of undertaking the assessment process in a manner which makes appropriate use of professional skills.

Summary

The process of choosing a therapy strategy for a case using family assessment can be considered as six distinct stages, summarized below.

1 Examining the practitioner's competencies and style:
   - list 'options' (in terms of the therapy approaches commonly used)
   - clarify the amount of perceived competence in each of these approaches – particularly, on what training and experience is that competency based?
   - clarify how well each of these approaches fits with the practitioner's own personal style.

2 Describing the family:
   - use a proper framework to describe the family (such as the dimensional scheme and associated assessment methods described within this book)
   - organize and interpret the information available into a formulation, with particular attention to the following issues:

     i   is the presented problem discrete or part of a broad pattern?
     ii if there are multiple problems, what causative links (circular or linear) can be perceived?
     iii does the assessment suggest a need for specific work or investigation with any particular individuals?

3 Fitting the practitioner and family together:
   - specify therapy options (see Stage 1)

- for each option, specify whether the particular family conditions (described in Stage 2) will facilitate or inhibit the therapy.

4 Understanding the family members' subjective views:
- use the concept of patient position to examine each family members views of the problem and other critical attitudes
- check which therapy options are more promising given these views of the problem (by selecting more motivated family members)
- compare and summarize family members views, particularly in relation to:

    i is there agreement within the family about the nature of the problem(s)?

    ii are there any major discrepancies in the information gained, arising from the context of disclosure? If so, why?

    iii what issues are seen as priorities by family members?

5 Comparing family versus practitioner views. If they are radically different, be clear about the ethics of any intervention considered.

6 Formulating an appropriate therapeutic contract. Formulate any offer of help in terms that fit as closely as possible to the family members views. Use a written report to the patient or family to follow up any verbal discussions.

Part III

BRIDGING THE GAP
BETWEEN SCIENCE AND
PRACTICE

The first part of this book reviewed the existing literature in order to demonstrate the need to understand the family context, describe some of the more important ideas that have emerged in relation to family work, and discuss the implications of these ideas for the process of assessment.

The second part of the book then described the practice of child and family assessment using ideas and methods designed to meet the needs of practitioners. The five chapters considered in turn the concepts used within the assessment, beginning the assessment, interviewing with families, additional assessment procedures, and the use of the information gained in the assessment in formulation, choosing a therapeutic strategy and communicating with the family. The system is intended to help practitioners (from various professions) develop a basic set of skills to understand and work with family groups in a flexible way. Since the system is intended to be used for basic training, Part II concentrated upon presenting practical and pragmatic advice in a clear way, with little reference to theory.

The final part of this book provides an overview of the assessment approach described in the book. The relationship between science, assessment and clinical practice is particularly complex in relation to children and families. Traditional scientific approaches to family assessment are difficult to apply because of the complexity of the variables involved, and the need for a pluralistic analysis. The DFAS was intended to provide this kind of analysis and function as an aid to training, and the evaluation of a training course based upon the system gave good results. Also, the concept of clinical guidelines can be considered as a bridge between science and practice. Clinical guidelines are intended to summarize the literature in relation to good practice and good professional ethics, to be based upon the evidence about what procedures are effective, to be applicable by multiple professions, and to encourage standardized practices. The book concludes by presenting a set of brief clinical guidelines for child and family assessment.

10

SCIENCE, LEARNING AND CLINICAL GUIDELINES

Science and the practitioner

Many authors have described how a 'traditional' conception of the nature of scientific activity stems from certain materialistic, mechanistic and reductionist assumptions. These can be traced back to the work of Galileo, Descartes and Newton, among others. Galileo provided an alternative view of the universe which did not rely on religious dogma; Descartes assumed that it was possible to render all that was unknown into rational knowledge, and Newton provided an explicit theoretical basis for the technological advances of the Industrial Revolution. The Industrial Revolution resulted in enormous social change and was also significant in that it *popularized* science. This seems to be because it enabled humanity to change the world to such a degree that the science which was the basis of this power was almost reified. Because many of the discoveries could be viewed as almost miraculous, science became a kind of oracle, the source of all truth. This process gathered pace when Darwin's explanation of the origin of the species gave a material explanation of the origin of humanity in a material world and challenged traditional religious explanations. The strength of this reductionist ideology is still evident today when television programmes popularizing science advance arguments that events are 'really only' the consequence of underlying reductionist concepts. (For example, that a rainbow is 'really only' the result of diffraction effects caused when light passes through droplets of rainwater.) In fact the reality is the rainbow – the reductionist concepts are models which help us, among other things, to predict when rainbows will occur.

One of the major dangers in this traditional and popular misconception is the notion that there can be such a thing as a universal scientific 'truth'. The assumption that there is some kind of absolute knowledge which a scientist can 'capture' is misleading, particularly within psychology and the social sciences where we are dealing with multiple versions of what is experienced. Furthermore, the notion of an absolute truth generates a great deal of conflict between proponents of different theories who assume that their theory is right in some absolute sense – and therefore that everyone else's must be wrong.

In the age of the post-industrial society, however, we must adjust to some rather different conceptions of science (derived from more recent advances in physics). Heisenberg's Uncertainty principle accepts that light can behave either as a wave or a particle. Quantum mechanics teaches us that sometimes nothing can be predicted concerning the behaviour of individual microparticles that goes beyond what can be said about the macrobehaviour of a whole collection of particles. The rather puzzling fact that light is always observed at a constant velocity is thought to be a result of the fact that light is the medium through which we view and interpret the world and thus upon which all our physics is based. Post-industrial science therefore offers multiple views of reality, suggests that context is all important, and has to accept that an absolute distinction between subject and object is impossible.

What has therefore emerged over the last few decades is a new and more sophisticated philosophy of science which is of great importance for psychology and the other social sciences. As discussed in Chapter 1, Manicas and Secord (1983) summarized the salient features of this new philosophy as:

- Acceptance that knowledge is a social and historical product with the suggestion that it is the task of science to invent theories to represent the world, which exists independently of cognizing experience.
- A non-reductionist view of the world – rather a 'stratified' approach suggesting that the world is best viewed at different levels and in different ways as a set of interacting, interwoven structures.
- Laws of absolute causation are rejected, rather it is accepted that events never occur under conditions of complete 'closure'; that events are 'always the outcome of complex causal configurations at the same and at many different levels'.
- Since only under complete closure are explanation and prediction symmetrical, events are not predictable with certainty in the real world (although this can be approached in the laboratory). They conclude with a suggestion that just as the application of physics requires engineering technology, so explaining the behaviour of a particular person requires not only psychological theory but also situational, biographical, and historical information.

Although the social sciences and psychology cannot yet be said to have eagerly embraced this new philosophy, shifts towards it can be identified. Farr (1987) demonstrated in his presidential address to the British Psychological Society a concern for a psychology which is scientific but also incorporates social and subjective phenomena. In clinical psychology there has been a gradual shift from purely 'objective' learning-theory based models towards cognitive, ecological and social models utilizing subjective and system-theory concepts.

Because the assessment system described in this book is founded upon the new philosophy of science, it contains a theory of human development and problem solving that is pluralistic. In particular, the theory takes account of both the individual person and his/her social world (in practice, the child and the family). From a developmental perspective neither can be understood without reference to the other. The implications of this philosophy also entail a need to view situations both subjectively and objectively, and from multiple perspectives. A number of concepts from behavioural, cognitive, developmental and family models of therapy have been blended to form an eclectic whole. As Doherty (1986) pointed out, light can only be fully understood as both wave and particle; human behaviour is no less complex.

In general, therefore, this book describes an attempt to apply a more modern and pluralistic philosophy of science to the practice of family assessment. The work was undertaken in a very typical public-service context in the UK over several years. It is also an example of practitioner-generated research and development. Health care generally relies upon both academic and practitioner developments, each of which is often evaluated in a two-stage process. Academic-generated developments usually arise from theory, and often lead immediately to academic research as a means of evaluation of the development. If this is satisfactory, the development is often accepted as scientific – but may not yet be proved to be practically applicable. The development must then be applied in practice settings where, effectively, the generalizability of those results is put to the test under non-ideal conditions (as an example of this process consider the development of behaviour therapy). Practitioner developments, on the other hand, arise from innovations in practice settings. They are generated less by theory and more by imaginative efforts to deal with the pressures of a particular working context. Sometimes they involve idiosyncratic approaches in therapy (as a classic example, Milton Erikson; see Haley, 1973) which initially are not supported by any scientific evidence. In this case the development arose from a special interest in assessment combining with pressures and trends in health care. Often practitioners are regarded as unscientific by academics and leading researchers. However, if such developments are clearly applicable, they are eventually taken up and evaluated scientifically by academic centres, as the second stage of the evaluation of practitioner-generated development. The topic of family assessment is a particularly complex one, however, in which traditional scientific approaches have not been easy to apply.

Measurement problems for family assessment

As a conclusion to their guide to methods and measures for family assessment Grotevant and Carlson (1989) identified several major problems:

1   a lack of theoretical consensus adding to a proliferation of different
    measures
2   poor links between theory and measurement in practice
3   a lack of empirical support for many measures
4   most research measures are not yet adequate for use by practitioners
5   measures also need to assess various levels of the family

To some extent these problems result from the political split between academics and practitioners (see Chapter 4). It is easy to add to this list. Most
of the family relationship concepts are inferred from group behaviour which
are likely to be very difficult to define and measure compared to aspects of
individual behaviour. Traditional scientific methods of assessing reliability
and validity within family assessment packages are likely to yield 'poor'
results because of the process of comparing data from different system
sources or different methods. This is a crucial point to bear in mind when
evaluating empirical studies. It is particularly important to consider
whether the method of assessment is appropriate for the purpose of the
research. The result of all this is that family and relationship measures
currently tend to be either scientifically respectable or clinically useful but
rarely both.

Learning about child and family psychology and therapy

One of the major problems for agencies working with children is that most
professional training is primarily adult focused so that basic training often
has a very small academic content about children and their development.
Hence for most professionals who work with children the most relevant
skills have to be developed after basic qualification. Similar problems apply
for training in family theory and therapy, partly because the topic overlaps
several academic disciplines; medical and other health personnel, psychology, sociology, social work, child development, and counselling and
psychotherapy. This makes it very difficult to delineate a core curriculum
since each discipline has its own priorities and emphases. Ganahl, Ferguson
and L'Abate (1985) made this and several other important points:

*   Because of a proliferation of theories of family therapy some means for
    integrating theories to provide an overview of theory-building should be
    an important aspect of training.
*   Academic training in family theory and therapy has been minimal. For
    example, there has been an appalling lack of attention given to the family
    in general psychology training courses. Most practitioners of whatever
    profession receive little or no training in family theory until after qualifi-
    cation. Even many practising family therapists in the UK have not
    completed a formal training course in the subject.

- Although there is an extensive literature on 'supervision' as the primary method of training therapists, there is little agreement about what is the best form of supervision. Ganahl *et al.* conclude that supervision should focus on the behaviour and skills of the therapist (technical aspects), on conceptual skills (relating theory to practice) and on the personality of the therapist in so far as this affects the implementation of their skills; they also suggest that live supervision should be the primary method of supervision for therapists in training but that this can be combined with other methods such as group supervision as skills develop.

In their review of family therapy efficacy Gurman *et al.* (1986) also examined the evidence on the efficacy of available training programmes. They reported only five replicable studies. All five demonstrated the acquisition of executive skills, two documented the enhancement of perceptual/conceptual skills, and one showed changes in relationship skills. They concluded that no direct evidence exists to prove that training experiences in marital and family therapy increase trainee effectiveness with families in the long term. In fact, Tucker and Pinsof (1984) did show some minor but significant changes in the clinical conceptualization and in-therapy behaviours of trainees over the first year of a two-year programme – but they were forced to conclude that 'training is a more gradual and sequential process than had been considered previously'. The most supportive evaluation of the long-term effects of family therapy training methods was provided by Byles, Bishop and Horn (1983) in relation to the McMaster model. In a study of twenty-four American social workers undergoing post-qualification training, they demonstrated stable changes using measures of perceptual and conceptual skills as well as ratings of job performance. They also noted (within their sample) the importance of continuing peer group meetings for support and discussion if the methods were to continue to be used in practice. In a review of methods of teaching therapeutic skills, Matarazzo and Patterson (1986) singled out the microcounselling method of Ivey (1971) as having repeatedly demonstrated its effectiveness when compared with no training controls or with less well specified programmes.

Although there has been a massive upsurge of interest in family therapy, interest in the formal assessment of the family has been remarkably limited (as was discussed in Chapter 4). From a training point of view, few courses are offered on the topic, and few publications are specific to this topic alone. This neglect stems mainly from a lack of distinction between assessment and therapy by many of the early family therapy writers and a tendency by psychologists (who are the main developers of assessment devices) to focus upon intra-psychic rather than social models. The state of the art in family assessment can perhaps best be summed up by reference to a book published by Pergamon Press in 1984 by Masson and O'Byrne. This book was purportedly a 'training manual' for family assessment and therapy. It was

based on work with one family, was filled with anecdotal speculation, displayed an ignorance of the available literature, and produced no empirical
evidence to support its claims.

Street (1988) commented that 'the training literature to date tends to
describe theoretical models with a considerable degree of vagueness. Many
articles refer to various amalgamations of models with no attempt to specify
the way in which these models have been combined. Those that are clear
about this combination process are rare (and demonstrate the degree of
conceptual clarity that needs to go into the exercise).'

The Darlington system as a training device

One aim of the assessment system was to produce a practical method that
would be useful in teaching and training, as this was felt to be a particular
need in child and family work. Instruments such as structured interviews are
particularly useful because they assist trainees to learn a core set of skills
and concepts far more rapidly than when using unstructured learning situations. Hence, once the system had begun to take a clear shape a training
course was designed which was intended to teach the most essential concepts and methods within the system. The general aims and content of the
course are described below. The exact content of the course has obviously
evolved somewhat over time and should vary according to the recipients
level of knowledge and skills.

Course Aims

The aims of the course were limited to teaching what were felt to be the core
principles of the DFAS. Since the teaching had to be time-limited and did
not allow for a detailed examination of individual skills, the course was also
orientated towards teaching perceptual and conceptual skills rather than
executive skills. The main aims of the course can be summarized as follows:

1   To teach a conceptual framework with which to understand and assess
    psychological problems in relation to the family. Since most trainee prac-
    titioners already had a grasp of the dimensional concepts used for the
    child, the parental, and the parent–child perspectives, the major effort
    was usually concentrated upon teaching the concepts of the family
    dimensions and their inter-relationship.
2   To accompany this theoretical framework for family assessment, the
    latter half of the course focused upon principles and practical skills that
    were most necessary to apply this understanding. General interviewing
    skills were examined in some detail before the use of the structured
    interview was demonstrated using a role play. The related topic of
    engaging and convening reluctant family members was also explored.

Furthermore, the technique of mapping family structure was explored as a means of summarizing and integrating information, leading to the formulation of hypotheses and the choice of a therapeutic strategy.

3   In particular the course was designed to highlight the necessity of clarifying both the therapist's view of the problem and the client's view, in order to formulate an appropriate therapeutic contract. The concepts of 'customerhood' and 'patient position' (Fisch *et al.*, 1982) were used to examine motivational issues and to clarify the differing views of the problem that are often held by different family members.

Methods of Training

The course was run as a small group workshop with six to eight trainees per group. This small number was deliberately chosen to allow the group to get to know each other relatively quickly, so that trainees would feel free to discuss the issues which concerned them and produce an interactive learning event. The manner and style of teaching also attempted to stimulate interactive learning by positively reinforcing participants who asked questions, made useful comments and responded to questions from other trainees in the group. The didactic component of the course was delivered not as 'the truth' but more with the qualification 'I have found these ideas very useful – I hope that you can find something of value in them yourself'.

The overall strategy used in the teaching, loosely based upon the micro-training model suggested by Ivey (1971) is shown in Figure 8.

Four specific methods were used within this general format. First, video-recordings were played to the group to demonstrate concepts (e.g. problem dimensions) to illustrate other crucial skills in practice, and to provide real case material for discussion. Some recordings were of expert therapists, whereas others were chosen by the author from his own work to show that

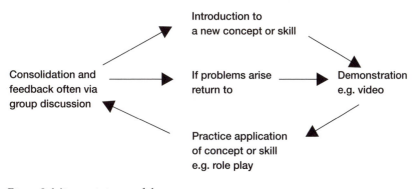

Figure 8 Microtraining model

mistakes could be made within the model. This was a deliberate emphasis to avoid making trainees feel 'de-skilled' in the face of too large a gap between themselves and the model presented. Discussion of particular topics in pairs was used to make trainees explore new concepts and clarify their own ideas (e.g. when setting personal agendas and expectations at the beginning of the course). Summaries of these discussions were then fed back to the whole group to clarify common themes. Role-play was used as a basic medium to practise applying the concepts and skills covered in the course. Initially this was done in pairs to minimize negative reactions to the use of role-play, with partners taking turns to interview and role-play clients using 'scripts' based on real cases. Provided that initial anxieties about role-play were overcome, a group role-play was used to illustrate the structured family interview.

Lastly, a number of written handouts were given to illustrate key concepts within sessions and to provide an opportunity for homework and consolidation of learning between the five sessions. A description of the main handouts used is given below.

Details of the training course

A course syllabus was sent to each participant prior to the start of the course. The general aims, content and teaching methods were described and a synopsis of each of the five sessions given (listing the main concepts covered in the session and the handouts that would be provided). A reading list was also provided.

SESSION 1

This session began with an introductory exercise in which participants (in pairs) discussed their own personal aims, doubts and strengths in relation to the course. The results of these discussions were fed back to the group and used to highlight specific issues from this 'agenda' as they arose during the course.

After briefly outlining the total dimensional structure, the rest of this session was devoted to examining two family-level concepts – power hierarchies, and closeness and distance. Since these concepts represent the means to understand family structure, two videos were shown which gave clear illustrations of structural problems within families. The first video was used to provoke a general group discussion of how structural issues can be inferred from interview behaviour. This provided a natural introduction to the topic of mapping, which was explained carefully with an accompanying handout. This handout described the symbols used by Minuchin (1974) to represent the various aspects of family structure. Each concept that can be symbolized (e.g. boundary, affiliation) was explained, and a number of examples given, to illustrate how the symbols can be used to represent complex situations within families. The second video was then used to pro-vide a case example for participants to map for themselves; the results of their efforts were fed back to the group for a further discussion of the benefits and difficulties of structural mapping.

As a homework exercise the family life-cycle table used in Chapter 2 was given for the participants to read before the next session. This handout (Table 1) summarizes the concept of the family life cycle in terms of the other three family problem dimensions (closeness and distance, power, and emotional rules).

SESSION 2

This session aimed to illustrate the other family-level problem dimensions and the inter-relationship of the problem dimensions. To begin the session, a short video showing a person looking back over the stages of their own life was used to stimulate a group discussion about the concept of the family life cycle, emphasizing the advantages and problems of a normative approach with related topics such as single-parent and step-families, cultural norms, and sexual stereotypes. Second, the concept of emotional atmosphere and rules was presented using Table 9 from Chapter 5 before illustrating with another video of a case example, in which difficulties in expressing conflict have led to conduct disorder in a child, as well as depression in the mother. To consolidate the understanding of the links between the problem dimen-sions participants were then asked to discuss and hypothesize about some of their own cases in these terms.

SESSION 3

This session aimed to explore the topic of interviewing with particular ref-erence to the understanding of the client's point of view. First, a group brainstorm was used to elicit a list of general interviewing skills and the participants were asked to comment upon their own strengths and difficul-ties. Second, two brief role-play scenarios were used to allow the partici-pants to explore some of their own skills. This role-play exercise was done by separating into pairs so that each participant had a chance to be both therapist and client. Scripts were based on real cases of individual family members presenting a complex problem with a degree of ambivalent motiv-ation. Before the role play, the concepts of 'customerhood' and 'patient position' were explained and participants were instructed to use these con-cepts to guide their interviewing. After each role play impressions were fed back to the group as a whole by both 'therapist' and 'patient'. Handouts on the two concepts were given to consolidate learning. As a preparation for the next session, the script of the structured family interview was given out to be read as a homework task.

SESSION 4

The aim of this session was to explore the topic of interviewing families as opposed to individuals. The DFIS was used as a vehicle to explore this topic by using a group role play. Two participants acted as interviewers, while the other members of the group acted out a role-played family situation based upon a real case. Prior to the interview several of the points discussed in Chapter 7 were discussed in the group, with a handout given for future reference. After the interview a long group discussion was held to fully explore the perceptions of 'family members' and 'therapists' with respect to the interview content and style. The rating scale was also distributed and completed with respect to the case used in the role-play.

SESSION 5

In earlier versions of the course, this session was used partly to provide an overview and integration of the course, and partly to explore any particular topics that participants were particularly interested in. To provide an overview participants were encouraged to discuss their own cases and certain other handouts containing material incorporated in Chapter 5 (e.g. problem severity, using the distinctions arising from the family life-cycle concept) were used to highlight issues arising from the group discussions. Exploration of other topics left space for an open agenda, provided the topic was relevant to the course.

In later versions of the course the final session began to address the topic of integrating and applying assessment information using materials incorporated in Chapter 9 in conjunction with actual case material.

Finally, verbal feedback was obtained from participants.

Evaluation of the training course and the DFAS

As part of the technical evaluation of the DFAS the impact of this training was formally evaluated. The details of the data can be found in Wilkinson and Stratton (1991) so that only a brief summary is given here.

The training course was evaluated both subjectively by the trainees and objectively by the experimenter. The trainees' subjective views about the course were obtained from a simple feedback questionnaire which asked for ratings about the value of the course and gave a space for free comments. Objectively, the DFAS training was compared both to a no-training control group and also to a control group which utilized placement experience (an unstructured learning experience). This was therefore a fairly stringent test of the training since the placement experiences (three to six months) were of much longer duration than the DFAS course (two and a half days). The design of this research is summarized below:

Design of the training study

Group A	Baseline exam	Training (DFAS course)	Exam 2
Group B	Baseline exam	No training	Exam 2
Group C	Baseline exam	DFAS + placement experience	Exam 2
Group D	Baseline exam	Placement experience only	Exam 2

Subjects were mostly trainees of mixed professional groups (psychiatrists, clinical psychologists, social work and probation officers, and nurses). Most were undergoing their basic professional training courses. In order to make a brief but efficient assessment of trainees' skills it was decided to utilise an exam-type procedure using standard materials (two videotapes of family interviews). After viewing each tape the trainee was given an examination paper about the family to be completed in 40 minutes. The results were marked by three separate external examiners who did not know the origin of each script or the content or purpose of the training, and who developed their own criteria of quality.

Subjects in experimental group A (training only) completed their two assessments at the beginning of, and immediately after, the training course. Subjects undergoing placement experiences (groups C and D) completed their two assessments as near as possible to the beginning and end of the placement. Control subjects in group B simply received the two skills assessment sessions which were separated by a period of two weeks.

The evaluation forms completed by subjects in the training groups gave generally positive feedback reflected in a high level of satisfaction with the value of the course for learning concepts and skills, and for creating some change in working practice. The free response section produced roughly two positive comments per person, most of which concerned four topics: theoretical concepts such as the family life cycle, applied concepts such as patient position, the teaching methods, and 'gaining skills' and 'gaining confidence'. Several asked for a longer or follow-up course and there were few critical comments.

First, the objective evaluation demonstrated a positive and significant effect of the training course which was equivalent to a mean improvement for each subject of a little under ten per cent of the exam total. This was a stronger effect than that of a placement experience. This suggests that training courses focused upon specific topics are effective in the short term, certainly for teaching perceptual and conceptual skills at an early stage of professional development. Second, the value of the course in terms of both subjective satisfaction and performance changes in trainees supports the functional validity of this assessment system; it is a 'workable reality'. However, it is impossible to reach specific conclusions about why it works. It could have been the teaching methods that were effective rather than the content; or the improvement could be due to a placebo effect due to enhanced confidence, rather than any intrinsic validity of the assessment system.

In summary, it can be safely concluded that the effect of training in the DFAS upon conceptual skills is significant, positive, and at least equally effective to that of an unstructured placement experience. Feedback from those receiving the training suggested that the benefits were due to the theoretical and applied concepts within the course, the teaching methods, and the confidence of having a clear model to follow (in that order). This can be interpreted as evidence that the DFAS has good construct validity.

Other evidence

The other evidence in support of the DFAS can be summed up as follows.

Significant but not high levels of reliability can be expected for data derived from the DFRS; this will drop when interviews are unstructured or when different interviewers are used. Given the difficulties of rating family characteristics, it seems fair to conclude that the DFRS displays consistent and significant levels of inter-rater reliability in its present form, but that the level of precise agreement can only be described as moderate. The main implication of this result for the rating scale is that it is best considered as a way of organizing information rather than as a psychometric tool.

Despite relatively small numbers of subjects, the dimensional scheme as a whole performed quite well. Within the sample of families studied, the majority of the problem dimension ratings showed significant associations with self-report measures of the problem. This was despite the limitations of having to use a battery of concurrent measures which had to be limited in size, which utilized mostly self-report rather than observational data, and which contained some measures that were designed to measure different concepts from those used in the DFAS. Strong associations occurred where there were clear external criteria to compare with the problem rating (e.g. for child development) or closely related measures with good psychometric properties (e.g. parental health with the GHQ). Weak associations occurred where other measures were not specifically designed to tap particular problem dimensions and had been adapted to do so (e.g. all the family dimensions) or where the problem rating tended to be based upon a different type of information (e.g. the child's social relationship rating could be strongly influenced by observations of behaviour in the interview rather than parental reports).

The majority of the problem dimension measures were also able to discriminate between the clinical and healthy families, although there were certain exceptions as well as a wide variation in the level of discrimination.

The most powerful discriminators between the clinical and healthy family groups were the child problem dimensions (mainly parental reports about the child) and the social support index. The discriminatory power of the child dimensions is not surprising in the context of a child clinic, to which parents bring children that they see as problems. The fact that the social support index also discriminates the groups so clearly suggests that social relationships are central features of psychological problems and exert a powerful protective influence against the impact of problems. The general pattern of the results shows that the measures used for the child perspective discriminate best, followed by those used for the parental perspective. The whole family measures show a weak but consistent level of discrimination.

In general, the discriminatory power of each problem dimension is likely to depend on the following factors:

1   the type of data and method of data collection used by the particular measure – i.e. whether the data were 'objective' or derived from subjective opinions;
2   the general psychometric quality or power of the measuring instrument or index used;
3   whether this characteristic varies widely within family samples;
4   whether this characteristic varies widely between family samples;
5   the likelihood of a problem being openly reported, denied, minimized or otherwise distorted, or not being acknowledged because of a lack of insight. (This last factor may have reduced the discrimination of the marital satisfaction scores.)

In comparing the four perspectives upon the family, the family problem dimensions gave poorer results for both concurrent and criterion validity than the dimensions from other perspectives. The low level of concurrent validity of the whole family concepts probably arises from comparing results derived from different methods of assessment. The low level of criterion validity probably arises from the fact that clinical groups may be clearly different at the level of individual measures but contain wide variation at the family level. Also, measures of whole family phenomena are likely to be less precise (harder to judge) than those for individual and dyadic phenomena. Nevertheless the family level problems were predictive of outcome (whereas the summary of problems from all perspectives was not). The dimensional scheme as a totality offers a powerful method for describing and differentiating families. The use of multiple measures should further add to the power of the assessment scheme when it is used in clinical practice.

The therapeutic work with the families following the assessment was also demonstrated to have positive and measurable effects, giving indirect support for the DFAS as a clinical tool. The heterogeneous mix of families and the eclectic approach make it impossible to be specific about exactly what factors were responsible for these benefits; but these two factors also make the result more generalizable since the work is typical of much clinical endeavour. It seems probable that careful and systematic assessment of family situations is likely to lead to a therapeutically effective service.

Clinical guidelines for child and family assessment

Some of the most important reforms in health care in recent years have been an emphasis upon understanding and using the views of the consumer (particularly in mental health settings) and the development of effective quality and audit initiatives. One of the central concepts is that of clinical guidelines for practice which help to identify and standardize good practice across different services. This book is in essence an elaborated set of clinical guidelines for child and family assessment. As such it is possible to summarize the main points in a short set of clinical guidelines which form the conclusion to this chapter and to the book as a whole.

Clinical guidelines are intended to summarize the literature in relation to good practice and good professional ethics, to be based upon the evidence about what procedures are effective, to be applicable by multiple professions, and to encourage standardized practices. These are the aims of this work.

CLINICAL GUIDELINES FOR CHILD AND FAMILY ASSESSMENT[1]

Using a comprehensive assessment framework

One of the major choice points in assessment is between client-centred versus more comprehensive assessments. An initial interview understanding patient and family views can be used to prepare for a contractual assessment (utilizing more formal assessment methods as the practitioner thinks appropriate, with family consent). The client-centered interview is used to select more specific assessments if required. The use of a broader or comprehensive view can also be important because in health contexts there is an implicit professional duty to screen for health problems. (The level of public awareness about children's mental health problems is also low, leading to a high rate of unrecognized problems.) Ethically, with unscreened and potentially serious problems then a more comprehensive assessment is preferable.

The following conceptual framework can be used to ensure that important problem issues are not omitted from the assessment. The framework provides a useful means of describing families and offers a way of generating hypotheses to link individual and relationship phenomena in problem-solving therapy. Where appropriate, the use of formal assessment methods should be considered as aids to the assessment process (some examples are given, see also the *Child Psychology Portfolio*, Scheme, 1997). The following areas should be considered:

THE CHILD OR ADOLESCENT AS AN INDIVIDUAL

Child development (e.g. British Ability Scales, WISC-R)
Current developmental behaviour and brief developmental history: especially the possibility of known developmental syndromes or learning disabilities.

Emotional disturbance (e.g. Children's Depression Scale)
The child's ongoing mood and affective behaviour, particularly in relation to anxiety, sadness and angry behaviour. Note the chronicity of any mood disturbance and distinguish from normal behaviours.

Patterns of relationships (e.g. Bene–Anthony Family Relations Test)
The child or young person's patterns of attachments and relationships within and outside the family, including relationships with siblings, peers, teachers and other adults.

---

1 These guidelines are intended for use with unscreened populations presenting to Child Mental Health or Psychological Clinics.

Behaviour and conduct problems (e.g. Child Behaviour checklist)
General patterns of ongoing behaviour and conduct: in relation to the socialization process within and without the family, and whether conduct is specific to one particular context or generalized to others.

Negative life events
The impact of particularly traumatic life events upon the child or young person: for example road traffic accidents, bereavements, witness to violence, and any known (or possible) child maltreatment.

Physical health
The impact of known physical illnesses upon the child's development, mood and behaviour. The possibility of undiagnosed physical conditions, which are known to affect development, mood or behaviour, for example temporal lobe epilepsy, diabetes.

PARENT-CENTRED PROBLEMS (e.g. Parenting Stress Index)

Particular problems encountered by the main carer or parent in that role can be secondary to:

Physical health

Psychological health
Especially formal psychiatric conditions.

Marital partnership
The impact of conflict or covert relationship problems within the marital partnership upon the child.

Social support
Social support available to parents or carers especially in relation to their needs for practical assistance and psychological support with the role of parenting.

Parenting history (e.g. Adult Attachment interview)
The parents' own experiences of being parented, their own early attachments and how these are understood (denied or resolved?).

CARER–CHILD INTERACTION (e.g. Parent–Child Game)

The quality of the attachment between the child or adolescent and their parent(s) or carer(s). The history of the attachment(s) over time is particularly important where there is intense conflict between the parent or carer and child. The style of parenting should be considered in relation to patterns of care (including over-involvement as well as neglect) and control (including under-control and over-control).

Some understanding of the family context in which the child's development has occurred is important, sometimes in order to understand problem development and also to predict the impact of interventions. It seems to be particularly important to understand:

Patterns of closeness and distance
The ongoing patterns of attachment and affiliations within the family, particularly in relation to unmet needs.

Power hierarchy
The nature of the family hierarchy in relation to patterns of authority and autonomy, conflict, and conflict avoidance.

Emotional atmosphere and rules
Ongoing patterns of affective behaviour within the family, particularly where there is a chronic atmosphere or mood present in family interaction. The expression of particular types of affect may be affected by implicit family rules, which can be particularly important for some problems, for example grief.

Contextual stresses
For some families there may be particular stresses associated with difficulties with the wider social context or other social systems, for example the impact of deprivation, poverty, prejudice, which may manifest in conflict with other agencies such as school.

Life stages and family development
Problems can often usefully be viewed in relation to the life stages of individuals within the family and the development of the family as a whole in relation to the family life cycle. In particular, how typical are the presenting problems for families at this stage of development?

Patient and family views of the problems

The expressed views, wishes and needs of the patient and other family members should also be considered carefully, particularly in relation to:

Child's or young person's views
In relation to children's rights.

Differences between family members' views
Views in the family in relation to agreements, disagreements and discrepancies from the information gathered. The meaning of any disagreements or discrepancies can be very important in therapy.

Expressed needs, priorities and language used
The way that the family members express their problems: any feedback
should be given in such a way that it is easier for the family members to
comprehend it and fit it within their own frame of reference.

Discrepancies between family and professional views
Critical points in the assessment may arise where family members' views are
markedly different from those of the professional undertaking the assessment. The need to acknowledge that people are experts about their own
experience will have to be balanced with the professional duty of care which
requires professionals to inform patients about the likely impact of problems. The timing of when and how to confront disagreements is a critical
issue which needs to be carefully considered.

Liaison and consultation with other people and professionals
It may be necessary to seek further information and views from other
people involved with the child or young person, within the limits of confidentiality that are appropriate for the case. In complex cases network
meetings should be considered.

Formulation of the problem

Once assessment information has been gathered, then a clear formulation of
the problem should be made which

- acknowledges and connects problems on different levels, uses a developmental framework to understand sequence, linear and circular
  causation, and problem maintenance
- is communicable to others involved.

Where the case is very complex so that formulation is difficult, or is otherwise causing grave concern, then further advice should be sought from more
experienced or specialized professionals. It is important to balance the need
for other professional frameworks or skills against the danger of passing
difficult problems on as a form of avoidance. Good supervision is essential,
which should consider conceptual skills (relating theory to practice), technical aspects (behaviour and skills) and the personal experience of the
therapist in so far as this affects their work. It should also consider possible
psychiatric diagnoses (such as ADHD, developing psychotic illness) and the
need for additional specialist advice or multi-professional work.

Communication of formulation

- It is particularly important to communicate the assessment and
  formulation to the child, young person or family (as appropriate to the

developmental level of the child, the issues of confidentiality involved, and any other risks).

- It is preferable that a clear version of the formulation is given back to the patient and/or family in an empowering manner, preferably in writing.
- The formulation of the assessment should make clear the choices that are available to the family in terms of further work, intervention, or referral to other professionals or other agencies.
- The need to pass this information on to others involved has to be considered in relation to the wishes of the patient and family in relation to confidentiality.

Summary

The relationship between science, assessment and clinical practice is particularly complex in relation to children and families. Traditional scientific approaches to family assessment are difficult to apply because of the complexity of the variables involved, and the need for a pluralistic analysis. The DFAS was intended to provide this and function as an aid to training; evaluation of a training course based upon the system gave good results in terms of both subjective satisfaction, and performance changes in trainees. The results supported the functional validity of this kind of assessment as a 'workable reality'. The opinions of the trainees about what was useful for them were highly supportive of the ideas underlying the assessment system.

The concept of clinical guidelines can be considered as a bridge between science and practice. Clinical guidelines are intended to summarize the literature in relation to good practice and good professional ethics, to be based upon the evidence about what procedures are effective, to be applicable by multiple professions, and to encourage standardized practices. The book concludes by presenting a set of brief clinical guidelines for child and family assessment.

REFERENCES

Aarons, M. and Gittens, T. (1987) *The Autistic Continuum: An Assessment and Intervention Schedule* (NFER-Nelson; Windsor).

Abidin, R. (1992) 'The determinants of parenting behaviour', *Journal of Clinical Child Psychology*, 21: 407–412.

Ables, B. and Brandsma, J. (1977) *Therapy for Couples* (Jossey-Bass; San Francisco).

Achenbach, T. (1986) 'The developmental study of psychopathology: implications for psychotherapy and behavior change', in S. Garfield and A. Bergin (eds) *Handbook of Psychotherapy and Behavior Change* (Wiley; New York).

Ainsworth, M., Blehar, M., Waters, E. and Wall, S. (1978) *Patterns of Attachment: A Psychological Study of the Strange Situation* (Erlbaum; Hillsdale, N.J.).

Akiskal, H.S. and McKinney, W.T. (1975) 'Overview of recent research in depression', *Archives of General Psychiatry*, 32: 285–305.

Akisker, J. and Stevenson-Hinde, J. (1991) 'Identifying families at risk: exploring the potential of the McMaster Family Assessment Device', *Journal of Family Therapy*, 13: 4, 411–421.

Alexander, J., Barton, C., Schiavo, R.S. and Parsons B.V. (1976) 'Systems-behavioural intervention with families of delinquents: therapist characteristics, family behaviour and outcome', *Journal of Consulting and Clinical Psychology*, 44: 656–664.

Andolfi, M. (1993) 'Mental health and community care', Presentation to Families at risk European conference, London, July.

Aragona, J. and Eyberg, S. (1981) 'Neglected children: mother's reports of child behaviour problems and observed verbal behaviour', *Child Development*, 52: 596–602.

Archer, R. (1992) *MMPI-A: Assessing Adolescent Psychopathology* (NCS; Minneapolis).

Axline, V. (1969) *Play Therapy* (Ballentine; New York).

Azrin, N.H., Naster, B.J. and Jones, R. (1973) 'Reciprocity counselling: a rapid learning-based procedure for marital counselling', *Behaviour Research and Therapy*, 11: 365–382.

Bailey, J. and Coppen, A. (1976) 'A comparison between the Hamilton rating scale and the Beck depression inventory in the measurement of depression', *British Journal of Psychiatry*, 128: 486–489.

Barkley, R. (1990) *Attention Deficit Hyperactivity Disorder* (Guilford; New York).

—— (1991) *Attention Deficit Hyperactivity Disorder: A Clinical Workbook* (Guilford; New York).

Barnhill, L. and Longo, D. (1978) 'Fixation and regression in the family life cycle', *Family Process*, 17: 469–478.

Bateson, G. (1970) 'A systems approach', *International Journal of Psychiatry*, 9: 242.

—— (1972) *Steps Toward an Ecology of Mind* (Ballentine; New York).

Battle, J. (1981) *Culture-Free SEI (self-esteem inventories) for Children and Adults* (Special Child Publications; Seattle).

Beavers, W.R. and Hampson, R.B. (1990) *Successful Families: Assessment and Intervention* (W.W. Norton; New York).

Beck, A.T. (1976) *Cognitive therapy and the emotional disorders* (International Universities Press; New York).

Belsky, J., and Nezworski, T. (eds) (1988) *Clinical Implications of Attachment* (Lawrence Erlbaum; New Jersey).

Belsky, J., Rovine, M. and Taylor, D. (1984) 'The Pennsylvania infant and family development project, III: the origins of individual differences in infant–mother attachment: maternal and infant contributions', *Child Development*, 55: 718–728.

Bene, E. (1978) *The Family Relations Test: Children's Version* (NFER-Nelson; Windsor).

Bentovim, A. (1989) 'A conceptual frame for describing families', Paper presented to the first World Family Therapy congress, Dublin.

Bentovim, A. and Kinston, W. (1978) 'Brief focal family therapy when the child is the referred patient: I. Clinical; II. Methodology and Results', *Journal of Child Psychology and Psychiatry*, 19: 1–12, 119–144.

Berger, A. (1985) 'Characteristics of abusing families', in L. L'Abate (ed.) *The Handbook of Family Psychology and Therapy* (Dorsey Press; Illinois).

Berkowitz, R. (1987) 'Rating expressed emotion from initial family therapy sessions (a pilot study)', *Journal of Family Therapy*, 9: 27–37.

Bertalannfy, L. Von, (1968) *General System Theory; Foundation, Developments, Applications* (Braziller; New York).

Binney, V. and Wright, J.C. (1997) 'The bag of feelings: an ideographic technique for the assessment and exploration of feelings in children and adolescents', *Clinical Child Psychology and Psychiatry*, 2(3): 449–462.

Bishop, D. (1987) 'McMaster Model of Family Therapy: Interview Proforma' (Personal communication).

Bloch, D.A. and Weiss, H.M. (1981) 'Training facilities in marital and family therapy', *Family Process*, 20: 133–146.

Bopp, M. and Weeks, G. (1984) 'Dialectical metatheory in family therapy', *Family Process*, 23: 49–61.

Borgatta, E.F. (1962) 'A systematic study of interaction process scores, peer and self assessments, personality and other variables' *Genetic Psychology Monographs*, 65: 219–291.

Boscolo, L. and Cecchin, G. (1989) 'Milan and post-Milan approaches', Paper presented to the first World Family Therapy congress, Dublin.

Boss, P.G. (1980) 'Normative family stress: family boundary changes across the life span', *Family Relations*, 29: 445–450.

Bowlby, J. (1977) 'The making and breaking of affectional bonds. I. Aetiology and psychopathology in the light of attachment theory', *British Journal of Psychiatry*, 130: 201–210.

—— (1988) *A Secure Base: Parent–Child Attachment and Healthy Human Development* (Basic Books; New York).

Bretherton, I. and Waters, E. (1985) 'Growing points of attachment theory and research', *Monographs of the Society for Research in Child Development* 50: Nos. 1 and 2.

Brown, G. and Harris, T. (1978) *Social Origins of Depression: A Study of Psychiatric Disorder in Women* (Tavistock; London).

Brown, G. and Prudo, R. (1981) 'Psychiatric disorder in a rural and urban population: I. Aetiology of depression', *Psychological Medicine*, 11: 581–599.

Brown, G. and Rutter, M. (1966) 'The measurement of family activities and relationships: a methodological study', *Human Relations*, 19: 241–263.

Budman, S. and Gurman, S. (1988) *Theory and Practice of Brief Psychotherapy* (Guilford Press; New York).

Byles, J., Bishop, D., and Horn, D. (1983) 'Evaluation of a family therapy training program', *Journal of Marital and Family Therapy*, 9: 299–304.

Byng-Hall, J. (1995) *Rewriting Family Scripts* (Guilford; New York).

Calam, R. (1997) 'Can computers help us talk to children?' *SIG Newsletter (children and young people) for clinical psychologists*, March, pp.7–10 (BPS; Leicester).

Cape, J. (1997) 'Clinical guidelines', Paper presented to the inaugural conference of CORE (Clinical Outcomes, Research and Effectiveness centre, London, April 1997).

——, Durrant, K., Graham, J., Patrick, M., Rouse, A. and Hartley, J. (1996) 'Counselling and psychological therapies' (Camden and Islington Medical Audit Advisory Group, London).

Caplan, G. (1981) 'Mastery of stress: psychosocial aspects', *American Journal of Psychiatry*, 138: 413–420.

Carlson, C. and Grotevant, H. (1987) 'A comparative review of family rating scales: guidelines for clinicians and researchers', *Journal of Family Psychology*, 1: 23–47.

Carpenter, J. (1986) 'And so they lived happily ever after: intimacy and the idealization of marriage. A comment on Birtchnell', *Journal of Family Therapy*, 8: 173–177.

—— and Treacher, A. (1983) 'On the neglected but related arts of convening and engaging families and their wider systems', *Journal of Family Therapy*, 5: 337–358.

Carpenter, J., Treacher, A., Jenkins, H. and O'Reilly, P. (1983) 'Oh no! Not the Smiths again! Part II' *Journal of Family Therapy*, 5: 81–96.

Carter, B. and McGoldrick, M. (eds) (1980) *The Family Life Cycle: a Framework for Family Therapy* (Gardner Press; New York).

Cattenach, A. (1994) *Play Therapy: Where the Sky Meets the Underworld* (Jessica Kingsley; London).

Chen, E. and Cobb, S. (1960) 'Family structure in relation to health and disease', *Journal of Chronic Disorders*, 12: 544–567.

Churven, P. (1978) 'Families: parental attitudes to family assessment in a child psychiatry setting', *Journal of Child Psychology and Psychiatry*, 19: 33–41.

Cochrane, R. (1983) *The Social Creation of Mental Illness* (Longman; New York).

Coleman, S., Kaplan, J. and Downing, R. (1986) 'Life cycle and loss – the spiritual vacuum of heroin addiction', *Family Process*, 25: 5–23.

Cox, A., Rutter, M. and Holbrook, D. (1981) 'Psychiatric interviewing techniques. V. Experimental study: eliciting factual information', *British Journal of Psychiatry*, 139: 29–37.

Crittenden, P. (1981) 'Abusing, neglecting, problematic and adequate dyads: differentiating by patterns of interaction', *Merrill-Palmer Quarterly*, 27: 1–18.

—— (1992) 'Quality of attachment in the pre-school years', *Development and Psychopathology*, 4: 209–241.

Cromwell, R.E. and Peterson, G.W. (1983) 'Multisystem–multimethod family assessment in clinical contexts', *Family Process*, 22: 147–163.

Cromwell, R.E., Olson, D.H.L. and Fournier, D.G. (1976) 'Tools and techniques for diagnosis and evaluation in marital and family therapy', *Family Process*, 15: 1–49.

Cronbach, L.J., Rajaratnam, N. and Gleser, G.C. (1963) 'Theory of generalisability: a liberalisation of reliability theory', *British Journal of Statistical Psychology*, 16: 137–163.

Crowley, R. and Mills, J. (1986) *Therapeutic Metaphors for the Child and the Child Within* (Brunner/Mazel; New York).

Davis, H. and Rushton, R. (1991) 'Counselling and supporting parents of children with developmental delay: a research evaluation', *Journal of Mental Deficiency Research*, 35: 89–112.

Day, L. and Reznikoff, M. (1980) 'Social class: the treatment process and parents and children's expectations about psychotherapy', *Journal of Clinical Child Psychology*, 9: 195–198.

Derogatis, L., Rickels, K. and Rock, A. (1976) 'The SCL-90 and MMPI: a step in the validation of a new self-report scale', *British Journal of Psychiatry*, 128: 280–290.

Dewitt, K. (1978) 'The effectiveness of family therapy: a review of research', *Archives of General Psychiatry*, 35: 549–561.

Dicks, H. (1968) 'Experiences with marital tensions seen in the psychological clinic', in J.G. Howells (ed.) *Theory and Practice of Family Psychiatry* (Brunner/Mazel; New York).

Doane, J. (1978) 'Family interaction and communication deviance in disturbed and normal families: a review of research', *Family Process*, 17: 357–394.

Doane, J., West, K., Goldstein, M., Rodnick, E., and Jones, J. (1981) 'Parental communication deviance and affective style: predictors of subsequent schizophrenia spectrum disorders in vulnerable adolescents', *Archives of General Psychiatry*, 38: 679–685.

Doherty, W. (1986) 'Quanta, quarks and families: implications of quantum physics for family research', *Family Process*, 25: 249–263.

Dohrenwend, B.P. and Dohrenwend, B.S. (1974) 'Social and cultural influences on psychopathology', *Annual Review of Psychology*, 25: 417–452.

Dominian, J. (1981) 'Causes of marital breakdown', Paper presented at Psychotherapy Workshop, London.

Dowdney, L., Mrazek, D., Quinton, D. and Rutter, M. (1984) 'Observation of parent–child interaction with two to three year olds', *Journal of Child Psychology and Psychiatry*, 25: 379–407.

Dunn, J. and McGuire, S. (1992) 'Sibling and peer relationships in childhood', *Journal of Child Psychology and Psychiatry*, 33: 1, 67–105.

Edelbrock, C., Costello, A., Dulcan, M., Conover, N. and Kala, R. (1986) 'Parent–child agreement on child psychiatric symptoms assessed via structured interview', *Journal of Child Psychology and Psychiatry*, 27: 181–190.

Ellis, A. (1962) *Reason and Emotion in Psychotherapy* (Lyle Stuart; New York).

Epstein, N.B. and Bishop, D.S. (1981) 'Problem-centered systems therapy of the family', in A. Gurman and D. Kniskern (eds) *Handbook of Family Therapy* (Brunner/Mazel; New York).

Epstein, N.B., Baldwin, L.M. and Bishop, D.S. (1983) 'The McMaster family assessment device', *Journal of Marital and Family Therapy*, 9: 171–180.

Erikson, E. (1963) *Childhood and Society* (2nd edn) (Norton; New York).

—— (1980) *Identity and the Life Cycle* (Norton; New York).

Eyberg, S.M. and Robinson, E.A. (1981) *The Dyadic Parent–Child Interaction Coding System: A Manual* (University of Washington; USA).

Eyberg, S.M. and Robinson, E.A. (1982) 'Parent–child interaction training: effects on family functioning', *Journal of Clinical Child Psychology*, 11: 130–137.

Eyberg, S.M. and Ross, A.W. (1978) 'Assessment of child behaviour problems: the validation of a new inventory', *Journal of Clinical Child Psychology*, 7: 113–116.

Falloon, I., Boyd, J. and McGill, C. (1984) *Family Care of Schizophrenia: A Problem-solving Approach to Mental Illness* (Guilford; London).

——, ——, ——, Razani, J., Moss, H. and Gilderman, A. (1982) 'Family management in the prevention of exacerbations of schizophrenia', *New England Journal of Medicine*, 306: 1437–1440.

Farley, F. and Patterson, J. (1979) 'Identifying a distressed marriage from the interactions between spouses: a structural analysis', *Family Therapy*, 6: 119–122.

Farr, R. (1987) 'The science of mental life: a social psychological perspective', *Bulletin of the British Psychological Society*, 40: 1–17.

Fielding, D. (1985) 'Chronic illness in children', in F. Watts (ed.) *New Developments in Clinical Psychology* (BPS; Leicester).

Filsinger, E. (ed.) (1983) *Marriage and Family Assessment* (Sage; London).

Fisch, R., Weakland, J. and Segal, L. (1982) *The Tactics of Change: Doing Therapy Briefly* (Jossey-Bass; London).

Fisher, L. (1976) 'Dimensions of family assessment', *Journal of Marriage and Family Counseling*, 4: 367–382.

—— (1977) 'On the classification of families', *Archives of General Psychiatry*, 34: 424–433.

——, Anderson, A., and Jones, J. (1981) 'Types of paradoxical intervention; indications and contra-indications for use in clinical practice', *Family Process*, 20: 25–35.

Fleck, S. (1980) 'Family functioning and family pathology', *Psychiatric Annals*, 10: 17–35.

Ford, F. (1983) 'Rules: the invisible family', *Family Process*, 22: 135–145.

Forehand, R. and Long, N. (1988) 'Out-patient treatment for the acting out child: procedures, long term follow-up dates, and clinical problems', *Advanced Behavioural Research and Therapy*, 10: 129–177.

Forehand, R. and McMahon, R. (1981) *Helping the Non-compliant Child: A Clinician's Guide to Parent Training* (Guilford Press; London).

Foster, M. and Berger, M. (1985) 'Research with families with handicapped children: a multilevel systemic perspective', in L. L'Abate (ed.) *The Handbook of Family Psychology and Therapy* (Dorsey; Illinois).

Freud, S. (1966) *The Complete Psychological Works of Sigmund Freud* (standard edn) (Hogarth; London).

Frydenberg, E. and Lewis, R. (1993) *Adolescent Coping Scale* (ACER; Melbourne).

Gaarder, J. (1996) *Sophie's World* (Phoenix; London).

Gale, A. (1979) 'Problems of outcome research in family therapy', in S. Walrond Skinner (ed.) *Family and Marital Psychotherapy* (Routledge and Kegan Paul; London).

Gale, A. (1985) 'On doing research: the dream and the reality', *Journal of Family Therapy*, 7: 187–211.

Ganahl, G., Ferguson, L., and L'Abate L. (1985) 'Training in family psychology', in L. L'Abate (ed.) *The Handbook of Family Psychology and Therapy* (Dorsey; Illinois).

Garfield, S. and Bergin, A. (eds) (1986) *Handbook of Psychotherapy and Behavior Change* (3rd edn) (Wiley; New York).

Gehring, T. and Marti, D. (1993) 'The family system test: differences in perception of family structures between nonclinical and clinical children', *Journal of Child Psychology and Psychiatry*, 34: 3, 363–377.

Gilbert, R. and Christensen, A. (1985) 'Observational assessment of marital and family interaction', in L. L'Abate (ed.) *The Handbook of Family Psychology and Therapy* (Dorsey; Illinois).

Ginsberg, B. (1976) 'Parents as therapeutic agents: the usefulness of filial therapy in a community mental health centre', *American Journal of Community Psychology*, 4: 47–54.

Goldberg, G. (1978) *Manual of the General Health Questionnaire* (NFER-Nelson; Windsor).

Griest, D. and Wells, K. (1983) 'Behavioural family therapy with conduct disorders in children', *Behaviour Therapy*, 14: 37–53.

Grolnick, L. (1972) 'A family perspective of psychosomatic factors in illness: a review of the literature', *Family Process*, 11: 457–486.

Grotevant, H. and Carlson, C. (1987) 'Family interaction coding systems: a descriptive review', *Family Process*, 26: 49–74.

—— and —— (1989) *Family Assessment: A Guide to Methods and Measures*, (Guilford; New York).

Gurman, A. and Kniskern, D. (1978a) 'Research on marital and family therapy: progress, perspective and prospect', in S. Garfield and A. Bergin (eds) *The Handbook of Psychotherapy and Behavior Change* (2nd edn) (Wiley; New York).

—— and —— (1978b) 'Deterioration in marital and family therapy: empirical, clinical and conceptual issues', *Family Process*, 17: 3–20.

——, —— and Pinsof, W. (1986) 'Research on the process and outcome of family therapy', in S. Garfield and A. Bergin (eds) *Handbook of Psychotherapy and Behavior Change* (3rd edn) (Wiley; New York).

HMSO (1973) *The Family in Society: Dimensions of Parenthood* (HMSO; London).

—— (1982) *Report of the Advisory Council on the Misuse of Drugs* (HMSO; London).

—— (1987) *Social Trends* (No. 17) (HMSO; London).

Haley, J. (1973) *Uncommon Therapy* (Norton; New York).

—— (1976) *Problem Solving Therapy* (Harper and Row; New York).

Halpern, H., Canale, J., Gant, B., and Bellamy, C. (1979) 'A systems-crisis approach to family treatment', *Journal of Marital and Family Therapy*, 5: 87–94.

Harlow, H. (1958) 'The nature of love', *American Journal of Psychology*, 13: 673–685.

Harrington, R. (1993) *Depressive Disorder in Childhood and Adolescence* (Wiley; New York).

Haynes, S. and Chavez, R. (1983) 'The interview in the assessment of marital distress', in E. Filsinger (ed.) *Marriage and Family Assessment* (Sage; London).

Heard, D. (1982) 'Family systems and the attachment dynamic', *Journal of Family Therapy*, 4: 99–116.

Herbert, M. (1993) *Working with Children and the Children Act* (BPS; Leicester).

Hodges, K., McKnew, D., Cytryn, L., Stern, L. and Kline, J. (1982) 'The child assessment schedule (CAS) diagnostic interview: a report on reliability and validity', *Journal of the American Academy of Child Psychiatry*, 21: 468–473.

Hoghughi, M., Dobson, C., Lyons, J., Muckley, A., and Swainston M. (1980) *Assessing Problem Children* (Burnett Books; London).

Hyams-Parish, T. (1995) 'Banished to the exclusion zone' *Childright*, 116: 11–15.

Ivey, A. (1971) *Microcounselling – Innovations in Interviewing Training* (Thomas; Springfield, Illinois).

Jackson, D. (1965) 'The study of the family', *Family Process*, 4: 1–20.

Jenkins, H. (1983) 'A life-cycle framework in the treatment of underorganised families', *Journal of Family Therapy*, 5: 359–377.

Jenner, S. (1992) 'The assessment and treatment of parenting skills and deficits: within the framework of child protection', *ACPP Newsletter*, 14: 228–233.

Jurkovic, G. and Ulrici, D. (1985) 'Empirical perspectives on adolescents and their families', in L. L'Abate (ed.) *The Handbook of Family Psychology and Therapy* (Dorsey Press; Illinois).

Kadushin, P. (1971) 'Towards a family diagnostic system', *Family Coordinator*, 20: 279–289.

Karpel, M. and Strauss, E. (1984) *Family Evaluation* (Gardner Press; London).

Kecks, S. and Sporakowski, M. (1982) 'Behavioural diagnosis and assessment in marital therapy', *Journal of Sex and Marital Therapy*, 8: 119–134.

Keeney, B. and Cromwell, R. (1977) 'Towards systemic diagnosis', *Family Therapy*, 3: 225–236.

Keeney, B. and Ross, J. (1985) *Mind in Therapy* (Basic Books; New York).

Kinston, W. (1988) 'A total framework for enquiry', *Systems Research*, 5: 9–25.

—— and Loader, P. (1984) 'Eliciting whole-family interaction with a standardised clinical interview', *Journal of Family Therapy*, 6: 347–363.

—— and —— (1986) 'Preliminary psychometric evaluation of a standardised clinical family interview', *Journal of Family Therapy*, 8: 351–369.

—— and —— (1988) 'The family task interview: a tool for clinical research in family interaction', *Journal of Marital and Family Therapy*, 14: 67–87.

——, —— and Miller, L. (1987) 'Quantifying the clinical assessment of family health', *Journal of Marital and Family Therapy*, 13: 49–67.

Kirkland, K. (1982) 'Assessment and treatment of family violence', *The Journal of Family Practice*, 14: 713–718.

Kopp, R. (1995) *Metaphor Therapy – Using Client Generated Metaphors in Psychotherapy* (Brunner/Mazel; New York).

Kuhn, T. (1962) *The Structure of Scientific Revolutions* (University of Chicago Press; Chicago).

L'Abate, L. (ed.) (1985) *The Handbook of Family Psychology and Therapy* (vols 1 and 2) (Dorsey Press; Illinois).

L'Abate, L. and Bagarozzi, D. (1992) *Sourcebook of Marriage and Family Evaluation* (Brunner/Mazel; New York).

Lambert, M., Shapiro, D. and Bergin, A. (1986) 'The effectiveness of psychotherapy', in S. Garfield and A. Bergin (eds) *Handbook of Psychotherapy and Behavior Change* (3rd edn) (Wiley; New York).

Lang, M. and Tisher, M. (1978) *Children's Depression Scale* (NFER-Nelson; Windsor).

Lange, A., Schaap, C. and Van Widenfelt, B. (1993) 'Family therapy and psycho-pathology: developments in research and approaches to treatment', *Journal of Family Therapy*, 15: 113–146.

Leff, J. and Vaughn, C. (1985) *Expressed Emotion in Families* (Guilford Press; London).

Leff, J., Kuipers, L., Berkowitz, R., Eberlein-Vries, R. and Sturgeon, D. (1982) 'A controlled trial of social intervention in the families of schizophrenic patients', *British Journal of Psychiatry*, 141: 121–134.

Levinson, D.J., Darrow, C., Klein, E., Levinson, M. and McKee, B. (1978) *The Seasons of a Man's Life* (Knopf; New York).

Ley, P. (1988) *Communicating with Patients* (Chapman and Hall; London).

Lewis, J., Beavers, W., Gossett, J. and Phillips, V. (1976) *No Single Thread – Psychological Health in Family Systems* (Brunner/Mazel; New York).

Lewis, M. and Rosenblum, L. (1975) *Friendships and Peer Relationships* (Wiley, New York).

Lickorish, J.R. (1968) 'The psychometric assessment of the family', in J. Howells (ed.) *Theory and Practice of Psychiatry* (Brunner/Mazel, New York).

Liddle, H. (1982) 'On the problems of eclecticism: a call for epistemologic clarification and human scale theories', *Family Process*, 21: 243–250.

Lieberman, S. (1979) *Transgenerational Family Therapy*, (Croom Helm; London).

Litman, T. (1966) 'The family and physical rehabilitation', *Journal of Chronic Disorders*, 19: 211–217.

Litman, T. and Venters, M. (1979) 'Research on health care and the family: a methodological overview', *Social Science and Medicine*, 13: 379–387.

Locke, H. and Wallace, K. (1959) 'Short marital adjustment and prediction tests: their reliability and validity', *Marriage and Family Living*, 21: 251–255.

Lowenfeld, M. (1979) *The World Technique* (George Allen and Unwin; London).

MPAG Report, (1990) *Clinical Psychology Report*, Manpower Planning and Advisory Group, Department of Health, London.

MacKinnon, L. (1983) 'Contrasting strategic and Milan therapies', *Family Process*, 22: 425–440.

McMahon, L. (1992) *Handbook of Play Therapy* (Routledge; London).

Mace, C. (1995) *The Art and Science of Assessment in Psychotherapy* (Routledge; London).

Madanes, C. (1980) 'Protection, paradox and pretending', *Family Process*, 9: 73–85.

Main, M., and Goldwyn, R. (1984) 'Predicting rejection of her infants from mother's representation of her own experience: implications for the abused–abusing inter-generational cycle', *International Journal of Child Abuse and Neglect*, 8: 203–217.

Manicas, P. and Secord, P. (1983) 'Implications for psychology of the new philosophy of science', *American Psychologist*, 38: 399–413.

Margolin, G. (1978) 'Relationships among marital assessment procedures – a correlational study', *Journal of Consulting and Clinical Psychology*, 46: 1556–1559.

—— and Fernandez, V. (1983) 'Other marriage and family questionnaires', in E. Filsinger (ed.) *Marriage and Family Assessment* (Sage; London).

Margules, A. and Havens, L. (1981) 'The initial encounter: what to do first?', *American Journal of Psychiatry*, 138: 421–428.

Masson, H. and O'Byrne, P. (1984) *Applying Family Therapy* (Pergamon Press; Oxford).

Maston, A. (1979) 'Family therapy as a treatment for children: a critical review of outcome research', *Family Process*, 18: 323–335.

Matarazzo, R. and Patterson, D. (1986) 'Methods of teaching therapeutic skill', in S. Garfield and A. Bergin (eds) *Handbook of Psychotherapy and Behavior Change* (3rd edn) (Wiley; New York).

Meier, S. (1994) *The Crisis in Psychological Measurement and Assessment* (Academic Press; San Diego).

Meissner, W. (1966) 'Family dynamics and psychosomatic processes', *Family Process*, 5: 142–161.

Middleberg, C. and Gross, S. (1979) 'Families' affective rules and their relationship to the families' adjustment', *American Journal of Family Therapy*, 7: 37–45.

Miklowitz, D., Goldstein, M., Falloon, I. and Doane, J. (1984) 'Interactional correlates of expressed emotion in the families of schizophrenics', *British Journal of Psychiatry*, 144: 482–487.

Miller, D. and Westman, J. (1966) 'Family teamwork and psychotherapy', *Family Process*, 5: 49–59.

Millon, T. (1993) *Millon Adolescent Clinical Inventory* (NCS; Minneapolis).

Mind Report (1975) *The Assessment of Children and their Families* (National Association for Mental Health; London).

Minuchin, S. (1974) *Families and Family Therapy* (Tavistock; London).

—— and Fishman, C. (1981) *Family Therapy Techniques* (Harvard University Press).

Moos, R. and Moos, B. (1976) 'A typology of family social environments', *Family Process*, 15: 375–371.

—— and —— (1986) *Family Environment Scale Manual* (2nd edn) (Consulting Psychologists' Press; California).

Mrazek, D.A. and Mrazek, P.B. (1981) 'Psychosexual development within the family', in P. Mrazek and C. Kempe (eds) *Sexually Abused Children and their Families* (Pergamon Press; Oxford).

Nichols, W. and Everett, C. (1986) *Systemic Family Therapy: An Integrative Approach* (Guilford; New York).

Norcross, J. and Goldfried, M. (1992) *The Handbook of Psychotherapy Integration* (Basic Books; New York).

North, P. (1980) *People in Society* (2nd edn) (Longman; Essex).

O'Hanlon, W. (1989) 'No guru, no method, no teacher; if you meet Erikson on the road, kill him', Paper presented to the first World Family Therapy congress, Dublin.

Oliveri, M. and Reiss, D. (1984) 'Family concepts and their measurement: things are seldom what they seem', *Family Process*, 23: 33–48.

Olson, D. (1986) 'Circumplex model VII: validation studies and FACES III', *Family Process*, 25: 337–351.

——, Sprenkle, D. and Russell, C. (1979) 'Circumplex model of marital and family systems. I. Cohesion and adaptability dimensions, family types and clinical applications', *Family Process*, 18: 3–28.

Palazolli, M., Boscolo, L., Cecchin, G. and Prata, G. (1978) *Paradox and Counterparadox* (Aronson; New York).

——, ——, —— and —— (1980) 'Hypothesizing – circularity – neutrality: three guidelines for the conductor of the session', *Family Process*, 19: 3–12.

Parker, G., Tuckling, H., and Brown, L. (1979) 'A parental bonding instrument', *British Journal of Medical Psychology*, 52: 1–11.

Parkes, C.M. (1972) *Bereavement: Studies of Grief in Adult Life* (Tavistock; London).

Patterson, G., Cobb, J. and Ray, R. (1973) 'A social engineering technology for retraining the families of aggressive boys', in H. Adams and J. Unikel (eds) *Issues and Trends in Behaviour Therapy* (Thomas; Illinois).

Pearce, B. and Cronen, V. (1980) *Communication, Action and Meaning: The Creation of Social Realities* (Praeger; New York).

Peterson, G. and Cromwell, R. (1983) 'A clarification of multisystem–multimethod (MSMM) assessment: reductionism versus holism', *Family Process*, 22: 173–177.

Pinsoff, W.M. (1979) 'The family therapist behaviour scales (FTBS): development and evaluation of a coding system', *Family Process*, 18: 451–461.

Pirotta, S. (1984) 'Milan revisited: a comparison of the two Milan schools', *Journal of Strategic and Systemic Therapies*, 3: 3–15.

Pless, I. and Satterwhite, B. (1973) 'A measure of family functioning and its application', *Social Science and Medicine*, 7: 613–621.

Pless, I., Roghmann, K. and Haggerty, R. (1972) 'Chronic illness, family functioning and psychological adjustment: a model for the allocation of preventive mental health services', *International Journal of Epidemiology*, 1: 271–278.

Power, M., Champion, L. and Aris, S. (1988) 'The development of a measure of social support: the Significant Others (SOS) scale', *British Journal of Clinical Psychology*, 27: 349–358.

Prior, M. (1992) 'Childhood Temperament', *Journal of Child Psychology and Psychiatry*, 33: 1, 249–279.

Reder, P. (1986) 'Multi-agency family systems', *Journal of Family Therapy*, 8: 139–152.

—— and Lacey, C. (eds) (1995) *Assessment of Parenting* (Routledge; London).

Reid, J.B. (1970) 'Reliability of observation data: a possible methodological problem', *Child Development*, 41: 1143–1150.

Reinecke, M., Dattilio, F. and Freeman, R. (eds) (1995) *Cognitive therapy with children and adolescents* (Guilford; New York).

Reiss, D. (1983) 'Sensory extenders versus meters and predictors: clarifying strategies for the use of objective tests in family therapy', *Family Process*, 22: 165–171.

—— and Oliveri, M. (1980) 'Family paradigm and family coping', *Family Relations*, 29: 431–444.

Richman, N. and Graham, P. (1971) 'A behavioural screening questionnaire for use with three-year-old children', *Journal of Child Psychology and Psychiatry*, 12: 5–33.

Richman, N., Stevenson, J. and Graham, P. (1982) *Pre-school to School: A Behavioural Study* (Academic Press; London).

Robinson, E. and Eyberg, S.M. (1981) 'The dyadic parent–child interaction coding system: standardization and validation', *Journal of Consulting and Clinical Psychology*, 49: 245–250.

Robinson, E., Eyberg, S. and Ross, A. (1980) 'The standardization of an inventory of child conduct problem behaviours', *Journal of Clinical Child Psychology*, 9: 22–29.

Rogers, C. (1951) *Client-Centred Therapy* (Houghton; Boston).

Rosen, G., Kleinman, A. and Katon, W. (1982) 'Somatization in family practice: a biopsychosocial approach', *The Journal of Family Practice*, 14: 493–502.

Russell, C., Olson, D., Sprenkle, D. and Atilano, R. (1983) 'From family symptoms to family system: a review of family therapy research', *American Journal of Family Therapy*, 11: 3–13.

Rust, J. and Golombok, S. (1986) 'The GRISS: a psychometric instrument for the assessment of sexual dysfunction', *Archives of Sexual Behaviour*, 15: 153–161.

Rust, J., Bennun, I., Crowe, M., and Golombok, S. (1988) *The Golombok – Rust Inventory of Marital State (GRIMS)* (NFER-Nelson; Windsor).

Rutter, M., Shaffer, D. and Shepherd, P. (1975) *Multiaxial Classification of Child Psychiatric Disorders* (WHO; Geneva).

Rutter, M., Taylor, E., and Hersov, L. (1994) *Child and Adolescent Psychiatry: Modern Approaches* (Blackwell; Oxford).

Sanders, M. (1992) 'Enhancing the impact of behavioural family intervention with children: emerging perspectives', *Behaviour Change*, 9: 3, 115–119.

Sanua, V. (1985) 'The family and sociocultural factors of psychopathology', in L. L'Abate (ed.) *The Handbook of Family Psychology and Therapy* (Dorsey Press; Illinois).

Satir, V., Stachowiack, J. and Tachsman, H. (1975) *Helping Families Change* (Aronson; New York).

Schaefer, E. (1959) 'A circumplex model for maternal behaviour', *Journal of Abnormal and Social Behaviour*, 59: 226–235.

Schwartzman, J. (1984) 'Family theory and the scientific method', *Family Process*, 23: 223–236.

Sclare, I. (ed.) (1997) *Child Psychology Portfolio* (NFER-Nelson; Windsor).

Seltzer, L. (1986) *Paradoxical Strategies in Psychotherapy* (Wiley; New York).

de Shazer, S. (1985) *Keys to Solution in Brief Therapy* (Norton; New York).

Sheehy, G. (1976) *Passages* (Bantam; London).

Shepherd, E. (1987) 'Telling experiences: conversations with child victims', Paper presented to BPS annual conference, Brighton, April.

—— (1993) 'Resistance in interviews: the contribution of police perceptions and behaviour', in P. Mathias (ed.) *Aspects of Police Interviewing, Issues in Criminological and Legal Psychology* series, No. 18. (Leicester; British Psychological Society).

Singer, M. and Wynne, L. (1963) 'Differentiating characteristics of parents of childhood schizophrenics, childhood neurotics, and young adult schizophrenics', *American Journal of Psychiatry*, 120: 234–243.

Sluzki, C.E. (1983) 'Process, structure and world views: towards an integrated view of systemic models in family therapy', *Family Process*, 22: 469–76.

Spence, S. (1980) *Social Skills Training with Children and Adolescents – A Counsellor's Manual* (NFER-Nelson; Windsor).

Stanton, M. (1981) 'An integrated structural/strategic approach to family therapy', *Journal of Marital and Family Therapy*, 6: 427–439.

—— and Todd, T. (1981) 'Engaging resistant families in treatment', *Family Process*, 20: 261–293.

——, ——, Steier, F., Van Deusen, J., Marder, L., Rosoff, R., Seaman, S. and

Skibinski, E. (1980) *Family Characteristics and Family Therapy of Heroin Addicts – Final Report* (Philadelphia Child Guidance Clinic; Pennsylvania).

Stedman's Medical Dictionary (1976) (Williams and Wilkins; Baltimore).

Steele, H. and Steele, M. (1994) 'Intergenerational patterns of attachment' in K. Bartholomew and D. Perlman (eds) *Attachment Processes in Adulthood* (Jessica Kingsley; London).

Steger, C. and Kotler, T. (1979) 'Contrasting resources in disturbed and non-disturbed family systems', *British Journal of Medical Psychology*, 52: 243–251.

Stratton, P., Heard, D., Hanks, H., Munton, A., Brewin C. and Davidson, C. (1986) 'Coding causal beliefs in natural discourse', *British Journal of Social Psychology*, 25: 299–313.

Strauss, M.A. (ed.) (1969) *Family Measurement Techniques* (University of Minnesota Press; Minneapolis).

Street, E. (1988) 'Family therapy training research: systems model and review', *Journal of Family Therapy*, 10: 383–402.

——, Downey, J. and Brazier, A. (1991) 'The development of therapeutic consultations in child-focused family work', *The Journal of Family Therapy*, 13 (3) 311–333.

Stuart, R. (1980) *Helping Couples Change* (Guilford; New York).

Tomm, K. (1987a) 'Interventive interviewing: I. Strategising as a fourth guideline for the therapist', *Family Process*, 26: 3–13.

—— (1987b) 'Interventive interviewing: II. Reflexive questioning as a means to enable self-healing', *Family Process*, 26: 167–183.

—— (1989) 'The New Paradigm: Ethical Postures', Paper presented to the first World Family Therapy congress, Dublin.

Treacher, A. (1984) 'Families and Networks, Prevention and Change', Opening Plenary of Family Therapy Association Training Meeting, York University, July.

—— and Carpenter, J. (1982) 'Oh no! Not the Smiths again! Part I', *Journal of Family Therapy*, 4: 285–305.

Tucker, S. and Pinsof, W. (1984) 'Empirical evaluation of family therapy training', *Family Process*, 23: 437–456.

Vaughn, C.E. and Leff, J. (1976) 'The measurement of expressed emotion in the families of psychiatric patients', *British Journal of Social and Clinical Psychology*, 15: 157–165.

Vetere, A. (1987) 'General system theory and the family: a critical evaluation', in A. Vetere and A. Gale (eds) *Ecological Studies of Family Life* (Wiley; Chichester).

—— and Gale, A. (eds) (1987) *Ecological Studies of Family Life*, (Wiley; Chichester).

Visher, E. and Visher, J. (1980) *Stepfamilies: Myths and Realities* (Citadel Press; Secaucus, N.C.).

Vostanis, P. and Nicholls, J. (1995) 'The Family Environment Scale: comparison with the construct of expressed emotion', *Journal of Family Therapy*, 17: 3, 299–315.

Walker, L., Thompson, N. and Lindsay, W. (1984) 'Assessing family relationships: a multi-method, multi-situational approach', *British Journal of Psychiatry*, 144: 387–394.

Walrond-Skinner, S. (1984) 'Whither family therapy? Twenty years on', *Journal of Family Therapy*, 6: 1–16.

Walsh, F. (1982) *Normal Family Processes* (Guilford; New York).

—— (1993) *Normal Family Processes* (2nd edn) (Guilford; New York).

Watzlawick, P. (1966) 'A structured family interview', *Family Process*, 5: 256–271.

Watzlawick, P., Beavin, J. and Jackson, D. (1967) *The Pragmatics of Human Communication* (Norton; New York).

Watzlawick, P., Weakland, J., and Fisch, R. (1974) *Change: Principles of Problem Formation and Problem Resolution* (Norton; New York).

Weakland, J., Fisch, R., Watzlawick, P. and Bodin, A. (1974) 'Brief therapy: focused problem solution', *Family Process*, 13: 141–168.

Wertheim, E. (1975) 'The science and typology of family systems. II. Further theoretical and practical considerations', *Family Process*, 14: 285–309.

Westley, W. and Epstein, N. (1969) *The Silent Majority* (Jossey-Bass; San Fransisco).

White, M. and Epston, D. (1990) *Narrative Means to Therapeutic Ends* (W.W. Norton; London).

Widiger, T. and Costa, P. (1994) 'Personality and personality disorders', *Journal of Abnormal Psychology*, 103: 1, 78–91.

Wilkinson, I. (1987) 'Family assessment: a review', *Journal of Family Therapy*, 9: 367–380.

—— (1993) *Family Assessment: A Basic Manual* (Gardner Press; New York).

—— and Stratton, P. (1991) 'The reliability and validity of a system for family assessment', *Journal of Family Therapy*, 13: 73–94.

Will, D. and Wrate, R. (1985) *Integrated Family Therapy: A Problem-centred Psychodynamic Approach* (Tavistock; London).

Wing, J., Cooper, J. and Sartorius, N. (1974) *The Measurement and Classification of Psychiatric Symptoms* (Cambridge University Press; London).

Winnicott, D.W. (1971) *Playing and Reality* (Tavistock; London).

Wynne, L., Jones, J. and Al-Khayyal, M. (1982) 'Healthy family communication patterns: observations in families at risk for psychopathology', in F. Walsh (ed.) *Normal Family Processes* (Guilford; New York).

Wynne, L., McDaniels, S. and Weber, T. (eds) (1986) *Systems Consultation: A New Perspective for Family Therapy* (Guilford; New York).

INDEX

Note: Page numbers in *italic* type refer to tables. Page numbers in **bold** type refer to figures.